The Christian Agnostic

Leslie D. Weatherhead

The Christian Agnostic

Abingdon Press
Nashville

THE CHRISTIAN AGNOSTIC

Copyright © 1965 by Leslie D. Weatherhead

Second Printing 1990

This book is printed on acid-free paper.

Library of Congress Cataloging-in-Publication Data

Weatherhead, Leslie Dixon, 1893–
   The Christian agnostic / Leslie D. Weatherhead.
      p. cm.—(Abingdon classics)
   Includes indexes.
   ISBN 0-687-06980-7 (acid-free paper)
   1. Theology, Doctrinal—Popular works. 2. Apologetics—20th century. I. Title.
II. Series.
BT77.W39 1990
230—dc20   90-35764
                                                  CIP

Formerly published under ISBN 0-687-06979-3, 0-687-06978-5, 0-687-06977-7.

"A Creed" reprinted with permission of The Macmillan Co., from *The Story of a Round House* by John Masefield. Copyright 1912 by   Macmillan Co., renewed 1940 by John Masefield.

MANUFACTURED IN THE UNITED   AMERICA

To
KINGSLEY
my son and
my friend

ACKNOWLEDGMENTS

The author wishes to thank the following publishers for giving permission to quote from their books:

Methuen & Co. Ltd. for quotations from Sir Oliver Lodge's *Raymond*, Whately Carington's *Telepathy*, and J. A. Hadfield's *Psychology and Morals*

Cassell and Co. Ltd. for a quotation from the poem "Christ in the Universe" by Alice Meynell from the *Anthology of Jesus* by Sir James Marchant

Ernest Benn Ltd. for a quotation from Sir Oliver Lodge's *My Philosophy*

Cambridge University Press for quotations from H. A. Williams in *Soundings*, Dr. John Oman's *Paradox of the World* and John S. Whale's *Christian Doctrine*

Herbert Jenkins Ltd. for a quotation from *Religion and Modern Society* by J. Chiari

English Universities Press Ltd. for a quotation from Dr. Raynor Johnson's *Psychical Research*

Victor Gollancz Ltd. for a quotation from Dr. Geoffrey Parrinder's *The Christian Debate*

Jonathan Cape Ltd. for a quotation from C. Day Lewis's *Collected Poems*

Oxford University Press for a quotation from *A Sleep of Prisoners* by Christopher Fry

The Clarendon Press, Oxford, for quotations from Richard Robinson's *An Atheist's Values* and from *The Testament of Beauty* by Robert Bridges

Edward Arnold Ltd. for a quotation from W. Macneile Dixon's *The Human Situation*

Macmillan & Co. Ltd. for a quotation from A. E. Taylor's *Does God Exist?*

Chatto and Windus Ltd. for a quotation from *Ends and Means* by Aldous Huxley

S.C.M. Press Ltd. for quotations from *Honest to God* by the Bishop of Woolwich, Dr. John A. T. Robinson

Neville Spearman Ltd. for quotations from Tudor Pole's *The Silent Road*

The Saint Andrew Press for a quotation from Dr. William Barclay's *The Gospel of St. John*, Vol I (The Daily Study Bible)

John Gifford Ltd. for a quotation from R. Gheyselinck's *The Restless Earth*

Gerald Duckworth & Co. Ltd. for a quotation from Dr. Nathaniel Micklem's *Faith and Reason*

Oxford and Cambridge University Presses for quotations from *The New English Bible, New Testament*

Routledge and Kegan Paul Ltd. for a quotation from C. G. Jung's *Memories, Dreams, Reflections*

Rider & Co. Ltd. for a quotation from *The Problem of Rebirth* by Ralph Shirley

The author would also like to thank the following newspapers and periodicals for allowing him to quote extracts:

The Daily Telegraph for an extract of August 28, 1964

The British Weekly for a quotation from Professor J. Alexander Findlay's article of November 26, 1942

The Guardian for extracts published on August 10, 1963 and May 16, 1964

The Sunday Times for three extracts published on December 3, 1961, March 25, 1962 and March 15, 1964

The Times for two extracts published on December 4, 1954 and August 8, 1964

Acknowledgments

The Spectator for an extract from W. C. Edgar's article, "The Adventure of Dying," published on February 11, 1928

The Daily Mail for extracts from Monica Furlong's article which appeared there on December 24, 1962

The Observer for an extract published on April 7, 1963

The People for permission to refer to an article which appeared on April 19, 1959

Lastly, the author would like to thank the following agencies, societies and persons for granting him their permission to quote:

A. D. Peters & Co. for permission to quote from *Johnson Over Jordan* by J. B. Priestley, published by William Heinemann Ltd.

A. P. Watt & Son, Mrs. George Bambridge, Methuen & Co. Ltd. and the Macmillan Company of Canada Ltd. for permission to quote verses from "The Explorer" by Rudyard Kipling, first published in *The Five Nations*

The Society for Psychical Research for permission to quote from an article published in the *Proceedings of the S.P.R.* Vol. 33

The Rev. Austin Farrer and William Collins Sons & Co. Ltd. for permission to quote from his books, *Saving Belief* and *Love Almighty and Ills Unlimited*

Dr. Raynor Johnson and Hodder and Stoughton Ltd. for permission to quote from *A Religious Outlook for Modern Man*

Miss Helen Macnicol for permission to quote Hymn No. 159, translated by Nicol Macnicol, in the *Methodist Hymn Book*

Miss Margaret Chaplin Anderson for permission to quote from her poem "A Wail from a Distressed Soul"

Miss Monica Furlong and Hodder and Stoughton Ltd. for permission to quote from *With Love to the Church*

Mr. John Freeman and the B.B.C. for a quotation from a B.B.C. television series interview between Mr. Freeman and Lord Birkett

Mr. Bernard Canter, Editor of *The Friend,* for a quotation from his article of September 11, 1964

The Society of Authors and Dr. John Masefield, O.M. for a quotation from his poem, "A Creed," published in *Collected Poems*

Mrs. Magdalen Goffin and Constable and Co. Ltd. for permission to quote from *Objections to Roman Catholicism*

Source references for shorter quotations appear on the relevant pages.

CONTENTS

"If we have faith and courage to seek it, we shall be shown new truths in the Gospel of real and immediate relevance to our own time, and we shall be given new insight to understand the unexampled problems which arise, almost every day, at home and abroad."

Her Majesty Queen Elizabeth II, at the Special Assembly of The Church of Scotland in 1960 to mark the Fourth Centenary of the Scottish Reformation

"Not only do I leave the door open for the Christian message, but I consider it of central importance for Western Man. It needs however to be seen in a new light, in accordance with the changes wrought by the contemporary spirit. Otherwise, it stands apart from the times and has no effect on man's wholeness."

Jung
(*Memories, Dreams and Reflections.*)

"The comparative science of religion compels us to recognize religion as the master force of human culture. Religion makes man do the biggest things he is capable of, and it does for man what nothing else can do; it gives him peace and happiness, harmony and a sense of purpose; and it gives all this in an absolute form."

Malinowski

"A theological system is supposed to satisfy two basic needs: the statement of the Christian message and the interpretation of this truth for every new generation. Theology moves back and forth between two poles, the eternal truth of its foundation and the temporal situation in which the eternal truth must be perceived."

Paul Tillich
(*Systematic Theology*)

PREFACE

THIS book had a checkered history before its publication. Through the kindly offices of his sister—then a university student in Leeds who attended my Friday Fellowship for young people—I met, some forty years ago, Dr. Raynor Johnson, of London University, who was then teaching physics at King's College. We became friends at sight and our friendship has deepened through the following years, though he is now Master of Queen's College in the University of Melbourne, in Australia.

In 1951, with my daughter Margaret, I spent three months in his home, and, among many other matters, we discussed the possibility of writing a book together which sought to commend Christianity to the modern, thoughtful layman who is so acutely dissatisfied by the conventional presentation of the Christian religion. We even got to the point of working out a rough table of contents for the proposed book.

However, while I was still the Minister of the City Temple, in London, this was impossible, and even after retirement in 1960, I had so many commitments in preaching, lecturing, writing and interviewing, that we both realized that to wait for my contribution would delay publication, particularly if we had to meet to discuss the points on which we differed and to decide who should write the various sections.

So Dr. Johnson went ahead, and in 1963 his book, called *A Religious Outlook for Modern Man*, was published by

13

Hodder and Stoughton, and to it I merely contributed a foreword.

As a certain amount of leisure became mine in retirement, I started to write this book and I called it *The Christian Agnostic*. Just before his death, I had a long conversation with Lork Birkett whom I had known for many years. We spoke quite frankly together about our doubt and dissatisfaction in the field of religion, and then he, who had been a Methodist lay preacher, and a prospective candidate for the Methodist Ministry, said, "I think now I should describe myself as a 'Christian Agnostic'." The phrase stuck in my mind, and I determined to make it my title. I have always been attracted by those lovable men and women who rarely have anything to do with organized churches but who would never act dishonorably or meanly, who are full of generosity and helpfulness if ever one is in trouble or need, who bear their own troubles with magnificent courage, who never complain or grumble or gossip or run other people down. I wanted to write for them.

Many of them feel that the church services are dull, boring and irrelevant. Many have been put off by the frailties of church members. Many men, I am sure, hate hypocrisy more than anything, and rather than fall below the profession of being Christians which going to church involves, they will profess nothing and thus be "better than their creed." Many wives are unwilling alone to join the fellowship of the church. Many, both husbands and wives, no longer believe the creeds of the church and feel that their intellectual integrity would be impugned by association with the church. In fact, many professing agnostics are nearer belief in the true God than are many conventional church-goers who believe in a bogy that does not exist whom they miscall God.

I feel that it is no sin to be an agnostic. By "agnostic" I do not of course mean the atheist, who declares that there is no God. The simplest reader of this book will realize that no one can prove a negative like that. Robinson Crusoe could prove that there *was* a man on his island. He could never have proved there was not. For a man might have hidden behind the only trees he did not search, or dodged there when he was not looking! To me it seems a strange mentality by which a man can look up into the starlit sky or even down into a humble flower or listen to a haunting tune or watch a sunset, meditate on some deed of utter self-sacrifice or on the mystery of human love, and say, "I *know* that in this whole universe there cannot possibly be God." Since I have talked with many self-styled "atheists," I have come to believe that the true species does not exist, and that atheism, so-called, is either an emotional deviation in the same category as neurotic illness and with a similar causation, or else the denial of the existence of a mythical figure who certainly does not exist. The latter type of "atheist" is welcome, for he helps us to find the true God and to exclude false ideas about him.

Nor by "agnostic" do I mean—to quote my dictionary—"one who holds that *nothing* is known or likely to be known of the existence of a God or of anything beyond material phenomena."

I am writing for the "Christian agnostic," by which I mean a person who is immensely attracted by Christ and who seeks to show his spirit, to meet the challenges, hardships and sorrows of life in the light of that spirit, but who, though he is sure of many Christian truths, feels that he cannot honestly and conscientiously "sign on the dotted line" that he believes certain theological ideas about which some branches of the church dogmatize; churches from which he feels excluded because he cannot "believe." His intellectual integrity makes him say about many things, "It may be so. I do not know."

So I am calling the book *The Christian Agnostic*. I wrote an article in *The Sunday Times* under this title, only to find, later, that, quite independently, my old friend, the Rev. Joseph McCulloch, Rector of the Church of St. Mary-le-Bow, Cheapside, London, had not only started a journal with this title but had gathered round him a group of highly intelligent people who call themselves "Christian Agnostics" and whom I have had the privilege of meeting and addressing. It is with his written and generous permission to do so that I use this title.

I believe passionately that Christianity is a way of life, not a theological system with which one must be in intellectual agreement. I feel that Christ would admit into discipleship anyone who sincerely desired to follow him, and allow that disciple to make his creed out of his experience; to listen, to consider, to pray, to follow, and ultimately to believe only those convictions about which the experience of fellowship made him sure.

This is how a man falls in love. He could not write a creed about the loved one at the beginning. He finds someone whose life he would like to share, and, if she is willing to do so, as fellowship deepens, he comes to believe certain things about her. Then he can write his creed, and it is of far more value, and much more his own, than if it were imposed upon him by someone else at the beginning as a condition of belonging to her. In my opinion, the beginnings of the Christian life have much in common with falling in love.

As things are, we are losing from the churches thoughtful and immensely worth-while folk, who do not feel at home in most churches because the language used either cannot be accepted by them, or else can only be used by making private mental reservations and interpretations which seem a species of intellectual dishonesty; of making words mean something quite different from the meaning in the minds of those who first wrote them down, such as, "I believe in the resurrection of the body." Originally men believed that the particles of the physical body magically rose from the grave, were knit into a heavenly body and went to live up in the sky. Even the learned St. Augustine taught that if, in a cannibal orgy, A devoured B, the flesh of B would be restored. He wrote, "The flesh of the man that was eaten shall return to the first owner from whom the famished man who ate it, does but, as it were, borrow it and must repay it again." [1] One wonders how long we shall be imprisoned in outworn ideas.

"I would not have believed," says Canon Harold Anson, Master of the Temple, in his autobiography, "If I had not heard it from a reliable witness, that a modern bishop could have said, in consecrating a churchyard in a particularly beautiful spot, 'How delightful for you all to know that at the last day you will rise to have this beautiful scene as your first view on the resurrection morning!' " [2] One wonders how the bishop would have regarded men lost at sea whose bodies were devoured by herrings which were afterwards devoured by other people! The degree of superstition still in religion is almost incredible.

"Because they cannot believe it [physical resurrection]," writes Sir Richard Acland, "they stay outside the church, even when they find the Spirit of Christ almost irresistibly magnetic." [3] Alas! that sentence is true of a dozen tenets of the church besides physical resurrection.

When we say, "Oh, but *we* mean, 'I believe in the survival of personality',", the modern layman wonders why we don't say so, since he lives in a world where he tries to make words mean what they say. Like Oliver Wendell Holmes he wonders what would happen to mathematics if two meant two to him, but twenty-two to another, and two hundred to a third, or if a chemist recited as a creed what I was taught as a boy, namely, that an atom is the smallest conceivable part of an element, with the mental reservation that by "atom" he meant "electron" or whatever label the smallest part of an atom now bears. He knows that religion is very different from science and that many words can only be symbols, but

[1] *City of God*, 22:20.
[2] Harold Anson, *Looking Forward*, p. 294 (Heinemann, 1938).
[3] Acland, *We Teach them Wrong*, p. 187 (International Publications Service, 1963).

he sees no point in reciting words that distort meaning and unnecessarily confuse his mind.[4]

With J. A. Froude, the historian, I wonder what the state of the health of this country would be like if, four hundred years ago, a committee of physicians had written down thirty-nine articles and demanded that, for ever after, physicians should prescribe according to them. Yet we have thirty-nine articles which every Anglican clergyman declares that he believes, containing among other credos that, "Christ did truly rise again from death and took again His body with flesh and bones, . . . wherewith He ascended into Heaven and there sitteth until He return to judge all men at the last day." [5] Further, the Prayer Book makes a preliminary declaration "prohibiting the least difference from the said articles" and demanding that they believed in their "true, usual and literal meaning." To make the point still clearer, and to preclude any from putting their tongue in their cheek, I read this, "No man hereafter shall either print or preach to draw the article aside in any way, but shall submit to it in the plain and full meaning thereof and shall not put his own sense or comment to be the meaning of the article but shall take it in the literal and grammatical sense." Why *do* men hug words to their hearts after the living truth has long since fled from them? Cries Stevie Smith,

> *Oh what do you mean, what do you mean?*
> *You never answer our difficulties.*[6]

[4] Since I wrote this preface, a leading article in *The Times* appeared containing the following (8/8/64), "It is not a sign of wickedness or even of irreligion for a man to confess that he does not believe in the Virgin Birth or the Resurrection. But there must appear something fundamentally false about such a man who will recite the Nicene Creed at the head of his congregation. The ordinary layman quite properly feels that if a man does not believe in the creed he should give up saying it. The modern churchman cannot expect ordinary men to respond to the patent insincerity of reciting the words regularly and then maintaining that they do not mean what they say."

[5] Article iv, "Of the Resurrection of Christ."

[6] *The Guardian*, May 16, 1964.

This book contains no sneer at the creeds and ancient statements of what some men used to believe. But they were written down to rebut current charges, not to impose formulae on future generations. Though not as important as loving, believing certainly matters. It matters so much that, if it has any relevance to the business of living, it must be born in the individual mind, not thrust by church authorities on others. Our young Davids cannot fight Goliath in Saul's armor.

This book is not an attempt to remove from the Christian religion all those things which the modern man finds it hard to believe, and to present, as it were, a theology easier on the mind, tailored to fit a nuclear age. Certainly I would not be any party to softening the stern challenge of Christ, as long as I was sure that the stern words really were Christ's and not the bad temper of his reporters.

The thoughtful layman often feels, however, that the churches are far more concerned to defend a hoary tradition than to follow the moving light of new insights and understanding; far more concerned to defend historic language than to discover truth. We talk much of the "faith which was once for all delivered to the saints." It is a dangerous phrase taken from the obscure book of Jude, which goes on to discuss Michael the Archangel contending with the devil and disputing with him about the body of Moses! [7] One remembers that electricity was "once for all" revealed to scientists, but they were not content to regard it only as a phenomenon produced by rubbing amber with the skin of a dead cat!

Unless we can break out of the prison of old-fashioned expressions, creeds and formularies, we shall never be free to find the far more glorious truths which are inherent in the Christian religion.

Here is a sentence from a letter addressed to me by a thoughtful layman, dated February 6, 1963. I have his written permission to quote, "I was brought up, christened and con-

[7] Jude 3 and 9.

firmed in the Church of England, but for many years I have been unable to cope with the dogma as set out in the Apostles' Creed. Try as I may, I am unable to accept the doctrine of the Holy Trinity except in a symbolic way, nor can I accept the Virgin Birth or the complete divinity of Jesus Christ or the physical resurrection of the body."

Dr. Whately Carington spoke for thousands when he wrote, "The churches are so deeply committed to a set of technical propositions, bound to appear either incredible, or offensive, or irrelevant to any reasonable man, that they alienate rather than attract just those whose support they most desire." He goes on to say, "As I see it, all questions regarding the factual accuracy of Biblical statements—notably such 'miraculous' events as Virgin Birth, Resurrection, etc.—are wholly irrelevant to the true issues. Indeed, I should go so far as to say myself that the whole value of the Gospel story to mankind —and it is very great—lies *not* in its historical but in its legendary, mythical, or 'typical' character. It is not, I think, the Sermon on the Mount—or at least not this alone—that constitutes the peculiar contribution of Christianity to human thought, for very similar maxims are to be found elsewhere, and in any event could be deduced from first principles. It is to be found, rather, in the affirmation that all that is best and highest in man, as typified in the person of Jesus, is bound to arouse opposition, is often persecuted and apparently destroyed—yet is in fact indestructible and does perennially 'rise again' triumphant over seeming disaster. It is because this affirmation is (as I believe) profoundly true, and because mankind has dimly yet tenaciously perceived it to be true, and because the Christian conception of the 'best in man' (as in the Sermon) is more advanced than that associated with the usual hero myths (physical prowess, etc.) that true Christianity can claim to be a faith worth holding." [8]

[8] Whately Carington, *Telepathy*, pp. 145-46 (Methuen, 1945).

This book would say to the modern layman, "Don't exclude yourself from the fellowship of Christ's followers because of mental difficulties. If you love Christ and are seeking to follow him, take an attitude of Christian agnosticism to intellectual problems at least for the present. Read this book to see if the essentials of the Christian religion are clarified for you and only accept those things which gradually seem to you to be true. Leave the rest in a mental box labeled, 'awaiting further light.' In the meantime, join in with us in trying to show and to spread Christ's spirit, for this, we feel, is the most important thing in the world."

No one can set out the truth about our most holy religion so that it is acceptable to all, and one wonders whether a religion whose profundities did not go deeper than all language, and, indeed, all thought, would suffice for man. Each thinker has the right to do what Paul did, to set forth truth as he sees it, in the thought-forms of his own day and generation, as long as he does not willfully distort truth merely to fit his own ideas. We have the right to do this too, and in many ways to disagree with Paul, who was admittedly inspired, but not more inspired than later thinkers in any sense which made him a finalist in his way of putting things.

In so many situations the church seems to be talking to itself, and as William Purcell so well said: "No church can afford to go on indefinitely talking to itself, once it has become concerned with meaning and no longer largely dependent on mystery. The mediaeval worshipper did not have to understand the Latin mutter of the Mass. The mutter itself was enough. But once the Scriptures and the language of worship have been translated into the vernacular, the question of meaning arises." [9]

Every effort made to express the Christian religion will be full of mistakes and half-truths and there must be large

---

[9] William Purcell, biography of *Woodbine Willie*, p. 130 (Hodder and Stoughton, 1962).

patches of reverent agnosticism in which the seeker is bound to say, "I just don't know," but we can say with Browning:

> God's gift was that man should conceive of truth
> And yearn to gain it, catching at mistake
> As midway help till he reach fact indeed.[10]

But it will be long before man does reach final truth, for as has been well said by Le Roy, "If dogmas formulated absolute truth in adequate terms, they would be unintelligible to us." The glorious fact is that the truth cannot be overthrown, and will more and more emerge as man's fearless questing brings him insight.

In this book I have used, where relevant, my studies in psychical research. I agree with Dr. Arthur Guirdham, "Man is at the present moment in the process of changing his nature. He is passing through a phase of evolution which will enable him to live on a more psychic plane. . . . He is preparing himself to live in a new and psychic dimension." [11] Few writers on Christianity have taken psychic factors into account, presumably because formerly the whole subject was bedeviled by cranks, cheats, fanatics and the self-deluded, and even now the standards by which evidence is assessed are far too low. But I prophesy that when this field is explored more fully by those who overcome their stony reluctance to enter the field of psychic research and who bring to its investigation the disciplines and methods of the real scientist, the reward for religion will be far greater than our present flirtation with physics. After all, the New Testament opens with a story about angels, continues with stories of telepathic communication and evil spirits cast out, relates an interview between our Lord and Moses and Elijah who had been dead for centuries, and is crowned by an account of one who rose from the dead, could pass through closed doors, appear and disappear, and

---

[10] Robert Browning, *A Death in the Desert.*
[11] *The Nature of Healing,* pp. 9-10 (Hillary, 1964).

who was seen after his death by hundreds of the faithful. Surely if there is one field of inquiry, not itself essentially religious, relevant to Christian understanding, it is that of serious psychical research. As Julian Huxley says, "We must follow up all clues to the existence of untapped possibilities like extra-sensory perception. They may prove to be as important and extraordinary as the once unsuspected electrical possibilities of matter," [12] and Professor H. J. Eysenck has commented that to call all psychic phenomena fraudulent is to imply that there is "a gigantic conspiracy involving some thirty University departments all over the world and several hundred respectable scientists in various fields." [13] I can only hope that what I have written may bring a reader a bit nearer to concepts of truth in which no violence is done to his mental processes; in which his mind can rest, his will be freed and his heart kindled. So may he find a closer bond with the living Christ, whose will is our mental peace and in whose service we find fulfillment.

I have made use of many footnotes. Some of them indicate my indebtedness to others. Some of them were put in after the first draft of the book had been typed. They gave me the comfort of the support of other writers! Footnotes attract me more than does a bibliography at the end of the book, to which readers rarely refer.

My wife, and my secretary, Miss E. B. Thompson, have given me unstinted and immense help in preparing this book for the Press. My younger son, Professor A. Kingsley Weatherhead, M.A., Ph.D., of the Department of English, in the University of Oregon, U.S.A., has read the manuscript of this book, and I am grateful for having had the chance of discussing it with him, and for some valuable suggestions which I have adopted. My son-in-law, Dr. Anthony D. Caunt,

[12] Sir Julian Huxley, article on "The Destiny of Man," (*The Sunday Times,* September 7, 1958).
[13] Professor H. J. Eysenck, *Sense and Nonsense in Psychology,* p. 131 (Pelican Books, 1957).

23

a scientist engaged in research, kindly read the book in proof, and I am also grateful to him for certain suggestions. My friends Sir James Barnes, K.C.B., K.B.E., and Mr. Norman French were kind enough to read the manuscript also, and to give me the benefit of their most valuable comments. But, of course, the responsibility for the views expressed in what follows is mine alone.

LESLIE D. WEATHERHEAD

CHAPTER I

DISSATISFACTION AND DISAPPOINTMENT

"O preacher, holy man, hear my heart weeping;
I long to stand and shout my protests:
Where is your power? and where is your message?
Where is the gospel of mercy and love?
Your words are nothingness! nothingness! nothingness!
We who have come to listen are betrayed.

Servant of God, I am bitter and desolate.
What do I care for perfection of phrase?
Cursed be your humour, your poise, your diction.
See how my soul turns to ashes within me.
You who have vowed to declare your Redeemer.
Give me the words that would save."

Margaret Chaplin Anderson
(A Wail from a Distressed Soul)

"If only we could have got down to basic principles more, we might now be able to argue with agnostics and atheists, instead of all being bested in argument and our faith laughed at."

Student at a teacher training college, quoted in
Dr. J. W. Daines' Enquiry into Religious Education.

"The human heart can go the lengths of God
Dark and cold we may be, but this
Is no winter now. The frozen misery
Of centuries breaks, cracks, begins to move;
The thunder is the thunder of the floes,
The thaw, the flood, the upstart Spring.
Thank God our time is now, when wrong
Comes up to face us everywhere,
Never to leave us till we take
The longest stride of soul men ever took,
Affairs are now soul size.
The enterprize
Is exploration into God.
Where are you making for? It takes
So many thousand years to wake,
But will you wake for pity's sake?"

Christopher Fry
(A Sleep of Prisoners)

I

DISSATISFACTION AND DISAPPOINTMENT

WE hear much these days of angry young men and women. I am an angry old man, and I feel I must get the fire out of my bones, as John Wesley would say, before I die. In 1960 I retired from the ministry of the City Temple, London, after over twenty-four years, and from the active Methodist ministry after forty-five years, and in my retirement I have had more time to listen, to study and to meditate. I have visited churches of every denomination and have talked with the men and women who belong to them. I have also talked with those who have no use for any of the churches, and I am sad and angry at the same time.

Not for much longer will the world put up with the lies, the superstitions and the distortions with which the joyous and essentially simple message of Christ has been overlaid. One thinks of the legend about the pipe which Moses the shepherd played when he gathered Jethro's sheep on the hillsides of Midian. As the years passed, it was treasured and revered and became a relic to be adored. For this, its simple structure seemed too plain, so workmen overlaid it with gold. It was highly respected but it could not be played. Its clear note was ruined and as a musical instrument it was useless. So the message of Galilee is overlaid with creeds and ceremonies and doctrines, and what with denominational squabbles, mutual disapprovals and intolerances, one can hardly catch the message of the Son of Man or be lifted up and strengthened by its beauty and power.

27

Every declaration of that message should bring the listener into communion with the living Christ and into touch with the unseen world of the spirit. If it did, that listener would find love kindled in his heart for every man, woman and child in the world. He would find that his pride and self-assertion, his cleverness and his wealth had become all but meaningless to him. He would feel humbled to the dust and yet exalted to the stars. He would know that his sins were forgiven, and he would feel that even his pain could be woven into a plan. All resentment, all rebellion, all grievance would just vanish. He would know that he was in the presence of one who so called forth his adoration and love that he could put down all his problems knowing that a mighty purpose enfolded all lives and would bring them at last to a goal, not just satisfying, but glorious beyond his power to imagine or conceive.

Christianity is a love relationship with Christ far below—or above, if you like—differences of belief or different ways of worshiping, far above differences of language or of color. The Christianity of tomorrow will embrace all truth wherever it is found or however men have come to apprehend it, whether through specifically Christian teaching or through Buddhism or Mohammedanism, Hinduism, Confucianism, Taoism, Zoroastrianism or even through the bleak desert of apparent atheism. Many of our greatest minds pass through the latter, feeling that to deny all is nearer the truth than to be identified with those who deny all approaches to truth save their own, and in their narrowness and exclusiveness deny love which is more fundamental than anything else.

Every denomination within organized Christianity contains a valuable truth, but none contains all truth. Each mirrors at its best something of Christ but all are only caricatures of him. The only value I can see in these endless conferences on unity is that we should grow to understand and love one another more truly and believe in one another. After all, a man's denomination is nearly always emotionally, not rationally, determined. Who among us has made a close study of Presbyterianism, Methodism, Anglicanism, Congregationalism, Roman Catholicism, and the Baptist position and then said, "Truth is here and to this branch of Christ's church I will give my adherence"? In the cases of nearly all of us, what our fathers were, we are, and we make up our reasons afterwards. There are a few exceptions like Newman going into Rome and John Tettemer coming out of it, but I know if I had been brought up in the Anglican Church I should now be a clergyman. If I had been brought up in the Baptist denomination I should have been a Baptist and argued that it is much more reasonable to follow the practice of baptism to which Jesus submitted, than to base an alleged essential sacrament of the church on one occasion when our Lord gathered a few kiddies up in his arms and cuddled them.

The essential in Christianity, past, present and future, is loving Christ and one another, and if the Quaker finds God in the silence and the Salvation Army in the band, the Roman Catholic in the Mass and the Baptist in immersion; if the High Anglican likes incense and ceremonial, and the Methodist puts his emphasis on personal experience, the fellowship of the authentic class meeting and Charles Wesley's hymns, why talk of disunity? The Air Force, the Navy and the Army can all serve the Queen, and, in the churches, what matters most is love of Christ, tolerance of one another and a passionate togetherness against every form of evil.

Frankly, I think that theological opinion is comparatively unimportant. If Christ can—and he does—hold in utter loyalty the hearts of St. Francis and John Knox, of Calvin and St. Theresa, of General Booth and Pope John, of Billy Graham and Albert Schweitzer, who hold irreconcilably different beliefs about him, how can belief and uniformity of belief be vitally important? Further, where in the Gospels are we ever told that Christ demanded belief in some theological proposition before he would admit a seeker into discipleship? The answer is that he never did. Belief *in* a person, yes. I believe *in* a host of my friends. I love them and I am certain that they would never do a mean or dirty trick or let me down by a breach of friendship. But friendship does not involve my agreeing with the intellectual positions which they hold. "I am confident," says Dr. J. H. Oldham in his splendid book, *Life Is Commitment*, "that if a single ray of light reaches a man from Christ, penetrates into his being and influences his way of living, he is further along the road towards true belief in Him than if he gave his unreflecting assent to a multitude of orthodox propositions which have no perceptible effect upon his conduct." [1]

Peter—as I see it—was a Christian the moment he accepted the invitation of Christ, "Follow me." "A Christian is someone who responds to the call of Christ. First and always Christianity is a relationship to a Person." [2] Peter knew nothing of, far less did he believe in, the Virgin Birth, the Trinity and many theological improbabilities which some men have demanded from their fellows before they allowed them the label, "Christian." This is far indeed from the attitude of Christ.

When people said to me, "I should like to be a member of the City Temple, what must I believe?" I used to say, "Only those things which appear to you to be true. These may increase or decrease as your discipleship deepens, but only loyalty to the Truth *as it authenticates itself* in your mind is asked from you. For one thing, believing theological dogmas was not Christ's test of those who sought to be his disciples, and for another very important and fundamental fact, you cannot *believe* a thing because you are told to believe it." Let me recall a favorite quotation from *Alice in Wonderland*. The Queen asserts that she is a hundred and one years, five months and one day old. "I can't believe that," said Alice. "Can't you?" said the Queen. "Try again. Draw a long breath and shut your eyes." Only by such a method can many a

[1] P. 70 (Student Christian Movement Press, 1952).
[2] A. Leonard Griffith, *What Is a Christian?* p. 11 (Abingdon Press, 1962).

Christian accept the improbabilities of his religion. You can *assent*, because you are afraid, or want to please, or haven't the energy or skill to think a thing out, but belief is a triumph of one's own mind. When I really believe a thing, I mean that its truth *possesses* me. "The penny drops," as we say! I do not have truth imposed on me. I don't impose it on myself. Truth is self-authenticating, and when it possesses me, nothing can shake it from its enthronement until some greater truth displaces it or gives it less prominence.

Christ called his disciples to follow him, to enter into a friendship with him. As their experience deepened certain great truths were born in their minds from observation, meditation, discussion and experience. These truths became their creeds, but they were not imposed on them by Christ or by the fellowship as a condition of "belonging." I am sure this is still the way for us, for no truth is of any value in personality until it is perceived to be true and received as a possession of the mind.

Yet recently, in a television interview, a distinguished and thoughtful layman, who seemed to me hungry for all that Christ can give a man, was brushed off by an eminent dignitary of a certain denomination, because the layman said he could not accept the Virgin Birth. Jesus would not thus have turned him away. Jesus never mentioned the Virgin Birth, neither was it for centuries any part of the missionary message of the church. We still make of prime importance matters about which Jesus said nothing. How can a matter be fundamental in a religion when the founder of the religion never mentioned it? And all this goes, not for the Virgin Birth only, but for a dozen improbabilities about which not even a reverent agnosticism is allowed by the die-hard Scribes and Pharisees of today, and the sad result is that we lose from Christian discipleship some of the ablest minds of our time.

Said Brunner, in an indignation which I share, "Who can establish criteria to judge whether or not the Holy Ghost is really active in a human heart to which God is only just

31

beginning to reveal Himself? Who would wish to propose criteria of membership which in certain circumstances would exclude precisely those whom God in secret has begun to draw unto Himself? The boundaries of the church face to face with the world must therefore remain invisible to the eyes of men; a full dogmatic confession can deceive just as much as the entire absence of any such thing." [3]

It is this unfair demand that to be a Christian one must "believe" this and that intellectual proposition which has put so many thoughtful and lovable people off. "Must" and "believe" are words that should never go together. We blame people for not going to church, and we call them pagan, or indifferent, or materialistic, or careless, but the truth is that Christianity as purveyed does not seem relevant to their needs or their outlook.

This is a book for laymen, and my aim is, in complete loyalty to Christ and what I believe to be essential Christianity, to win back some of the finest men and women I have ever known who are estranged from both, because, being intellectually honest, they cannot "sign on the dotted line" that they believe certain theological dogmas. As one wrote to me on March 8, 1963, "I feel that it is morally wrong to stand up in God's house and say you believe in something which you do not." Many laymen hate the idea of saying one thing and meaning another, making dishonest mental reservations or putting their tongues in their cheeks when they are required to recite the creeds and follow language which needs a theological education to be understood. As Sir Julian Huxley said recently, "The old ideas will no longer serve; the old ideological framework can no longer be tinkered up to bear the weight of the facts and a radical reconstruction becomes necessary." [4] As Professor Henry Chadwick of Christ Church, Oxford, says in the Gifford Lectures given at St. Andrew's

[3] Brunner, *Misunderstanding of the Church*, p. 109, quoted from *Soundings*, ed. Vidler, p. 260 (Cambridge University Press, 1962).
The Observer, March 31, 1963.

University on April 25, 1963: "The central theme of Christian doctrine is God and His self-manifestation not only in the creation but also in particular in Christ as the expression of God in terms of a personal life and the unique model for our relation to God.

"From the earliest time it has been characteristic for Christian believers to "confess" their faith in the form of credal or quasi-credal affirmation. The primary function of the affirmation was not so much to test the correctness of an individual's doctrinal beliefs as to act as a pledge of loyalty and expression of confidence in God.

"The temper of the ancient church was not initially favourable to the imposition of doctrinal tests. Testing orthodoxy by creeds was a secondary function which came into much prominence during the unhappy controversy of the fourth and fifth centuries; and by many important theologians of the time the process was regarded as a most regrettable necessity."

Well, as for me, I acknowledge no such necessity. Christ did not do so. He drew word-pictures called parables with such winsome clarity that men, gazing upon them and meditating on them, could SEE the truth. No argument or logic carries the same degree of conviction as *insight*, and it is the kind of conviction by which we know that dawn over the Alps on a perfect morning is beautiful. Argument cannot produce it and doubt cannot remove it. The outward beauty meets the inward recognition and in our hearts we *know*.

CHAPTER II

AGNOSTICISM AND DOUBT

"All intelligent faith in God has behind it a background of humble agnosticism."

The Rev. Dr. Harry Emerson Fosdick
(*Dear Mr. Brown*)

"I believe that one should be agnostic when belief one way or the other is mere idle speculation, incapable of verification; when belief is held merely to gratify desires, however deep-seated, and not because it is forced on us by evidence; and when belief may be taken by others to be more firmly grounded than it really is, and so come to encourage false hopes or wrong attitudes of mind."

Sir Julian Huxley
(*Religion Without Revelation*)

"I am astonished at the boldness with which people undertake to speak of God."

Pascal
(*Pensées*)

"Many a humble agnostic, worshipping an unknown God, is nearer to the Kingdom of God than is a theologian confident in *his* theology. . . . Many an 'atheist' is rejecting false conceptions of God which he assumes to be Christian beliefs about Him. Many an agnostic has a reverence for the unknown God which puts to shame the pride of a superficial dogmatist."

Principal the Rev. Dr. Frederic Greeves,
Ex-President of the Methodist Conference
(*The Meaning of Sin*)

"The mistake which 'orthodox' people make is to suppose that they have all the truth and that nothing more can be known."

The Rev. Dr. W. R. Matthews,
The Dean of St. Paul's

"As one goes on, it is the things one doesn't believe, and finds one doesn't have to believe, which are as liberating as the things one does."

The Bishop of Woolwich
(*Honest to God*)

"The real breakthrough began when I realised that I had far more in common with the honest agnostic than with the average Christian."

A Free Church Minister
(*The Honest to God Debate*)

"Consciously, I was religious in the Christian sense, though always with the reservation: 'But it is not so certain as all that.'"

C. G. Jung
(*Memories, Dreams, Reflections*)

II

AGNOSTICISM AND DOUBT

I SHALL be accused in this book of paring down Christianity to meet the inability of the modern man to believe anything he cannot prove; of diminishing its august doctrines in order to make it easier for men to receive it.

I am awake to this danger and do not think I have fallen into it. I claim rather that an immense amount has been added to the true teaching of Jesus—which surely must determine what is essential Christianity—and that accretions to it have, in many cases, become substitutes for it. A message which could be likened to a magnificent steed, on which a man might ride in splendid adventure to the end of the world, has been so weighed down by saddle and cloth, so restrained by bridle and bit, that the horse can hardly move, and indeed, in the modern world, except in the case of a few live centers and secret saints, hardly does carry anyone anywhere. "It is of the greatest importance," said Sir Julian Huxley, "that humanity should now and again take out its beliefs for spring-cleaning." [1]

There is much about God and his dealings with men concerning which I feel I can say, "I know." There are basic certainties which have possessed my mind with such powerful tenacity that I feel that their denial, or the assertion of their opposites, finds no answering echo in my mind. Indeed, concerning some things, denial would outrage the

[1] Sir Julian Huxley, *Religion Without Revelation*, p. 121 (Max Parrish, 2nd ed., 1959).

workings of my mind. The "feeling" part of my mind, as well as my intellect, have made them a part of myself.

These certainties will emerge as this book proceeds. They are summarized in the last chapter. But when one lets one's mind meditate on the universe that is now being unfolded to us by one staggering discovery after another, how can one possibly believe that man, by any form of words, based on any possible kind of authority or revelation, can imprison all the activities of its Creator?

I live now near the sea. My garden gate is a hundred and fifty yards from the beach. I can see the sea from this desk at which I write, and in the deep midnight I can hear its ceaseless music as I lie in bed. I have only to walk down to the shore and get a beaker full of water and have it chemically analyzed to know the *nature* of the vast Atlantic of which it is a part. But what can a beaker of salt water tell me about what goes on in the vast, silent depths of the ocean, or of the majestic, terrifying storms which sweep across it, or of its incredible power?

Jesus, if one may be allowed so to express the matter reverently, was a vessel full of God. Any man, to the extent to which he is good, reveals the nature of God. Christ tells me as much about the *nature* of God as I need to know or am capable of knowing. But because he remains man he cannot tell me everything about the *activities* of God, nor could I receive it if he could, Jesus, if one may so put it, contained as much of God as can be poured into a man without disrupting his humanity and making him a monstrosity, but because he maintained his unbroken humanity I cannot, even from him, learn all I should like to know about God's activities. There are limitations in human nature, however glorified by the Divine, as there are limitations in a beaker when one seeks to explore all the secrets of the Atlantic. But I know the sea is salt even from the contents of a homely vessel and I know that God is love even by contemplating the man, Christ Jesus.

Added to the limitations of Christ, because of his humanity, are the limitations of the receiving human brain when finite man seeks to follow the activities of an Infinite God, and the creature seeks to comprehend the Creator.

I spoke to my people at the City Temple about an ant which I found crawling along the cushions on the edge of the pulpit while I was preaching there. It came to a gap where one cushion almost touched another, paused and hesitated, looked this way and that, and then descended the slope of one cushion edge, crossed and mounted the other. I wish now that I had helped it across the gap, but I might only have frightened it and muddled it up! I could only imagine its sense of triumph, and hope that it wasn't late home for lunch! I meditated on it often. It had no idea of *my* relationship to it, or indeed of my existence. It did not know it was in one of the most famous pulpits in the world! The concept "cushion" had no meaning, let alone "pulpit" or "City Temple" or "London" or "England" or "Europe" or "the world"! It had never heard of the *raison d'être* of a church. It had no object, let us imagine, save to get home.

Man is very precious to God, so I believe, and can be in a close and loving relationship with Him, but *intellectually* man probably knows as little of the vast, far-reaching activities of God as that ant knows about preaching, let alone about the wider life of the world. How can man, an insect on a wayside planet, which is itself of no size or importance, amid a million galaxies that baffle the imagination, put the tiny tape of words around the doings of this august and unimaginable Being who created all that is in the heavens and the heaven of heavens. There are, it is said, 100,000 million stars per galaxy, and in the visible universe 100,000 million galaxies. Their Creator, as Job said, "maketh the Bear, Orion and the Pleiades Who doeth great things past finding out, yea marvellous things without number." [2] I know he must be love

[2] Job 9:9-10.

just as I know the sea is salt, but I have no possibility of knowing all his activities any more than, from a beaker of water, I can understand the mystery of the tides. I was intrigued by a story told by a correspondent in *The Observer* (April 7, 1963). "Imagine," he said, "a family of mice who lived all their lives in a large piano, just as we live our lives in our fragment of the universe. And to them in their piano-world came the music of the instrument, filling all the dark spaces with sound and harmony. At first the mice were very much impressed by it. They drew comfort and wonder from the thought that there was Someone who made the music—though invisible to them—above, yet close to them. And they loved to think of the Great Player whom they could not see. Then one day a daring mouse climbed up part of the piano and returned very thoughtful. He had found out how the music was made. Wires were the secret; tightly stretched wires of graduated lengths which trembled and vibrated. They must revise all their old beliefs: none but the most conservative could any longer believe in the Unseen Player. Later, another explorer carried the explanation further. Hammers were now the secret, numbers of hammers dancing and leaping on the wires. This was a more complicated theory, but it all went to show that they lived in a purely mechanical and mathematical world. The Unseen Player came to be thought of as a myth.—But the pianist continued to play the piano."

A million planets, for all I know, may be inhabited. How childish to think ours is the only one! "Venus," said an astronomer lately, "may be now in the condition the earth was once in, and the mist around it may be caused by a cooling process similar to what the earth has known." [3] Life like our own may develop on it in another five hundred million years. It would be as foolish to deny this as it was once foolish to

---

[3] Francis Jackson in a B.B.C. program, December 16, 1962, said that 5,000 million years ago the earth was much like Venus is now. He added: "Life is probably widely spread throughout the universe."

suppose that the earth was the center of the solar system
or that the sun traveled obsequiously round it.

Sir Bernard Lovell, one of our greatest living astronomers,
said in Moscow on July 15, 1963, that he believed there were
many communities of other beings in different parts of the
universe (*The Times,* July 16, 1963), and he spoke in a television program on March 3, 1963, of the "high degree of
probability of life on other planets." Soviet scientists, Mr.
Mates Agrest, and a scientific writer, Mr. Alexander Kazant-
sev, claim to have discovered "tectites," pieces of a fused glass-
like substance which, they say, could not have appeared without causative factors outside the earth. They claim that space
travelers visited the earth in prehistoric times and that the
ruins of an ancient shrine at Baalbek in the Lebanons are the
remains of a "spacedrome built by travelers from the cosmos."
Perhaps, after all, the "flying saucers" exist! There is a mass
of evidence of unidentified objects having been seen in the
sky.

May not God, then, be working among men on other
planets? "Incarnation" may not be the appropriate word, for
it implies "flesh," but may God not have clothed himself on
other planets with whatever means of self-manifestation those
who live on them use? To deny this possibility goes far beyond our right and our knowledge. It is the mentality which
persecuted Galileo. But if it *is* possible, what happens to the
doctrine of the Trinity? God may not be three in one but
three million in one. And how can we speak of the "*only-*
begotten Son of God"? Can man ever use the word "only"
unless all is known? May not a hundred or a thousand Sons
of God have carried God's message of love to other planets?
To me this glorifies the Gospel, not diminishes it.

> No planet knows that this
> Our wayside planet, carrying land and wave,
> Love and life multiplied, and pain and bliss
> Bears, as chief treasure, one forsaken grave . . .

> *O be prepared, my soul!*
> *To read the inconceivable, to scan*
> *The million forms of God those stars unroll*
> *When, in our turn, we show to them a Man.*[4]

Surely a reverent agnosticism is the only possible attitude here.

How childish in this context the Athanasian Creed sounds! Here is part of it: "Whosoever will be saved before all things it is necessary that he hold the Catholic Faith, which Faith except everyone do keep whole and undefiled, without doubt he shall perish everlastingly. And the Catholic Faith is this: That we worship one God in Trinity, and Trinity in Unity; neither confounding the Persons, nor dividing the Substance. For there is one Person of the Father, another of the Son and another of the Holy Ghost . . . the Father uncreate, the Son uncreate and the Holy Ghost uncreate. The Father incomprehensible, the Son incomprehensible and the Holy Ghost incomprehensible. . . . There are not three incomprehensibles nor three uncreated, but one uncreated and one incomprehensible. . . . He therefore that will be saved must thus think of the Trinity."

Many I fear will be unsaved—whatever that means—for few "thus think of the Trinity," and all students with common sense let alone a knowledge of psychology know that "must think" is an impossible marriage of incompatible words. Their divorce is certain immediately in any normal and unfrightened intelligence. Thought must be free to range as it likes over all phenomena and philosophy, unhampered by compulsions. A man cannot be bludgeoned by vulgar threats of damnation, into accepting that what other people say is true.

How much more impressive to modern ears are the reverent words of Hooker! "Dangerous it were, for the feeble brain of man to wade far into the doings of the Most High, whom, although to know be life, and joy to make mention of His

---

[4] Alice Meynell, *Christ in the Universe.*

name, yet our soundest knowledge is to know that we know Him not as indeed He is, neither can know Him. Our safest eloquence concerning Him is our silence when we confess without confession that His glory is inexplicable, His greatness above our capacity and reach. He is above, and we upon earth, therefore it behoveth our words to be wary and few." [5] Professor H. R. Mackintosh speaks of "the audacious and contemptible illusion that we have fathomed or surrounded God by our eager cogitations." [6] "It is difficult to conceive of God," said Gregory of Nazianzus, "but to define Him in words is an impossibility . . . It is impossible to express Him, and yet more impossible to conceive Him."

How finely Cecil Day Lewis protests, in one of his poems, against the conceit of supposing that we can comprehend God.

> *God is a proposition*
> *And we that prove Him are His priests, His chosen.*
> *From base hypothesis*
> *Of strata and wind, of stars and tides, watch me*
> *Construct His universe*
> *A working model of my majestic notions.*
> *A sum done in the head.*
> *Last week I measured the Light, His little finger,*
> *The rest is a matter of time.* [7]

Why, even a little child of five, knowing himself loved, cannot understand or be made to understand the activities of his father. Supposing the latter is a surgeon. Supposing some ill-intentioned person says to the boy, "Your father has people made unconscious with a drug, and then, when they are helpless, he has them stretched on a table, cuts their bodies with knives and then sends them a bill!" What could a boy do but rest in the certainty of the love-relationship, believe by faith based on other evidence that his father was doing good,

---

[5] *Ecclesiastical Polity*, Book I, Chap. ii, Section 3, p. 201. Seventh edition.
[6] *The Person of Christ*, p. 518.
[7] Cecil Day Lewis, *Collected Poems* (Hogarth Press).

and, in a humble agnosticism, leave the intellectual problem unsolved? How monstrous it would be to tell the boy that he "must think" this or that about his father, or to cast him out of the family because he could not honestly do so. Yet the church at her worst does something like this to some of the earth's finest men and women. "You must think this or that," it thunders. You "must believe" or be cast out. But surely, in so many matters, a reverent agnosticism is the only place where the Christian can rest his mind, remembering that the gap between a child's comprehension and his father's activities is nothing compared with the gap between the wisest man's understanding and the scope of God's activity. The former gap will close as the child grows up. It is hard to believe that the latter gap will ever close unless men become gods. We move mentally in a twilight of wonder. Beauty, truth and goodness seem to speak of him, but, if we are wise, we confess with Job: "These are but the fringes of His ways. How small a whisper do we hear of Him." [8]

If God's purposes in the world were complete, to understand them would be beyond man's puny intellect, but we have it on the highest authority that God has only made a beginning with us. No wonder then that to us the world is unintelligible and the problem of evil insoluble. As the New English Bible translates a most pregnant saying of Jesus, we read, "My Father has never yet ceased His work and I am working too." [9] So that, added to the problem of understanding made difficult because we are like tiny children, is the further complication that we are not looking at a completed piece of work, but at the first half-dozen moments in a long play. Who can judge a play or understand its plot until the curtain falls? Those who are so certain that they can understand God's ways with us, sufficiently to deny any purpose in them, seem to me like toddlers who drift into a theatre as the curtain rises, watch the stage for five minutes, hear an incom-

[8] Job 26:14   [9] John 5:17

prehensible dialogue, and then drift out to tell their fellow infants that it is all nonsense and means nothing.

The certainties of the Christian Faith are very precious to me. They are what I call the essentials, and they are very few. Yet they are sufficient. To add to them and embroider them and then to demand belief in what has been added, as well as in the fundamentals, seems to me a criminal activity which has lost for us, and is still losing, some of the finest minds the world has known.

Let me instance the case of Darwin. In his autobiography [10] there is a sad passage in which he says that he was "very unwilling to give up" his belief in Christianity, but at last, he wrote, "disbelief crept over me at a very slow rate, but was at last complete." He adds this sentence: "I can hardly see how anyone ought to wish Christianity to be true; for, if so, the plain language of the text seems to show that the men who do not believe—and this would include my father, brother, and almost all my best friends—will be everlastingly punished. And this is a damnable doctrine."

I am sure we can only re-commend Christianity to the thoughtful men of today by a restatement which admits a large degree of agnosticism, eliminates magic, dispenses with imposed authority, and abolishes, from our conception of God, horror and cruelty which would degrade a man, let alone God. Such a restatement should not put up credal walls, let alone allow them to exclude loving souls who seek to follow Christ. He never demanded from anyone support for theological propositions, but told us to love God and our fellows and to react in all crises in the spirit which animated him, and which still calls forth our worship and adoration.

[10] *The Autobiography of Charles Darwin*, ed. by Nora Barlow, pp. 86-87 (Collins, 1958).

CHAPTER III

AUTHORITY AND CERTAINTY

"Let us seek to fathom those things that are fathomable and reserve those things which are unfathomable for reverence in quietude."

Goethe

"All we know is still infinitely less than all that still remains unknown. . . . The studious and good never think it unworthy of them to change their opinion, if truth and undoubted demonstration require them so to do; nor do they deem it discreditable to desert error, though sanctioned by the highest antiquity."

Dr. William Harvey
(*An Anatomical Disquisition on the Motion of the Heart and Blood of Animals*)

Broadcast interview between John Freeman and Lord Birkett.

" 'What sort of upbringing did you have in childhood?' Mr. Freeman continued his line of questioning. 'I mean, were your family puritanical and stern?'

" 'Well, my father and mother, they were Wesleyan Methodists,' Birkett answered, 'and I suppose one would say they were very, very devoted people. I shall always be grateful for my home life and for the chapel life to which they led me. My knowledge of the Authorised Version and the hymns of Wesley and Watts are certainly some of my very greatest possessions, and at the most formative period of my life I shall never cease to be grateful for the training I had in religious things.'

" 'Do you still hold these beliefs yourself?'

" 'No. You know, as one grows older one rather grows out of certain ideas, and, although I have my own very strong views about the conduct of life and the qualities which are necessary for the conduct of life, the great doctrinal things rather perplex me and trouble me.'

"Mr. Freeman now posed a most pertinent question.

" 'Would you in fact describe yourself as a Christian, or not?'

Birkett paused for a moment or two before replying, 'I would call myself a Christian,' he said, 'but, of course, as it was once said, you've got to define your terms. If you mean, do I believe in what are called *Christian* qualities, I most certainly do.'

" 'But not perhaps in the Thirty-Nine Articles?'

" 'I sometimes would like to say that I called myself a Christian agnostic,' said Birkett to this question, 'but I don't know whether that term is permissible.' "

H. Montgomery Hyde
(*Norman Birkett, The Life of Lord Birkett of Ulverston*)

III

AUTHORITY AND CERTAINTY

IN view of all which was written in the last chapter on agnosticism, the reader will naturally ask: "Must we then give up certainty in religion? Can we be said to know anything for sure, and if so, how do we reach certainty?"

For myself, I can say that I am quite certain about what I regard as the essential basis of the Christian religion. But the more I think about it the more I am convinced that there is only one authority in this field, and that is the authority which truth itself possesses when it is perceived to be true by the individual concerned; or, in other words, when it authenticates itself.

I know this view will be violently contested. I shall be told that to assess what is true by such a method is far too subjective; that it makes truth far too dependent on the powers, vision and decision of the individual, and so on. But the alternative procedure, the delegation to external authority, must itself follow an individual's subjective decision. It is *I* who finally decides to submit to the authority, say of the Bible or the Pope or the creeds. Of course, I realize that very many things may be true which *I* cannot perceive to be such, and that which I feel to be true may be only partially so. But to be *told* they are true has no *authority* at all though I may reverence deeply the person who tells me they seem true to him. Religious truth has no authority, no value in personality, until it authenticates itself, until the mind leaps up and sees it true, and accepts it, not because its truth is *imposed*, or its

49

refusal dreaded, but because it is *seen* to be true. "I have *seen*," said the saintly St. Thomas Aquinas, "that which makes all that I have previously taught and written seem as chaff to me." To be told I am forgiven by God does not bring me release of mind unless I accept readily and embrace in my secret heart the truth that God forgives.

In a Y.M.C.A. tent pitched on the banks of the Tigris, in Mesopotamia, one night early in 1918, returning after a long sojourn in the desert where, as a young staff-officer, I had lived with Arabs, there came to me, who had long assented to the idea of forgiveness and offered it to others, a sudden overwhelming sense of being possessed by this truth for the first time. No outward authority or teaching of the church had brought me the authority which that experience brought. It was utterly convincing and final and no one could take it from me.

This is a matter of such tremendous importance that I shall take a chapter to expound it. Men glibly turn to an infallible Bible, or an infallible church, or an infallible Pope, or an infallible conscience, or an infallible Christ, and say that that authority is sufficient for them and enables them to accept truth. I believe all that kind of talk is false. It is false psychology or a failure of insight, and it is the fruit of mental laziness; a refusal to think things through. The most important convictions in religion cannot really be *reached* on the word of another. We can *assent* to propositions out of laziness of thought, or a desire to please, or an inability to argue, but one of the reasons why, in a crisis, men often feel let down by their religion is that they glibly assented to this and that, and falsely called their assent "belief." The facts to which they had assented clearly had no authority to convince, though many such facts had been repeated every Sunday in church and the worshipers had falsely supposed that such a process would give them certainty. They had let a whole army of ideas march through the country of their minds, but the army had never conquered the country, never taken over the running of it, directing its economy and ordering its life. To take a painful example, many supposed that because they were Christians their homes would escape destruction by bombing during the Second World War. Were they not devout readers of the Bible, and had not the Bible final authority, and did not the Bible say, "There shall no evil befall thee nor shall any hurt come nigh thy dwelling"? [1] On the night they escaped, they felt that their religious faith was justified. Though others suffered the loss of home and loved ones, did not the Bible say, "A thousand shall fall at thy side and ten thousand at thy right hand but it shall not come nigh thee"? On the night their house *was* struck they not only lost their house but their faith as well. And many were made to doubt the whole value and truth of religion. Having accepted ideas merely because they wished they were true, and which they had found in the Bible, and having found those ideas repudiated by bitter experience, they threw away the baby of any religious certainty about anything with the bathwater of superstition. Into this matter of authority in religion, then, we must look with some care.

A good place to start is a definition. I suggest that authority is the power to coerce one into acceptance. The policeman has authority. He holds up his hand and coerces the motorist into acceptance of the idea that he must stop! Similarly the teacher in a school has authority, the power to make one do things. Years ago, parents had authority also, and could coerce children into accepting their will!

In matters of religion I hold the view that authority lies only in the perception of truth by the individual, a perception which is not a matter of facts or arguments thrust on the mind from without, but is the mind's intuitive recognition of those facts as true, an activity of the mind from within. As Browning said of Guido in "The Ring and the Book":

[1] Psalm 91:10.

> *So shall the truth be flashed out in one blow,*
> *And Guido see one instant and be saved.*

In his book, *Irrational Man, a Study in Existential Philosophy*, Professor William Barrett of New York University points out that the Greek word for "I know," *oida*, is the perfect of the verb "to see," and means, "I have seen." "He who knows is the man who has seen." [2] I hold that the self-authentication of truth, or, in other words, *seeing*, is the authority, and the *only* authority there is in the field of religion. A passage from Browning's "Paracelsus" puts the matter wonderfully:

> *Truth is within ourselves; it takes no rise*
> *From outward things, whate'er you may believe.*
> *There is an inmost centre in us all*
> *Where truth abides in fulness; and around,*
> *Wall upon wall, the gross flesh hems it in,*
> *This perfect, clear perception—which is truth.*
> *A baffling and perverting carnal mesh*
> *Binds it and makes all error, and to know*
> *Rather consists in opening out a way*
> *Whence the imprisoned splendour may escape*
> *Than in effecting entry for a light*
> *Supposed to be without.*

The same idea is in the old Latin tag, "*Non foras ire, in interiore homine habitat veritas.*" (Go not without, for within man dwells the truth.)

Now here religion is different from many other spheres of human interest and thought. In science, for example, we talk about "consulting our authorities," and if they are sufficiently eminent and unanimous, they have power to coerce our opinion, though not always to the point of acceptance. This is particularly true in a science like astronomy in which we ourselves have no equipment to judge the evidence or to check the consclusions, or to put forward an opposite view. There-

---

[2] P. 72. Heinemann (1961) and in Mercury Books (1964).

fore, if one astronomer says a star is ten million light-years from another, we, unless we are astronomers, accept his authority. He has power to coerce our judgment and we leave the matter there, perhaps subconsciously comforted by the thought that he is not merely guessing; that *if* we had the ability, training and equipment we could check up on what he says.

But now I want to ask the reader to consider what I think is a most important point: Where personal emotion is involved, a different kind of tension from that set up by a clash of intellectual opinions follows. It is a tension between the opinion of the authority and our own. In other words, where our emotions are involved, what *we* think begins to count. In astronomy I am content to accept the authority of the expert. His conclusion does not touch my personal emotion at all, save perhaps that the emotions of awe and wonder are stimulated. But when the matter comes close to my personal life, and affects me emotionally, my own opinion rears its head and demands to be heard.

We say that the mathematician is a scientist and that his authority must be respected. But supposing we give him a sum to do and he works it out and tells us that the answer is $50. If personal emotion is not involved, we tend to accept the result as right and authoritative. But supposing the answer to the sum is the amount an aunt has left us, might we not challenge it thus: "That can't be right, I am sure she left me much more than that. Do you mind working it out again?"— when, let us hope, the answer is found to be $5,000!

The factor that makes us question the authority of the expert is that we are personally emotionally involved in the result.

Take another illustration. In regard to the physical condition of our hearts, we might say that the heart specialist is the expert. He speaks with authority. We do not understand the physical working of a human heart as he does. Certainly we do not understand the situation created by heart disease. We call him in. We ask his opinion and he gives it with authority. But if, concerning our dearest, he says, "She has only a short time to live," immediately we resist his authority and say: "But that is incredible. I must have another opinion." In other words, we challenge the authority and remain unconvinced because we are personally and emotionally involved.

Our illustrations reach a climax when we try to imagine that someone is in love and talks to an expert. Supposing the expert says: "Listen! I know a lot about love. I have written books about love. I have been consulted by hundreds of people in love, and I am telling you, on my authority, that you are not in love." What lover would accept such "authority"?

If we turn for a moment to music and art and literature, I think the matter becomes clearer still, because all these things involve personal emotion. Let us imagine that someone sits down at a grand piano and perfectly plays a sonata of Beethoven. It is frankly no use anyone saying to me: "You *must* enjoy this because it is by Beethoven. He is an undisputed authority in music, and who are you, anyway?" I can be made to feel very ashamed and humiliated that I do not enjoy it, and it is fair that I should be told that so many people do enjoy it, that I ought to listen repeatedly until its beauty enters my nature and captures my conviction. But you just cannot impose Beethoven's authority on a non-musical person. There is a great gulf, which, for the time being is "fixed." He is not convinced by the so-called authority. It is not authoritative because it does not convince.

There are art galleries to which people go and buy a catalogue which not only describes the pictures and tells you who painted them, but it tells you which pictures to enjoy! So you will see a lot of people gathered round a picture they are told is a great picture, and you may overhear them vaporing about it with shallow, superficial comments, when, in truth, they would not know any difference if it were turned upside down! A friend of mine, I rather think for fun, actually sent a daub of his own into an exhibition and said it was in the

Picasso style. He actually saw it in the exhibition upside down! Yet he sold it for $10. Somebody had been told by somebody else that it was a good picture. I believe the painter did it in ten minutes!

So it is with literature. People will pretend that they enjoy a sonnet of Shakespeare, but if they did not know Shakespeare had written it, they would exhibit the boredom they still secretly feel. You cannot say, "This is by Shakespeare, an artist whose creative ability is indubitable, therefore you must enjoy it."

I hope that by now a principle of authority is emerging. These things, music, art and literature, have no authority *in themselves*. They have no power to convince. They involve our emotions, and therefore we resist being convinced, if we are honest, until some faculty within us responds with a response which is *authoritative*.

In all these three things, *following training*, something that the artist has done, as it were, leaps out of the work of art, and is grasped by our own inner apprehension, and, in that intuitive leap of the mind by which it grasps beauty and possesses it, is the *authority* of beauty.

Now let us turn to religion, and do distinguish between religion and theology, just as you distinguish between the enjoyment of flowers and botany. Religion is an intensely personal and emotional matter. If being in love with another *human person* is emotional, isn't it likely that religion has an intense personal content? The very word "*religio*" from "*re-ligare*," to bind, means a link—a ligament—between the soul and God—in a sense, being in love with God. *The authority, then, in religion, is my inner response to the religious truth put before me.*

Some writers express the same idea when they write of truth "finding them." Thus Professor Moffatt, in the *Approach to the New Testament*, quotes Origen in the third century saying, "The words of the Bible *find me* at greater depths of my being; and whatever finds me brings with it an irresistible evidence of its having proceeded from the Divine Spirit." Coleridge, in the nineteenth century, used almost the same language as Origen. He says: "I have found words for my inmost thoughts, songs for my joy, utterances for my hidden griefs, and pleadings for my shame and feebleness. In short, whatever *finds me* bears witness for itself that it has proceeded from the Holy Spirit." And later still, Dr. A. T. Cadoux wrote in one of his essays, "When we ask how we are to know what writings are inspired we are driven to find the criterion in the response they evoke from something within us."

In theology I may be told many things and accept them on the authority of the theologian, for he may speak of facts which do not have any personal emotional content at all. I frankly do not mind who wrote the first five books of the Bible or the Psalms. The claim that Jesus was Virgin born does not stir me emotionally in the least. But when you talk to me about the love of God, his care for the individual, his readiness to forgive my sins, his offer of a transforming friendship and so on, then I am personally and emotionally involved and authority will not lie with the speaker, nor will it lie with the hearer. It will lie in a clinch between what both offer: the idea presented and *its perception by personality*, its intuitive grasp by the mind.

The reader may counter all this by saying, "Truth is truth whatever *you* happen to think about it, and it is conceited and egotistical of you so to stress *your* apprehension of it."

I am saying that truth may certainly be true whatever my opinion may be, but it has no *authority* with me until I perceive it to be true. When I do, reality has spoken to me. This is not conceit. As John Oman once said, "True humility is not submission to human authority but *total disregard of it when reality speaks to us*." [3]

Consider, in the light of these thoughts, the authority of

[3] Principal John Oman, *The Natural and the Supernatural*, p. 101 (Cambridge University Press). Italics mine.

the church. Surely, one might argue, the scholars and doctors of the church are better equipped than I to decide the truth.[4] Who am I to set up my poor judgment against them? Is there not a danger that we may reject the infallible church and the infallible book only to enthrone an infallible self?

I too feel the force of the point. But I can no more find authority, that is, power to convince me of the truth, *because* of the church's declarations, than I can be convinced that a sonata is beautiful because Beethoven wrote it. In both cases the fault may be with me and I must sit down again before both the alleged truth and the alleged beauty and let them impress a mind which I strive to free from bias. But no *authority* is experienced, I claim, in either case until truth and beauty are perceived. I love the story of Luther who asked a charcoal burner what he believed. The man replied, "What the church believes." "That is not believing," said Luther, "*It is not your own.*" It is interesting that the Upanishads distinguish between "received doctrine" (smriti) and "intuitively experienced truth" (sruti). Aldous Huxley expounds this fully in *The Perennial Philosophy*.

My plea is not for an impossible subjectivism. But the so-called infallible church or book has no power unless I *feel* that what it says is true. And who can decide that but myself? "The teaching," said Plotinus, "is of the path and the place. Seeing is the work of each soul for itself." Everything depends for authority on my inner response to the impact of the alleged "infallible" statement. The final authority is bound to be the "inner light." [5] "I do not know the truth," said Kierkegaard, "except when it becomes part of me."

I entirely agree with my friend, Dr. Raynor Johnson, when

[4] St. Ignatius in his *Exercises, Rules for Thinking with the Church* said that "if the Church told him what seemed purely white was black he would pronounce it black" (*Objections to Roman Catholicism*, ed. Michael de la Bedoyere, p. 44, Lippincott, 1965).

[5] For an excellent discussion of this point see the chapter, "The Ultimacy of the Inner Light" in Professor Cecil Cadoux's masterly and monumental tome entitled *Catholicism and Christianity*, pp. 117 ff. (George Allen and Unwin, 1928).

he said, "I am not prepared to hand over to any other person, though wise and learned, or to any institution however ancient or sure of its position, my inalienable right to search for ever-growing and ever-expanding truth. I believe the craving for security in belief is one which arises from within ourselves, and can only be met adequately from resources which are within ourselves. It seems to me that it is far more important for a soul in evolution to believe a few things because it has struggled, thought and suffered to discover and possess them, than it is for it to have a comfortable and orderly faith which it has adopted from any source outside itself." [6] Dr. Oman would agree. "You must choose," he said, "by what you know to be true, and not merely by what you feel to be edifying." [7]

I value the historic teaching of the church immensely. If it did not exist, then the "right to private judgment" might lead me into exaggerated individualism and land me in half-baked ideas evolved from undisciplined speculation and private preference. I might end in undetected nonsense. I reject *unchecked* subjectivism as the authority in religion. No one can suppose that the final authority in religion is what the individual happens to think is true, unless his decision is preceded by long meditation, the weighing of all the available evidence and the prayer for guidance. Tomorrow he may think something else is true. Such "authority" is no authority at all. We should be at the mercy of what Sartre called "manufactured values" peculiar to the individual and altered and repudiated at the individual's whim. "We must not regard as important only what happens to be congenial to us, or select as the 'essence' of Christianity what is consistent with our own prejudices and try to explain the rest away." [8]

[6] *A Religious Outlook for Modern Man*, pp. 122-23 (Hodder and Stoughton, 1962).

[7] John Oman, *The Paradox of the World*, p. 124 (Cambridge University Press, 1921).

[8] J. N. Sanders, "The Meaning and Authority of the New Testament," in *Soundings*, pp. 140-41 (Cambridge University Press, 1962).

On one occasion I was made to feel the strength of the Roman position concerning authority. It was an amusing incident, but illuminating as well. A Methodist youth had fallen in love with a Roman Catholic girl, and as his parents disapproved of such a marriage, he wrote a naïve letter asking me if I would interview them both and, to use his own words, "convert the girl to Methodism"! I was happy to interview them both to see what would happen. That girl had been well instructed. Whenever she was confronted with a difficult situation, she fell back on the phrase, "Well, our church teaches so and so." In effect, she said to me this: "Who am I, a young, uninstructed, uneducated girl, to decide what is to be believed? For hundreds of years the great theologians, the great scholars of my church, adequately educated and magnificently equipped, have wrestled with these problems and come to certain conclusions. I, an untrained girl, can only accept what they say. I believe in what my church teaches." As Dr. Vincent Taylor once said, "No wonder Rome makes converts. It is all so simple once we have committed mental suicide by agreeing that the church cannot err." [9] Concerning some doctrines which are almost as remote from the business of living as astronomy, no doubt the girl's position is sound enough. The doctrine of the Trinity, for example, or the doctrine of the Virgin Birth, does not come anywhere near to everyday living, but a doctrine like the doctrine of the Forgiveness of Sins comes very close to daily living, and I would say that a truth received because it is imposed upon us by an external authority has no value for personality. As Dr. Taylor said later in the same article: "There *are* no external authorities. Thank God!"

If that last sentence sounds difficult, turn again to the doctrine of Forgiveness. We may remember that John Wesley went out to Georgia as a fully ordained clergyman in the Church of England. He had had a theological training, and

---

[9] In an article called, "Authority and Belief," *Methodist Recorder*, October 30, 1952.

no doubt he could have expounded the doctrine of Forgiveness. No doubt he had accepted the external authority of the church for believing it. But all students of Wesley tell us that his mind was forever questing. On board the ship on which he sailed to Georgia, the experience of the Moravians, so much deeper and more real than anything which his adopted orthodox beliefs had brought him, gave him pause and made him think and pray. After his return to England, sitting in the famous little room in Aldersgate Street, his heart, as all the world knows, was "strangely warmed" and he wrote these famous words: "An assurance was given me that He had taken away my sins, even mine, and saved *me* from the law of sin and death." The cynic might say, "Well, didn't he know that before?" Have we not here an illustration of the point I am trying to make? The experience of Aldersgate Street meant that the inner authority based on experience and the outer authority of the church met, and the doctrine of Forgiveness for Wesley ever afterwards had the highest authority man ever knows in religion. For Wesley, there occurred that intuitive leap which possesses truth or is possessed by it. In Oman's phrase, "Reality spoke to him."

In a very small way I had an illustration of my point in the course of my own work. A young man consulted me about some great difficulty through which he felt he could not see his way alone. At the end of the interview he said, "You have only confirmed my own judgment." He went away happy because he felt that such exterior authority as I might seem to possess had confirmed the inner decision he felt was right.

It is one thing to be told that Jesus is the Savior of the World, and to accept that truth with the intellect. It is another thing to sing, both with heart and mind: "Rock of Ages, cleft for *me*," and really to believe it. It is one thing to be told that the Bible has authority because it is divinely inspired, and another thing to feel one's heart leap out and grasp its truth. The doctrines of Christianity that mean most to men are those which concern their emotions, and where our emotions are concerned the external, imposed authority of the church is not enough; the inner light must shine as well. And the reason why religion for so many does not seem to possess the power it ought to have is that they have accepted the external authority of the church, but never made the inner response of the heart. So, in the hour of calamity the comfort does not flow, the assurance is not given, the power is not released. They have assented as one assents to astronomical facts, but truth has not become what Shelley called, "a truth of the emotions" *as well.*

Christianity is a way of life, not a system of theological doctrines which must be "believed." But though, by using the authority of the church, we must not thrust beliefs on people, belaboring their minds to try to make them accept orthodoxy, we may set these same beliefs before people, showing them the rich truth which we have found and which they may come to receive as their questing mind develops and grows. We say, in effect, not, "You *must* believe this and this," but, "Here is the body of Christian doctrine which you may believe as your mind contemplates it." We want them to *see* and then they will believe. The fact that thousands do so believe is one of the strands of the evidence to be considered, and considered with reverence.

It was thus that Christian belief grew up in the first place. Christ never said, "You must believe this and that." He *did* say, according to Luke, "Why do you not of yourselves judge what is right?" [10] There he was to be contemplated, and the august truths of the Christian Faith grew up in the minds and hearts of men as they contemplated him and all the implications of what he was and had done. The external phenomenon was Christ. When the inner authority of men's minds and hearts grasped it, their faith was unshakable. "Thou art the Christ, the Son of the living God," said Peter, unprompted by his Master that this is what he *ought* to be-

[10] Luke 12:57.

lieve. On *such* a faith the church is still built. Here we see the weakness of the position of the Roman Catholic girl in the illustration already used. She need not think. She need not consider. The church will tell her what to believe and the church will tell her what to do. Here is a refusal to grow up: a mind that wants everything done for it, a spirit that shelters in the protection of the church. But not thus does the soul develop and grow, and not thus is the highest form of faith attainable. Every psychologist knows that when he is treating a neurotic, the patient will again and again clamor to be told what he ought to do. He wants the short cut. He wants decisions made for him. The wise psychologist will spread the whole situation before the patient, helping him to *see* it as he never saw it before, but resolutely refusing to be an infallible director. The choice we make for ourselves has far greater authority and power than the direction imposed upon us, and all that should be done by another, however eminent, is so to spread out the situation that something within the patient will grasp the truth and follow the right way.

Finally, let us look at Jesus. What wonderful insight lies behind the sentence written down about him! "He taught them as having authority, and not as the Scribes." [11] Why, the Scribes were the very people who *had* authority! But it was an imposed authority, and what with the meticulous attention to ceremonial detail and the scrupulous keeping of the jot and tittle of the law, we realize what a burden upon people's minds that imposed authority had become, and how the very nature of religion was crushed by it. Its beauty and freshness were suffocated by an external, imposed authority. But Jesus spoke in a different way. When he spoke, something in his hearers' hearts leapt out to receive the truth. The inward met the outward and joined with it in a wholehearted acceptance which released power.

In our small way we are to be like Jesus in this regard as

[11] Mark 1:22.

in others. I would like to be able with authority to present the case for believing in God, but I would far rather *be* an authoritative argument for believing in God. The saints are the best argument for Christianity. They have the highest authority in the world for they coerce us and yet our coercion is a willing one. They drive us along the way which in our best moments we want to go. When we read their lives, and even more when we touch their lives with our own in day-to-day living, we meet Christianity's unanswerable argument. We know, with an authority nothing can resist or overcome, that Christianity changes lives and that if Jesus Christ were given a chance he would change the world. We *know* that he is indeed the Savior of the World.[12] Here is certainty!

Two other words I would like to add: The first is to point out what a solemn and liberating moment it is when, concerning some idea of immense importance, the mind leaps out, possesses it and *knows* it is true. I love the words of T. H. Huxley in one of his letters to Charles Kingsley, where he says, "The most sacred act of a man's life is to say and to feel, 'I believe such and such to be true.'" And what a releasing moment of freedom it is when, having been hampered by being told we *ought* to believe some improbable thesis because the church teaches it, or the Bible states it, we throw it away and discard it forever as the nonsense it has really always been!

Let me quote here some words of the Buddha:

> "Believe nothing because a so-called wise man said it.
> Believe nothing because a belief is generally held.
> Believe nothing because it is written in ancient books.
> Believe nothing because it is said to be of divine origin.
> Believe nothing because someone else believes it.
> Believe only what you yourself judge to be true."

These words can be misunderstood and be twisted to make the reader suppose that his own judgment is to be trusted

---

[12] Cf. John 4:42.

and is incapable of being wrong, but he must be willing to move on as more and more truth is revealed. If we believe that the Spirit of Truth is always guiding us into the truth, we shall see clearly that he who is not willing to move cannot be guided anywhere. I certainly may accept today what I reject tomorrow. If further light dawns on my dark mind, this must be so. A little humility would befit us here. No one knows all the truth. We only get a glimpse of partial facets of it. But I cannot tell you how proud I am that in the Free Churches we are not committed to creeds. We do not try by repetition to make our minds accept words which other people have written down and about which a sincere person must continually make private reservations and secret mental interpretations of his own. Such reservations play havoc with our intellectual honesty.

All this makes me want to add a word which may seem to some daring and heretical. I feel that this resistance to the domination of others, this claim to believe only that which I see to be true, should go through all our interpretation of the Scriptures. I am interested in what Paul said, and a very high degree of inspiration is to be attached to much of his writing. He was such a splendid missionary and scholar, and had such spiritual insight that if I differ from him I feel like a man who does not see beauty in the music of Beethoven, or the pictures of Raphael. But, for myself, I can no more take as authoritative what Paul says is true than I would take what any other saint says. Indeed, in several matters—such as our understanding of Christ's death and his "second coming" —Paul and the author of "Hebrews," have, in my opinion, misled men's thought for two thousand years. A moment's thought shows us that the process of collecting together the writings now called the Bible had to be stayed and a halt called, but if one imagines that the canon had not been closed, then the writings of Archbishop Temple, for example, might well have been part of the Bible. Why is the inspiration of Paul regarded as any greater than the inspiration of that great, unselfish servant of God called William Temple? For myself, I refuse mentally to close the canon as if inspiration had run out! Why should we follow traditional thought more than modern thought? My heart responds to a cry in one of Emerson's essays: "Why should not we have a poetry and philosophy of insight and not of tradition, and *a religion by revelation to us,* and not the history of theirs? The sun shines today also. . . . Let us demand our own works and laws and worship."

Among the letters which passed between T. H. Huxley (grandfather of Sir Julian) and Charles Kingsley, the English clergyman, poet and novelist, we may remember the one which Kingsley wrote to Huxley when the latter lost his little son, aged four. To this letter Huxley replied thanking Kingsley for his letter, and then he added this:

"As I stood behind the coffin of my little son the other day, with my mind bent on anything but disputation, the officiating minister read, as a part of his duty, the words, 'If the dead rise not again, let us eat and drink, for tomorrow we die.' " (This passage unfortunately still occurs in the funeral service of the Anglican Church.) Huxley went on, "I cannot tell you how inexpressibly they shocked me. Paul must have known that his alternative involved a blasphemy against all that was best and noblest in human nature. I could have laughed with scorn. What! Because I am face to face with irreparable loss, because I have given back to the source from whence it came the cause of a great happiness, still retaining through all my life the blessings which have sprung and will spring from that cause, I am to renounce my manhood, and, howling, grovel in bestiality? Why, the very apes know better, and if you shoot their young, the poor brutes grieve their grief out and do not immediately seek distraction in a gorge."

How passionately I agree with Huxley! With what relief I mentally part with some of the views of Paul! He said what he thought and could do no other, but there is no reason why his ideas should be fastened on our minds or be regarde₁ as if they had the authority of truth.

A statement is not true because it is in the Bible, let alone in the Prayer Book. It is not true because Paul says so, or the Pope says so, or because John Wesley says so. It has the *authority* of the truth only when our own individual insight can leap up and recognize it and possess it as our own.

So when we come to the sayings of Jesus himself, I, frankly, do not believe that Jesus ever said, "*All* that came before Me are thieves and robbers." [13] Does he mean John the Baptist and Isaiah? Immediately, we make our own interpretation and refuse the stark authority of the actual words reported. We *feel* that such language is out of character.

I do not believe that Jesus ever said, "No one cometh unto the Father but by Me." [14] Did not the Psalmist ever get near the Father when he said, "Like as a Father pitieth his children, so the Lord pitieth them that fear Him"? [15] or, "Cast me not away from Thy presence; and take not Thy holy spirit from me." [16] Are all the great saints of the Old Testament, and indeed, the great saints and seers of other religions, excluded from the presence of the Father because they had never heard of Jesus Christ? The supposition is ridiculous. [17]

I do not believe that Jesus ever said that any sin was unpardonable (Mark 3:28, Matthew 12:31). The supposition that he did, has, to my knowledge, made people mentally ill. The nature of sin and the nature of love make every sin pardonable if he who commits it seeks in penitence the forgiveness of God. Some misunderstanding, one is certain, has arisen. We must resolutely refuse to judge Jesus by the

---

[13] John 10:8   [14] John 14:6   [15] Psalm 103:13   [16] Psalm 51:11

[17] Probably the first quotation means that some of the earlier would-be deliverers of Israel were political revolutionaries. The word "thief" should have been translated thus. The thief on the cross was such, and no thief at all in our sense. The second quotation means probably that no one understands the nature of God more completely than it is revealed in Jesus. What one rejects, because they are so unlike Jesus, are the stark, unexplained words in the Gospel. We reject the authority because we are emotionally concerned.

Bible. We must judge the Bible by Jesus; by the total effect of a consistent personality made upon us from all sources, including our own experience. The one who is reported as saying, "Him that cometh to Me I will in no way cast out" (John 6:37) could not refuse forgiveness to a penitent sinner, whatever his sin.

So, we find ourselves rejecting the authority even of the alleged words of Christ, because in a matter so full of personal concern and emotion, we cannot be convinced by another. I shall return to this point when we discuss the words of Christ (pp. 95 ff.). It is sufficient here to quote a saying of Archbishop Temple, "There is no single deed or saying of which we can be perfectly sure that Christ said or did precisely this or that." [18]

May I suggest to you, my reader, that in some quiet hour you write out your own creed? Do not copy anybody else's. Do not try and make yourself believe what to you seems absurd. Do not have anything foisted on you at all. Write out what for *you* is true.

For myself, my creed is a very small one, but it is my own, and let me add this. Nothing that somebody else says is true will be of use to any of us in an hour of trial. Nothing will hold us as an anchor in a stormy sea save that little bit of the truth of God which we have made our very own. The very Greek word for "authority" is *"exousia,"* namely, "out of that which is one's very own." But what we have made our own will hold us. Nothing can ever destroy truth. To possess it we may have to part with the old traditional, dearly loved, conventional teaching, and the prejudices we have imbibed from childhood. In our quest we shall be met by opposition. Sentences will be hurled at us that begin, "The Bible teaches that . . ." or, "Everybody knows that . . ." "Do you imagine that you know better than the learned theologians who determined what the orthodox Christian should believe?" There

---

[18] "Revelation," quoted by John Baillie, *The Idea of Revelation in Recent Thought,* p. 114 (Oxford University Press, 1956).

are some people to whom the words of Coleridge the poet apply! "He who begins by loving [orthodox] Christianity better than Truth, will proceed by loving his own sect or church better than Christianity and end in loving himself better than all." For myself, I will refuse to say words that I intuitively feel are false, and I will not hug to my heart expressions and forms from which, for me, the truth has departed. Truth can be a lonely and bleak rock. But it *is* a rock, and only on a rock that will not move can one safely anchor in a stormy sea. And, God knows, the sea of ideas is stormy enough today to frighten anyone. But there is a ground where safe anchorage can be found. It is the ground of the tiny bit of truth we have discovered and made our own.

"Fixed on this ground will I remain."

CHAPTER IV

GOD AND OUR GUESSES

"I do not know what I may appear to the world, but to myself I seem to have been only a boy playing on the seashore, and diverting myself in now and then finding a smoother pebble, or a prettier shell than ordinary, whilst the great ocean of truth lay, all undiscovered before me."

Isaac Newton (1642-1727)

"Let me exhort everyone to their utmost to think outside and beyond our present circle of ideas."

Richard Jefferies

"Whatever the humblest men affirm from their own experience is always worth listening to, but what even the cleverest of men, in their ignorance, deny, is never worth a moment's attention."

Sir William Barrett

IV

GOD AND OUR GUESSES

THERE is something almost ludicrous in sitting down at a desk and writing the word "God" at the top of a sheet of foolscap paper and then being presumptuous enough to add anything. So the ant (see page 39), or the mouse (see page 40) might be imagined sitting down to write about man! Having just written the word "God," I feel that the most appropriate thing to do would be to leave half a dozen blank sheets of paper! The device would not be popular with my publisher or helpful to my reader, and yet to add anything to the one word "God" is to do him an injustice, for to describe is to limit and to mar. Paul at Athens was impressed by an altar inscribed, *"Agnosto Theo,"* "To the unknown God," and it was this word "agnostic" of which Thomas Huxley made use to describe his own attitude a hundred years ago. A high Buddhist authority wrote to a friend of mine, "The idea of God is quite acceptable to us, but we do not encourage the use of the word lest it should be tainted." I can understand this. No language can do other than belittle. No words can be other than caricature. The Hebrew writers were reluctant to use the name of God and there was a Hebrew saying, "If a word is worth one shekel, silence is worth two." At the same time, there is another side to the matter. Jesus spoke much about God, and his followers throughout the ages have done the same. We would not willingly lose what the saints and mystics have written of him, and the humblest testimony from *experience* seems to me of immense value.

71

I compromise by calling the chapter, "God and Our Guesses."

"The Catholic tradition has always claimed that God's existence can be proved," [1] but to prove his existence is impossible if the word "prove" is used in any scientific, unanswerable sense. To quote "authorities" is futile. Nowhere is what I have written in the last chapter about authority better substantiated than here. There *is* no authority for God's existence except the inward conviction that is born of mystical experience. And to prove the existence of God is a bit like proving that your wife loves you, with all the same difficulties of rebutting one who says she does not really love you, but acts the way she does because life is easier for both that way, or she wants you to like her, or hopes you will leave her your money!

I could quote the words of learned men who believe in God. I think of Einstein and Schweitzer, of Temple, Barnes, Father Ronald Knox and Dean Inge, of Professor Butterfield and Professor Coulson of Cambridge, both Methodist lay preachers. I think of a brilliant philosopher like A. E. Taylor and of his splendid little book, *Does God Exist?* [2] with its unmistakable affirmative answer. But then I think of equally brilliant men like Professor A. J. Ayer of Oxford, courteous and tolerant to a degree, and yet seeing no grounds for believing in God. I fancy that Sir Julian Huxley and many other scientists and philosophers would place themselves in the list of those who do not believe in the existence of God, and I secretly hope that, like C. S. Lewis, Cyril Joad and Frank Morison, so-called atheists for years, they may, before long, think differently, and write the kind of valuable apologetic literature which, in the eyes of many, is the more convincing because of the years during which the authors so passionately denied, and in some cases sneered at, the views they ultimately held.

[1] O. Fielding Clarke, *For Christ's Sake*, p. 9 (Morehouse-Barlow Co., 1963).

[2] Macmillan and Co., 1947.

It is interesting, in passing, to note how, even in science, men come back to accept what once was ridiculed. The word "lunatic" refers to the ancient belief that the moon had an influence on man's mental health. For years this has been scorned as an old wives' tale. But listen to Professor A. C. Lovell writing in *The Sunday Times* of March 15, 1964, "An account was given by Professors H. Friedman, R. O. Becker and C. H. Bachman of New York," [in *Nature*, 16, xii. 63] "of their attempts to find some factors correlating with suicides and admissions to mental hospitals. They investigated 28,642 admissions to eight psychiatric hospitals in New York State between 1957 and 1961 and found a significant correlation with magnetic storms. Thus in the last few years some strange and inexplicable links appear to be emerging between lunar phase, rainfall, meteoric impact, magnetic storms and mental disturbance. *It almost seems that we are moving through a series of scientific fantasies to a proof of the ancient belief in the connection between the moon and lunacy.*" [8]

In a similar way, many who have sneered at religion, denied the existence of God and ridiculed the teachings of the church, have, before old age set in, had some experience, or, I want to say, some *encounter*, which has turned them round and made them sure forever that the universe does not end at the point at which we cease to record it by our five senses; that the heart has reasons which the intellect may for a time deny, and that old wives' tales and "mother's knee stuff" may turn out to contain an inescapable amount of truth. When men meditate they intuitively feel out for something or Someone beyond the world known through the senses. Even the most daring, imaginative thought cannot reach out to what this is, but man's thought-life is incomplete if it is left out of what one could call his mental furniture. There is what has been called, "the pull of the invisible." When a boy whose kite had soared out of sight was asked how he knew it was still there, he said, "I feel the pull of it." Otto, in *The Idea*

[8] Italics mine.

of the Holy used the word "numinous" (from the Latin *"numen,"* a divinity to be worshiped). He believed that there is "an ultimate category of religious experience which is defined by this sense of mystery and awe," and R. W. Hepburn, in his *Christianity and Paradox,* agrees in regarding the numinous as the "irreducible hard core of religious experience." [4] Similarly, H. G. Wells wrote, "At times in the silence of the night and in rare, lonely moments, I experience a sort of communion of myself with Something Great that is not myself."

Recently my eye caught the words of a writer to the *Daily Mail* who said this, "I regard belief in God as something everyone should and must question furiously until a moment comes in their life when they can question no longer; when, in fact, they find themselves saying, like Jung, 'I don't believe, I *know*.' This moment came for me some years ago when I had an experience of God so vivid and so shattering that I knew that either God existed or I must be stark, staring mad. And I didn't *feel* mad, only much happier than I have ever felt in my life before or since. . . . The brief moment I refer to seemed, and still seems to me, the most real thing in my life; the pearl of great price compared to which everything and everyone else I value, however dearly, is a copy which makes me homesick for the original." [5]

I could not call myself a mystic, but on half a dozen occasions I have had experiences which *for me* made me certain of the reality of some supernatural Entity which, or whom, I label "God." One was among the foothills of the Himalayas near Simla, one at Vauxhall Station, one on a railway bridge at Woolwich, one in the lounge at a Swanwick Conference, once during the writing of a sermon in my own study, and once at a Holy Communion service when the bombs were

---

[4] I am indebted here to Sir Julian Huxley's *Religion Without Revelation,* p. 109 (Parrish, 2nd edition, 1959).
[5] Monica Furlong in the *Daily Mail* of December 24, 1962. The writer refers to this experience in her recent book, which I should like to recommend: *With Love to the Church* (Hodder and Stoughton, 1965).

falling near us, and we (the members of the City Temple Friday Fellowship) knelt on the rough boards of an upper room off Fleet Street lent to us by the Vicar of St. Bride's Church, the City Temple having been burned to the ground by incendiary bombs.

It would be boring to describe them all, but they all had similar characteristics. I will try to describe one. Vauxhall Station on a murky November Saturday evening is not the setting one would choose for a revelation of God! I was a young theological student aged nineteen, being sent from Richmond Theological College (London University) to take the services somewhere—I cannot remember where—for some minister in a Greater London church who had fallen ill. The third-class compartment was full. I cannot remember any particular thought processes which may have led up to the great moment. It is possible that I was ruminating over the sermons I had prepared, and feeling—what I have always felt —how inadequate they were to "get over" to others what I really felt about the Christian religion and its glorious message.

But the great moment came and when, years later, I read C. S. Lewis' *Surprised by Joy*[6] I thought, "Yes, I know exactly how he felt. I felt like that." For a few seconds only, I suppose, the whole compartment was filled with light. This is the only way I know in which to describe the moment, for there was nothing to *see* at all. I felt caught up into some tremendous sense of being within a loving, triumphant and shining purpose. I never felt more humble. I never felt more exalted. A most curious, but overwhelming sense possessed me and filled me with ecstasy. I felt that all was well for all mankind—how poor the words seem! The word "well" is so poverty stricken. All men were shining and glorious beings who in the end would enter incredible joy. Beauty, music, joy, love immeasurable and a glory unspeakable, all this they

* P. 22, published by Geoffrey Bles in 1955.

would inherit. Of this they were heirs. My puny message, if I passed my exams and qualified as a minister, would contribute only an infinitesimal drop to the ocean of love and truth which God wanted men to enjoy, but my message was of the same *nature* as that ocean. I was right to want to be a minister. I had wanted to be a doctor and the conflict had been intense, but in that hour I knew the ministry was the right path for me. For me it was right, right, right. . . . An indescribable joy possessed me. . . .

All this happened over fifty years ago but even now I can see myself in the corner of that dingy, third-class compartment with the feeble lights of inverted gas mantles overhead and the Vauxhall platforms outside with milk cans standing there. In a few moments the glory had departed—all but one curious, lingering feeling. I *loved* everybody in that compartment. It sounds silly now, and indeed I blush to write it, but at that moment I think I would have died for any one of the people in that compartment. They seemed—all of them—immensely lovable and valuable. I seemed to sense the golden worth in them all. I knew then—and believe now—that God would not allow any one of his children finally to miss the ecstatic happiness and joy towards which every human life, in spite of a million deviations, hindrances, wrong choices and the following of false signposts, is moving. I knew then that I *had* to move along that road, and that my life was to be spent in helping men and women to find the way to God, and in finding it in greater and greater measure myself.

I know that all this—which I have never disclosed before —can be laughed at and derided as evidence of God, or can be "explained" in terms of subjectivism. No doubt analytical psychologists could tear it all to bits and explain it in the jargon of this or that psychological school. Critics could trample on my dreams and say that it was too much in the realm of feeling to have any value, but so is falling in love. Is that not real, and highly significant, and life-changing? So is the state of mind induced by music, or by some of the glories of Nature, or by some of the works of man. "When I heard Beethoven's Ninth Symphony," said Claudel, "I *knew* there was joy at the heart of the universe." All I can say is that to *me* it was an experience of God, never to be denied. It happened fifty years ago. It is as authentic as if it had happened yesterday, and even to think of it is to feel a curious, reassuring sense of safety, comfort and well-being; in George Macdonald's lovely phrase, "to be haunted with the scent of unseen roses," to feel that the whole world and everyone in it is in the hands of a Mysterious Power which is utterly friendly, the Source of all the deepest joy man ever feels or is capable of feeling, and the Fount and Origin and Sustainer of all those values which man at his best seeks to establish and maintain.

Some words of Professor A. N. Whitehead come to mind. He wrote, "Only at rare intervals does the deeper and vaster world come through into conscious thought or expression, but they are the memorable moments of life. It is then, if ever, that the door to the invisible world silently swings open, and something of the wonder and greatness of the spiritual universe is flashed upon the soul." No one who has had such an experience can ever doubt but that in the end good will triumph over every form of evil, and that every life, however humble, frustrated, indifferent or even careless, is in the care of this Power and within a Plan, vast beyond our power to imagine, which will work out in a blessedness which brings utter satisfaction and a quality of bliss for which there are no words.

Some words of Paul Tillich read recently echo so closely my thought at that time. He says, "We experience moments in which we accept ourselves, because we feel that we have been accepted by that which is greater than we. If only more such moments were given us! For it is such moments that make us love our life, that make us accept ourselves, not in our goodness and self-complacency, but in our certainty of the eternal meaning of our life." [7]

Such an experience is like a message from the unseen. I can understand Joseph Nemes, who was beaten up by the Russians and hourly expecting death, writing thus: "At the sixteenth chapter of St. Matthew's Gospel I began to read. As I was doing it, all of a sudden light came to me. *It was as if a very important message had been flashed to me from another world*, and this light made it easy for me to turn into myself and find the way out victoriously." [8] I can understand Tertullian's sentence, "If I give you a rose you will not doubt God any more," but of course the rose has to unlock a mystical insight and appreciation within man. I can understand a wonderful passage from Rabindranath Tagore, "We still live in exile while the insolent spirit of worldly prosperity tempts us with allurements. In the meantime, the flower comes across with a message from the other shore and whispers in our ears, 'I am come. He has sent me. He will draw thee unto him and make thee his own.'" I can understand the conviction in the heart of Alfred Noyes, the poet, when he wrote: "Anyone who doubts the Christian Faith should see my father's face when he returns from his early Communion."

Many readers will feel dissatisfied with all this. They will say: "I have never had any experience of this kind and am not likely to have. So is there any way by which I can feel certain that God exists?"

This is an entirely fair comment. A reader can say, "This never happened to me," but he must not say, "Neither did it happen to you. You are deluded or making it all up." When we say we "know" anything, the condition of our mind is one of deep satisfaction. I can only say that experiences, such as the one I have tried to describe above, produce in my mind exactly the same feelings as are produced by other ways of being sure. It is, for example, like being sure of one's wife's

[7] *The Shaking of the Foundations*, p. 164 (Pelican Books, 1963).
[8] *Signs in the Storm*, p. 208 (Abingdon Press, 1957). Italics mine.

fidelity. "Of the three ways of acquiring knowledge—authority, reasoning and experience," said Roger Bacon, "only the last is effective."

The reader who says he never has any experiences of this sort—and indeed, they cannot be engineered or induced—must get as near to that sense of mental satisfaction as other ways of knowing bring him. He must pursue the way of argument as far as it can take him, and then make a leap of faith in the direction of the trend of the evidence, acting *as though* it were sound. Reason will take us so far on firm ground. But then there must be the leap *in the same direction*, if the truth of those facts in religion which are only reached by faith are to be enjoyed. Faith is not a leap in the dark, or, as the schoolboy said, "believing what you know to be untrue," or treading a road that is contrary to reason and superstitiously running in another direction. It is taking the road of evidence as far as it will go and then, with the energy provided by meditating on the character of God as Christ revealed him, making a leap of faith, only to land finally in a conviction as strong as proof can supply.

For myself, the old argument which seeks to prove God's existence from design, if rather differently stated, is still convincing. The argument would not fall to the ground, it seems to me, even if it could be proved that the universe had no beginning in time. The statement of a distinguished astronomer—Professor Hoyle of Cambridge—that hydrogen is still being "newly created," suggests that there was no beginning in time.

To return to the argument from design, it demands more of credulity to imagine that the universe was all a huge accident than to believe in the operation of a mind. How very strange that a ball of matter accidentally happening, and accidentally moving round the sun, should accidentally and purposelessly produce a man who purposefully seeks truth and purposefully asks how such an accident could happen, thus exhibiting a more profound degree of intelligence than that which accidentally produced this amazing universe, namely, to the atheist, mindless chance!

How and why should the world ever come into being unless behind the matter there was Mind? In imagination one watches breathlessly from some point beyond this world, a globe of incandescent gas cooling. One then imaginatively watches the earth spinning, when it is a red-hot mass of solid material on which nothing we know of as life can possibly exist, any more than it could at the heart of a furnace. One watches while the cooling process goes on, while boiling seas wash against hot rock and clouds of steam rise from the earth. Centuries and centuries pass and, without any activity of man, a new thing called an amoeba, a single cell, something which is alive, arrives in the warm sea. Something crawls at last out of that sea and life on dry land has begun. From that humble beginning all subsequent life emerges and a thousand strands of apparent purposefulness weave for man a home. Man's developing brain cooperates, until we have in civilized man one who is all but master of his environment and who is now dreaming of the mastery of the heavens.

Is all that accidental? If I leave my bed unmade, my bedroom a tangle of sheets, blankets and pillows, and returning, find that someone has made my bed, providing warmth for my body and a pillow where my head can rest, I deduce that a mind which can move and control matter has been at work. Is the long preparation for the appearance of man to be written down as unpurposed? "There is a coherent plan in the universe," said Professor Hoyle, "though I don't know what it's a plan for." [9] Says another scientist who is also a philosopher, "There is a wide measure of agreement which, on the physical side of science, approaches to unanimity, that the stream of scientific knowledge is heading towards a nonmechanical Reality." The scientist, Sir James Jeans, remarked that the universe begins to look more like a great thought than

[9] B.B.C./T.V. program on March 12, 1962.

a great machine. "Mind no longer appears as an Accidental Intruder into the realm of matter." [10]

Paley argued years ago that if he found a watch on the shore of a deserted island he would deduce from its structure that someone, a watchmaker, had made it in the first instance, and that however much man might understand of the working of a watch, he would not, by all his knowledge, make the watchmaker unnecessary.

As the philosopher, A. E. Taylor, wrote: "Mill meets and disables the well-known argument of Paley from the watch to the watchmaker by the retort that my only ground for reasoning from the discovery of the watch to the existence of a maker is that I already know that watches are the sort of things which men make. If I did not know this, I should have no more reason to say that a watch found on the shore of a deserted island must have been made by a man and brought to the island by a man, than to say the same thing about a curious shell on the beach. Yet I cannot but think that even if mankind should some day find out how to do without watches, and even in course of time, forget that such things have ever been, the discovery of a watch in an excavated city would be enough to satisfy intelligent antiquarians that they were dealing with a product of human intelligence. What would be felt to be conclusive is the way in which the various parts of the watch are co-adapted to produce a unitary result, and a result which cannot be effected until they are all assembled in a definite way. Even if the discoverers did not guess that the instrument was intended to measure the lapse of time, examination would at least be enough to show that its parts were all adjusted to bring about the single result that the hands on the dial revolve at a uniform rate, and it would be felt that either we must suppose this result to have been intended, and the watch therefore constructed for the purpose, or the happy conspiracy between the various parts

[10] Kenneth Walker, F.R.C.S., in *Health Education Journal*, November, 1963.

to effect this result must be due to an accumulation of coincidences which is antecedently enormously improbable. The overwhelming probability would be that we had before us a result of 'prospective contrivance.' And it might fairly be said that the thorough-going co-adaptation of the parts of organisms to contribute to a unitary result, which will only emerge when the organism is mature, may be ascribed to 'prospective contrivance' with an even higher degree of probability.

"The case stands thus. Throughout the organic realm at any rate, we find a thorough co-adaptation in advance of organs, or of individual members of species, in their structure and functioning, to results still lying in the future. We know with certainty of one cause which, if present, would account for this prospective co-adaptation—intelligent purpose; such prospective co-adaptation *is* characteristic of intelligence wherever it is found. We do not *know* of an alternative cause which works in this way, and if there is any such cause or causes, it (or they) work(s) in a way of which purely physical scientific laws consistently take no account. Refuse, if you like, to call this cause intelligent; call it X in order to avoid committing yourself. The question is whether, when you come to say how X operates, you are not in effect crediting it with exactly what we all recognise as the characteristic marks of intelligence, though you will not use the name but prefer to fall back on an alias. The mere name, to be sure, is a minor matter about which it would be idle to quarrel. *What is really important is that it seems impossible to give any account of nature which shall be true to the facts without recognising the presence of a power which works in the very way in which intelligence works in ourselves.*" [11]

In a recent book (1963) called *Law, Order, Cosmos, God*, sixteen scientists contribute sections to show that the existence of law and order in every area of the universe points to the reality of an organizing Intelligence. An astronomer speaks

[11] *Does God Exist?*, A. E. Taylor, pp. 103-5 (Macmillan, 1947). Italics mine.

of the billions of stars and the movements of the constellations. A physicist describes the infinitesimal electrons as orderly as the solar system. A biologist points to the orderly world of the cells. A chemist expresses the view that man may learn how to create life "because amino acids, which are the basis of life, are formed in the atmosphere by the mixture of gases exposed to an electrical charge like lightning," but even if life were thus created it would but be a repetition through human purposefulness of an earlier "experiment" by an earlier Mind. Dr. Orr Reynolds, an American scientist, told a reporter, so I read in the London *Evening Standard* (April 29, 1964), "I believe we shall create a cell which has the power to reproduce itself within the next ten years," and the journalist claimed triumphantly, "that life *needed no divine force to set it going.*" But where is his logic? God is not excluded by our learning some of his methods. I accept Dr. Reynolds' words that he "will create a cell which has the power to reproduce itself," but my wife and I did that forty years ago! We have grandchildren! But we do not exclude God from his own creative power by being allowed to understand it and to share in it.

In the making of man himself we find what I regard as evidence of purpose, marks of a planning mind. A single ovum within the mother-to-be is fertilized by a single sperm. The fertilized cell multiplies and a new life begins. What amazing accident is it by which cells differentiate! All the millions of cells have come from one fertilized ovum, yet in the end "some cells have changed their stuff and become rigid bone, or harder still, the enamel of a tooth; some become fluid as water, so to flow along tubes too fine for the eye to see. Some become clear as glass, some opaque as stone, some colourless, some red, some black. Some become factories of a furious chemistry, some become as inert as death. Some become engines of mechanical pull, some scaffoldings of static support, some a system transmitting electrical signs." Each cell is blind. It has no sense. It works in the dark. Yet "it is as if an immanent principle inspired each cell with knowledge for the carrying out of a design." [12]

Dr. Raynor Johnson, to whom I am indebted for the quotation, adds, "If the building of so complex a structure, capable of response to an environment which it will some day meet, is not evidence of purpose—highly intelligent purpose such as highly developed Mind might formulate—I confess I do not know the meaning of the word 'purpose.' " [13] That mind and love have somehow arisen by accident in a mindless machine seems to me fantastic.

It is not easy for one who, like myself is an ignorant layman where modern science is concerned, to keep up with what is going on in that field, but one's reading and discussion with scientists incline one to believe that no responsible scientist now holds that life and all its forms can be accounted for by the operation of mechanical forces acting without any guiding purpose. Both in astronomy and physics, what we could call mechanism does not account for all the observed phenomena. It did when Darwin's theory of evolution by natural selection was put forward a hundred years ago. It did when astronomy was ruled by the Newtonian conception of a balance of material forces which maintained the heavenly bodies wheeling through space. Small exceptions were regarded as explicable if mechanism were only more fully understood. The whole universe was regarded as a machine.

But in physics the nature of matter came to be regarded as "a flurry of electromagnetic forces whose spontaneous movements could not be explained by the analogy of the machine." [14] Einstein succeeded Newton, and Sir James Jeans crystallized the change in his famous phrase, already quoted, that the universe looked "less like a great machine and more

---

[12] Sir Charles Sherrington, *Man on His Nature*, Gifford Lectures, 1937-8 (Cambridge University Press), quoted from Raynor Johnson, *The Imprisoned Splendour*, p. 55 (Hodder and Stoughton, 1953).

[13] *Op. cit.*, p. 56.

[14] I owe the phrase and much else in this section to my friend, F. E. Christmas.

like a great thought." The idea that in astronomy or in physics phenomena can be wholly accounted for in mechanical terms has gone forever.

When biologists claim that the behavior of living creatures and the development of life through millions of years from the amoeba to the scientist can be wholly accounted for in mechanical terms, they seem curiously out of step with their brother scientists in other fields.

Further, it was believed that only on this planet we call earth had life developed. Life then could be regarded as the result of a trivial accident. Of trivial significance was this "accidental" happening on a trivial planet revolving round a trivial sun in a trivial galaxy. A freckle on a dying baby's nose was of similar importance! Here was life! So what? It was a meaningless incident which accidentally happened on a minor planet which itself only came into being as the result of a cosmic accident—the approach of some other sun sufficiently near to our own to pull out a stream of solar gases which went into orbit, cooled and condensed into planets.

But this theory that planets are the outcome of rare cosmic accidents has been abandoned. "More than 50% of the suns in the millions of galaxies throughout the universe must—according to calculations made possible by the use of computers—be accompanied by planets. Rational probability leaves little room for doubt that among this incredible welter of worlds, a large proportion must be capable of supporting life, or that upon them also life must have emerged and developed." [15]

Life then is no alien intruder into the universe but is native to it. Here is no mindless machine running down to inevitable extinction, and carrying, in one insignificant fragment, a solitary phenomenon called "life," which had happened by accident.

Is it unreasonable to suppose that as in astronomy and

[15] F. E. Christmas in a letter to the author, November 24, 1964.

physics the purely mechanistic explanation has broken down, so in biology the scientist will be led *through* mechanism to phenomena for which mechanism offers no explanation?

It is clear that mechanism possesses a *measure* of validity in the study of life and its development just as it possesses the clue to some problems in astronomy and physics. The biochemists and geneticists eloquently prove so much. But the idea that mechanism will explain life and its development from the speck of protein to the love and insight of a saint may be for some wishful thinking, but it has little encouragement from other sciences and none from the insights of religion.

I just cannot understand those who deny a purposing intelligence behind a mass of phenomena revealed in almost every science. And if mind itself "is the complex arrangement of non-mental elements which have been assembled in a fortuitous, that is in an unguided manner, it is impossible to suppose that the mind should be capable of discovering truth, since all its thoughts must be the outcome of non-mental causes. Hence we are reduced at once to complete scepticism. Everything, including the materialist theory, is ground out by the unthinking machine." [16]

Once the reader grants that the universe did not just happen accidentally but is the product of a mind, and that purposefulness is evidenced in it, the argument for God seems to me to leap ahead. That mind must be one *something* like my own, and possess *some* of the qualities of my mind, or else I should not be capable of recognizing purposefulness in what that greater mind brings about. I should not perceive design to be designed.

In our own bit of the universe, this world, there seems to me immense disorder. Calamity and disaster abound. I wonder what this Mind is doing and imagine that if I had the *power* I could make a much better world! But of course

[16] W. R. Matthews (Dean of St. Paul's), *The Christian Faith*, p. 80 (Eyre and Spottiswoode, 1936).

algebra, which appears orderly to me, might well seem disorderly nonsense to a savage on a lower level of mental activity. So what seems chaotic to me—as algebra to a savage—may be purpose to a higher mind. Cutting an unconscious man's body might seem, to a savage, purposeless cruelty. But a surgeon views it differently. So may the apparent disorder in the world confuse me and tempt me to call this Mind cruel, callous or stupid. But I do see *some* signs of order in the world and this cannot be *disorder* to a higher mind though it might be to a lower. As I said, *one* made bed in a dormitory full of unmade and disorderly beds is enough to prove purposefulness there on the part of someone. Even the biased atheist, Richard Robinson, in his jejune book, *An Atheist's Values*, writes, "Little bits of it [the world] appear to be designed." [17] And one bit of order, one proof of purposefulness in the whole universe is sufficient to show the activity of a mind that we can recognize as mind, and therefore is *a mind in some ways like our own.* Purpose anywhere must mean purpose everywhere, even if purpose is not yet discernible or not yet worked out fully or possibly hindered by evil intelligences. The atheist says the universe is purposeless and yet he himself is purposeful. This seems odd to me. When he says the universe is meaningless he claims to be saying something meaningful! If there is no purposefulness to be found anywhere in the universe, then it is the result of a colossal accident, and, as Edwin Conklin the biologist said, "The probability of life originating from accident is comparable to the probability of the unabridged dictionary resulting from an explosion in a printing shop."

It is difficult to assert that this mind is personal because we are again guilty of pushing our concept of it into the minute mold of our own personality. I should define a person as a self-conscious center of thinking, feeling and acting, and who is capable of responding to other "persons." But inasmuch

[17] P. 127 (Oxford, 1964).

as to be a person is man's highest achievement and lifts him immensely above being a thing or even an animal, we cannot deny personality to this mind in the sense of claiming that it is "it" rather than "he." If, however, we do think of him as a person it must be with the reservation that he must be far more than we are capable of meaning when we use the word "personal." We could say he is suprapersonal not infra-personal; more than we mean by personal, but certainly not less. Perhaps we could better say that he is not one Person among many, but, to invent a phrase, the Essence of personalness, the Ground of all that we call personality, a Being with whom we can enter into personal relationships.

Let us now give the name "God" to this Purposeful Mind and use the word "he," although "she" would be equally appropriate and misleading! If, instead, we call this Mind "the Ground of our Being," as the Bishop of Woolwich, Aldous Huxley and others do, or "the Absolute," or the "Final Reality," we evoke the idea of Something impersonal and then we are still further from the inexpressible truth.

The next question must be, "What is he like?" which is almost as important a question as, "Does he exist?" Here again I am aware of the poverty of language. What does "good" mean? Many people do things which are "good" in their own eyes but bad in the stricter eyes of others. However, if we know anything at all in this life we *know* that it is *better* (= more good) to be kind than cruel, *better* to love than to hate, *better* to be unselfish than selfish, *better* to care than to be indifferent, *better* to be humble than conceited, and so on.

It therefore seems to me sound to argue that if this august being we call God exists at all, his character must contain the qualities which, at my best, I admire. For if not, I am *better* than he is, unless my sense of values is utterly wrong. This would mean that something which the universe has produced is *better* in terms of moral qualities, than the Mind behind it, and that surely cannot be. This of course does not mean that everything is all right in the best of all possible worlds. Much that may be good we cannot yet see to be so. At the moment we could find in Nature as much evidence of a malign purpose as of a good one. As T. H. Huxley said in *Life and Letters*, "If we are to assume that anybody has designedly set this wonderful universe going, it is perfectly clear to me that he is no more entirely benevolent and just in any intelligible sense of the words, than he is malevolent and unjust." This statement is incontrovertibly true. But so might speak the surgeon's son (p. 43), whose father is kind to him at one point, and, at another, cutting the body of an unconscious patient. We are not old enough to understand. God is still at work in his world and has only made a beginning. He may have evil entities to overcome as well as the intransigence of man. While this is not yet the best of all possible worlds it may be the world of best possibilities, having regard to its Maker's ultimate purposes, and if we agree that Man at his best is what roughly we call "good" it is easier to believe that God must be good rather than any of its opposites—say cruel. Of course, if our sense of values is misleading; if there is no moral distinction between feeding a million famine-stricken people and murdering a million Jews in gas chambers; if being loving is really no "better" than being cruel, then God may be a cruel, unjust, obscene monster; the argument comes to an end, and we are left puzzling as to how a glorious thing like unselfish goodness has ever come to be on the earth.

Arguing still from man—which incidentally Jesus told us to do [18]—we know that a good man has a purpose concerning other lives. He seeks to ensure his wife's happiness and security, his children's probity and education. If his children took a false path, his purpose would be to point out to them some path along which they could find the realization and expression of all that was best within them.

If, behind all the perplexing phenomena and situations

[18] Luke 11:13.

with which we are confronted in this earthy journey, there is a Being who loves, cares and purposes, it would not be surprising to learn that he had done something to cope with sin and evil, with suffering and death, for these are, in the main, the factors which lead men to disbelieve either in his existence or in his qualities.

It would be odd indeed if a great Purposing Mind, loving and caring as well as planning, never disclosed such fragments of his purposes as man is capable of following, because, not only would such reticence be unworthy and uncharacteristic of the purposing mind of a human father, but it would be self-defeating. God plans that man shall slowly learn his purposes and cooperate with him for their fulfillment.

This brings us, however unworthily and incompetently, to meditate on Jesus Christ, and, as we move on, let us brood on his evidence. He believed in God, his existence and nature, and even on the cross he called God, "Father," when it looked as though everything had gone wrong and that God had let him down.

If a child who has just learned to play "The Joyful Peasant" with one hand, criticized Beethoven; if a boy who failed his General Certificate of Education in arithmetic said that Einstein was no mathematician; if a youth, who had just had his verses rejected by the local newspaper, said that Shakespeare had no idea of a sonnet, should we not complain that they had not the necessary equipment to deny? On the lowest level of assessment Jesus Christ was the greatest religious genius the world has ever known. Suppose that imaginatively we said to him: "When you were nailed on the Cross and said, "Father, into Thy hands I commit my spirit," you were quite wrong. There was no one there. You only wished you had a father. I know better than you. There isn't a God." Would it not be rather like telling Beethoven that he could not write music, Shakespeare that he was no artist, and Einstein that he had got his sums wrong?

CHAPTER V

CHRIST AND HIS ACHIEVEMENT

The British Council of Churches, in stating its theological basis, twice used the phrase that those who joined should "accept our Lord Jesus Christ as God and Saviour." Commenting on this in *The Friend* (September 11, 1964), Mr. Bernard Canter, the Editor, while only expressing his own opinion, wrote as follows:

"Every word that is here used—even the weak word 'accept,' and much more 'Lord,' 'Christ,' 'God' and 'Saviour'—nails down a precise decision as to who Jesus is, with the equally strong implication that all other views are 'out.'

"This is in itself a difficulty to the writer of this page. To him Jesus is someone he knows, and most deeply loves; and through this knowledge and love of Jesus, it would seem to him, he has come to know and love and live with God. This is in itself a pretty definite Christological and Theological statement. But as to going further, as to docketing and defining further, he feels at once a most strong reluctance: first because it seems a presumption and an impiety to attempt to reduce to the compass of his understanding, and his poor resources of language, so enormous a glory, and second because he wishes to be free, to the end of his life, freely to wonder with all his heart who Jesus is, and to arrange his speculations on Jesus in a different way, and in different language, for every day of his life—or on some days not to worry, just to love. When one falls in love with another person, one may delight to spend some time attempting to define and describe to oneself or to others his or her character, personality and significance. But, whatever little definitions one may reach, that has nothing to do with loving him or her. Directly one comes into a love relationship one is touching the vast eternal. So it is, but much more, with loving Jesus. In this matter the loving silence of Cordelia has something to commend it."

V

CHRIST AND HIS ACHIEVEMENT

IT is with a sense of deep humility and reverence, almost of awe, that I, having recently passed my seventieth birthday, sit down in this quiet study, within sight and sound of the sea, to write about the Person who has meant more to me than any other for over sixty years. As a child of nine I made my little act of dedication to him all alone on January 3, 1903, and determined to serve him for the rest of my life. I remember writing down the fact in red ink in a new diary someone had given me. Needless to say, I have gone back on him since then a thousand times, but always he has held my heart in thrall and I have known no peace outside his will and no joy to compare with the experience which I sincerely believe to be due to communion with him. I pray that I may write no word to lessen, for another, belief in that transforming, and available friendship.

It is presumptuous to give only one chapter to One about whom ten thousand books have been written, whose name is revered and whose Person is worshiped by men and women of every denomination and of none, in every race under heaven, and whose message has been translated into almost every known tongue.

Yet I am writing this book for the thoughtful layman who is immensely attracted by Jesus Christ and yet who is puzzled and bewildered by many of the things he is reported to have said and done, and even more bewildered by those claims which have been made by churches and sects on his behalf but which he never made for himself.

Lest what I am about to write seems, in the eyes of some, to strip from him those accretions—many of them cherished and precious to many—which men have added through the centuries, let me first state my own unshaken belief that compared with all other men he stood, and stands, in a unique relationship with God that he was and is truly human, and in one sense the most knowable and lovable of men, and yet that the word "human," as we usually use it, is not adequate to carry the heavy cargo of qualities which his words and deeds revealed. We use the word "divine" because the word "human" is not big enough. He is so much more like God than any other. But the word "divine" is really only an expression of Christian agnosticism. I am quite ready to say that I believe in the divinity of Christ, but I do not know what it means, nor can I find anyone who can explain what it means, least of all some of the theologians from Paul onwards. I sincerely believe that he is the Savior of the World, and if I am immediately challenged about what he saves men *from,* my answer is that he saves men from the utter despair which would fall upon a thoughtful man, who, conscious of high aims and immense possibilities within himself, was condemned to try to achieve them without any aid save his own, and the purely human help of his fellows. Seneca said that what men needed most of all was a hand let down from heaven to lift them up. God, I believe, came to man's rescue in Christ.

I have called him "knowable," and in one sense he is. Yet we know so little about him. He was only twenty-nine when he died, and of that short life we have records dealing with only three or four years. The records were written by human men, and although they were certainly "inspired," they were not thereby turned into dictaphones nor could they look at him, describe what he did, or report what he said, save as they looked through the tinted glasses of their own prejudices, their limited outlook, their complexes and their wishful thinking. The result is that there are few sentences we can take as the exact words he spoke, though we can and should read all four Gospels, get the total impact which his personality made, and then be in a position to say about the individual sentence, "This sounds just like him," or of other sentences, "No one would report an unlikely sentence like that unless he had said it." At the same time, some sentences which purport to have been spoken by him we must reject out of hand, or perhaps rather, put them in a mental drawer in our minds and label the drawer, "Awaiting further light."

This will sound to some an outrageous thing to say and they will angrily ask me if I do not believe the Bible record. I have tried to anticipate this objection by saying what I did in Chapter II about authority in the field of religion. The only convincing authority there, whether we are discussing something in the Bible or not, is the perceived and self-authenticating truth, and, although it sounds presumptuous, I cannot make myself believe that Jesus spoke certain words which are completely out of character with the total impact which his personality makes upon me, derived from all four Gospels, from the experiences of the saints, and from my own poor but sincere thought of him after half a century's meditation and experience. I must, I feel, judge the Bible by Jesus, not judge Jesus by the Bible, written, as it was, by fallible men who sometimes contradict one another,[1] and who must sometimes have been mistaken in their estimate of him. As a scholarly writer wrote in the London *Times* (December 4, 1954), "It ought to be stated roundly that the doctrine of textual infallibility is no part of orthodox Christianity and is in itself inherently untenable. The disruptive effect of mod-

---

[1] Those who believe in the infallible Bible and that every word was verbally inspired must be put to some difficulty when they realize that concerning the Resurrection narrative, Mark says a young man was present when the women arrived at the tomb, Matthew says it was an angel. Luke says two men. John says two angels.

ern critical study is due to the fact that popular objections still assume the theory of fundamentalism. If God did not converse with a snake in Hebrew, it follows, they think, that the Bible is untrue—and probably that there is no God at all. . . . Any attempt to hold on to that theory or to defend the neo-fundamentalism, of which there are disquieting signs today, must drive a wedge between Scriptural Christianity and the minds of educated men. To acclaim that the Bible *contains* the Word of God is not to say that all its words are the words of God."

Let me illustrate what I mean. Matthew tells us in his famous chapter about the sheep and the goats that Jesus will turn to those on his left-hand side—the goats—and say, "Depart from me ye cursed into the eternal fire which is prepared for the devil and his angels because I was an hungered and ye gave me no meat. . . ." [2] But Luke says that when Jesus was not just left hungry, but was being put to death, he said, "Father, forgive them for they know not what they do." [3] Both these sentences could not have come from the same lips.

We may rightly be told that Matthew's parable is a parable of the *nations*, not of individuals, that nations which fail to be instruments of God's purpose are scrapped and pass into age-long oblivion, and so on. But men, rightly in my judgment, seize on the lovely words in the same chapter, "Inasmuch as ye do it unto one of the least of these my brethren ye do it unto Me," and apply it to personal service. They ignore the passage about the place prepared for the devil and his angels. Clearly it is a psychological impossibility that the lips which said, "Father, forgive them," also said that those who made him hungry—even through inattention to his "little ones"—would eternally be tortured and share the same fate as the devil and his angels. So, by the very principle I set out in the chapter on authority we say, "He could not not possibly have said that." And the scholars vindicate us.

[2] Matthew 25:41-42 [3] Luke 23:34

The passage about the sheep and the goats only occurs in Matthew's Gospel. Moreover, an almost identical passage occurs in the apocryphal book of Enoch. "Surely," says Leckie, "it is evident that both owe their form to a common *imaginative* tradition." [4] So, when Jesus is reported as consigning to everlasting torture those who displease him or do not "believe" what he says, I *know* in my heart that there is something wrong somewhere. Either he is misreported or misunderstood, or else some bias or complex of the reporter has distorted his ideas, or the reporter is expressing—as some of his disciples were wont to do [5]—their desire that those who did not support him should meet some dire fate. So I put this alleged saying in my mental drawer awaiting further light, or else I reject it out of hand. By the judgment of a court within my own breast, more reliable than a theory of the inspiration of the Scriptures; by what I believe to be the leading of God's Spirit who promised that he would guide us into all truth, I reject such sayings. No one can believe—even on the evidence of a Biblical writer—that God is a despotic, cruel tyrant or that Jesus could support action which sounds more like Buchenwald and Belsen than the spirit which said, "Father, forgive them."

As I said earlier, into that same mental drawer go sentences like, "No one cometh unto the Father but by Me," [6] and, "All that ever came before Me were thieves and robbers." [7]

When we remember how difficult men find it to remember exactly what was said by anybody about anything a few hours after an occurrence, especially where strong feelings are involved, and then remember that though the Gospel writers had better memories than ourselves, who always keep pen

---

[4] Italics mine. J. H. Leckie, Kerr Lectures, *The World to Come and Final Destiny*, p. 110, T. & T. Clark, 1918, and also Streeter, *Immortality*, p. 197 (Macmillan, 1918) and Dougall and Emmet, *The Lord of Thought*, p. 170 (Student Christian Movement Press, 1922).

[5] E.g. "Lord wilt Thou that we bid fire to come down from Heaven and consume them?" (Luke 9:54)

[6] John 14:6   [7] John 10:8

and pad at the ready, yet it was in the A.D. 60's, perhaps A.D. 65, before the first Gospel—that of Mark—was written down —that is nearly forty years after the death of Christ—we are more ready to acknowledge that no claim can be pressed for accurate reporting. The Gospel of John may have been thirty years later still. Indeed, all reputable scholars agree that the fourth Gospel is rather the reflection of a very devout mind meditating on Jesus than any attempt at a verbatim report of what was said.

Yet we can be quite sure of the historicity of Jesus. This is vouched for by pagan historians who had no axe to grind and no interest in what Jesus said or did. Pliny (A.D. 61–114), Tacitus (55–120), Suetonius (75–150), and Josephus (37–100) make references in their works which prove indisputably that Jesus was a historical person. I cannot refrain from quoting a passage from Josephus, "About that time lived Jesus, a wise man, *if man He may be called*, for He did wonderful works—a teacher of those who joyfully received the truth. He won to Himself many Jews and many Greeks. He was the Christ, and though Pilatus condemned Him to death, He was our Messiah and appeared on the third day." [8] It is good to feel that the Christian religion is based on the objective reality of the historical Christ whose real existence in time and place is as well vouched for as that of Plato.

I shall deal now with four matters relative to the life of Christ which bother the thoughtful layman—the Virgin Birth, the miracles he is reported to have worked, the significance of his death and the manner of his resurrection.

Virgin Birth

For a great many Christians the manner of his birth is one of great importance. They attach immense significance, even

---

[8] Jewish Antiquities 18:3. Italics mine. Some scholars regard this either as an interpolation by a Christian apologist after the death of Josephus, or an evidence that the latter had become a Christian before writing the *Antiquities*.

sinlessness and divinity, to what is called the Virgin Birth, by which they mean that Jesus Christ had no human father but was conceived only by the Holy Ghost.

Here I should recommend the Christian layman to put the idea of the Virgin Birth into the imaginary mental drawer to be labeled, "Awaiting further light." For myself, I am quite sure that the doctrine, though of great interest, is of no *importance* at all. If it were, it would have been part of the missionary message of the Church. Mark, our earliest Gospel, never mentions it. Nor do Peter or Paul or "John." Divinity is not proved by having one parent instead of two. It could be argued that such a person is removed from us and could not have been truly man. As to sinlessness, we men are a wicked lot, but *all* the evil in our children does not come from us. Mothers can pass on evil as well as fathers, and sinlessness cannot be physically determined.

How can a doctrine be essential in a religion if the founder of the religion never mentions it, or teaches his apostles to pass it on? For myself, I neither believe it nor disbelieve it. Jesus is to me what he is, not because he entered the world in a special way or left it in a special way, but because of what he was and did and said while he was in the world, and because that being and doing, and those amazing words, give me the fullest clue available to the mysterious nature of God, and because he draws me near to God, as he said he would.[9] Every man, to the extent to which he is good, is a revelation of God. There is for me no fuller revelation than Jesus. From any significant action of his we feel we learn about the nature of God.

Virgin Birth, then, neither proves sinlessness, incarnation or divinity. We just do not know what divinity connotes, save that it implies a plus to his humanity, a plus which was both achieved and endowed. His sinlessness we assume, but of course we are not capable of proving it. Even I am not

[9] John 12:32.

tempted to steal the teaspoons when I go out to tea with the vicar, nor to run away with his wife, nor to get drunk. Christ was not tempted in all the *situations* in which I am tempted, He was tempted at all *points* as we are (Hebrews 4:15), namely at the point of his power, his weakness, his desires and so on. I suspect that, living on the moral and spiritual levels on which Christ lived, he must have had temptations so subtle that I should not have had enough spiritual sensitiveness to see them as temptations at all. Their subtle, insidious power is reflected in what otherwise sounds a rough answer to Peter, "You are a stumbling-block unto me." [10] Their reality is seen in what we call his temptations, which, since he was alone, he must have reported to his men. But I have often meditated on his swift rejoinder to the rich young ruler, "No one is good except God" [11]—a rejoinder, the authenticity of which seems proved in that no one would ever make up a sentence like that. The truth is we have no means of knowing if any trace of anything but perfection ever even momentarily invaded that peerless spirit. In my opinion, the strongest evidence of his sinlessness is that, if one had sinned, unless one were vicious, one would never let others think one sinless. It is reported that he asked, "Which of you convicteth me of sin?" [12] and that in the model prayer he said when YE pray, say, "Forgive us our trespasses." He never seems to have said, "In the eyes of God, I am a sinner too," as we should have done.

The doctrine of the Virgin Birth may have begun as a rumor. Buddha's birth is similarly accounted for. It may have received support from those who thought—as many still think —that the sex act is in itself wicked or at least animal,[13] and an expression of our lower nature, and that no one as glorious as Christ could be the fruit of sexual union. The word "vir-

[10] Matthew 16:23   [11] Luke 18:19
[12] John 8:46, though the New English Bible has, "Which of you can prove me in the wrong?"
[13] Cf. Psalm 51:5, "In sin did my mother conceive me."

gin," both in Hebrew *(almāh)* and Greek *(parthenos)*, simply means a mature young woman, not a *"virgo intacta,"* and more may have been deduced from the word than is warranted by its use. The text, "behold a virgin shall conceive and bear a son" (Isaiah 7:14) simply means that a mature young woman will have a baby! As I say, Mark, Peter, Paul and John show no knowledge of ever having heard of a virgin birth in the modern sense of the term, and Matthew goes out of his way to show that Jesus was descended through *Joseph* from David,[14] which seems rather meaningless if Joseph was not his father. Further, the New English Bible carries a footnote on Matthew 1:16 to the effect that the passage has been translated by one writer thus: "Joseph, to whom Mary, a virgin (= a young woman) was betrothed, was the father of Jesus called Messiah." The fourth Gospel (John) not only describes the Jews as calling Jesus the son of Joseph but says that the disciples did also.[15]

As Dr. Barclay—a great authority on the New Testament —wrote: "The Jews had a saying that in the birth of every child there were three partners, the father, the mother and the Spirit of God. They believed that no child could ever be born without the Spirit, and it may well be that the New Testament stories of the birth of Jesus are lovely, poetical ways of saying that even if he had a human father, the Holy Spirit of God was operative in his birth in the most unique and special way.[16]

On the other hand, we read that Joseph seemed shocked at Mary's pregnancy and was "minded to put her away privily" and was "not willing to make her a public example." [17] Unless he were a consummate hypocrite—which we can rule out, or Jesus would never have taught men to call God a

---

[14] Matthew 1:16, Luke 2:27, 41, 43, 4:22.
[15] John 6:42, Matthew 13:55, John 1:45.
[16] See Dr. William Barclay, *The Gospel of Luke,* p. 7 (St. Andrew Press, 1957).
[17] Matthew 1:18-19.

Father—the reference to his being "a righteous man" rules out premarital intimacy. Besides, if the child were his, Jewish law would have demanded his care for Mary and her unborn child. He would not have been allowed to "put her away privily." Indeed, it would not have entered his head to do so. Whence then came Mary's pregnancy? Can we suppose that some village rascal was responsible for her condition? I hold that the beauty of the peerless story rules this out. Read again the first chapter of St. Luke's Gospel and imagine a village maiden of sixteen or so, after some mystical experience beyond the power of any pen to describe, saying quietly, "Behold the slave-girl of the Lord; be it unto me according to Thy word!" [18]

If we are asked to believe that the incomparably beautiful narrative is a "cover up story" for some sordid sexual relationship in a back street in Nazareth, we are being asked to believe in a psychological miracle which strains credulity more impossibly than does belief in the alleged physiological miracle of the Virgin Birth. What genius made up that story? And how did he hush up the facts? No, that certainly will not do.

I do not ask the reader to accept the Virgin Birth if it offends his intellect. I do not ask him to reject it as impossible, but to hold it, *sub judice*, awaiting further light, to be a Christian agnostic about it.

One explanation of Mary's pregnancy has been put to me. I owe it to a scholarly correspondent, Mr. G. A. Wainwright, who, until his death in May, 1964, spent a lot of time at Oxford doing research work. He writes of the "sacred marriage" ceremony which was an ancient and widespread custom in the Near East, and indeed is also, as I recall from my own days in India, incorporated in certain Hindu practices.

In the ceremony of the "sacred marriage," either the high priest or the king played the part of a divine messenger. He

[18] Luke 1:38.

was "married" to a virgin with whom he cohabited. The offspring of such a union was regarded as a son of god, or a divine king, a divine personage or an "avatar" who incarnated god.[19]

Now Zacharias was the priest on duty in the temple at the relevant time. He "executed the priest's office before God in the order of his course" (Luke 1:8). We are told that, though old, Zacharias was not impotent, for he made his wife Elisabeth pregnant though she was past the normal time of childbearing. John the Baptist was their son.

We are also told that after Mary's visitation from the angel who told her she was to bear Jesus, Mary replied, "How shall this be, seeing I know not a man?" Mary was then reassured thus: "The Holy Ghost shall come upon thee, and the power of the Most High shall overshadow thee: wherefore also that which is to be born shall be called holy, the Son of God." (Luke 1:35.)

We have just seen, on Dr. Barclay's authority, that every birth was regarded as "overshadowed" by the Holy Spirit (p. 101), even if a human father also took part. We are then told that Mary entered the house of Zacharias (Luke 1:39-40), *stayed there three months,* and then returned to her own house (Luke 1:56).

In such a "sacred marriage" as I have described, a stay of three months was required in the house of the priest, or in the sacred precincts, to make sure that pregnancy was established.[20] This would explain why Mary stayed in the home of

---

[19] The origin of the 5th Dynasty in Egypt is said to have been in the birth of a child about 2500 B.C. to "the wife of a priest of Rê, Lord of Sakhebu." Ever afterwards the chief title of Pharaoh was "Son of Rê"— the Sun God. (See Erman, *The Literature of the Ancient Egyptians* [translated Blackman, p. 43], and Breasted, *Ancient Records of Egypt* [Vol. 2, pp. 196 ff.].). Frazer in *The Golden Bough* gives other examples (one vol. ed. pp. 142 ff.).

[20] Jewish law required a period of three months to certify the parentage of a child about to be born. A divorced woman could not marry for three months so as to assure the origin of any child subsequently born to her.

Zacharias for three months before returning to her own home. Indeed, what an otherwise strange reaction to Gabriel's message was her hurried journey *into* Zacharias' house! "Mary arose," we read, "and *went with haste* and entered the house of Zacharias" (Luke 1:39).

It is impossible to associate the birth of Jesus with some sordid affair between Mary and an unknown man. The Magnificat breathes the spirit of complete dedication to God on the part of an unsullied worshiper proud to label herself as the "slave-girl of the Lord." But of course such a process as I have suggested, far from being considered immoral behavior, would be regarded as the highest degree of spiritual dedication, just as in Hindu circles the most religious act a Hindu father of a girl could perform was to give his daughter as one of the *devadasi* of the temple, where she became what we should label a prostitute of the priests.

In ancient thought it would be an immense honor to a woman thus to bear a son, as well as requiring from her a supreme degree of dedication, and my correspondent points out that the expression used by the angel at the Annunciation, "Thou hast found favour with God" (Luke 1:30), is almost identical with the very words Herodotus uses of the Divine Bride at Babylon, where she is called, "a woman chosen by the god out of the whole nation."

We must allow that among the contemporary Scribes and Pharisees of the Temple in Jerusalem, and among the ecclesiastical authorities, the idea of the "sacred marriage" had disappeared and was disapproved of. But in the "hill country," to which we are specially told Mary went to seek out Zacharias and Elisabeth, decadent forms of religion—as we think of them—continued, just as Hindu practices like Suttee[21] still win approval in jungle villages in India, though both en-

---

[21] Suttee is the voluntary act of a Hindu woman who, on losing her husband, has herself burnt alive on a funeral pyre so that he shall have her company and affection in the life after death.

lightened Hindus and the law of the land have sough
banish them.

Scores of my friends, in their secret hearts, disbelieve in the
Virgin Birth, but they have no other explanation of the birth
of Jesus to put in its place. Here is another matter for Christian agnosticism; another matter for the mental drawer to
which I have referred. It is, of course, a speculation, but for
those who reject the Virgin Birth and are asked what alternative is possible, it seems to me a solution which meets such
evidence as we possess. Except for the opening chapters of
Matthew and Luke, the New Testament never mentions the
Virgin Birth again and bases nothing on it. In the important
document called *Doctrine in the Church of England*, which
has received far too little attention, we read, "There are some
among us who hold that a full belief in the historical incarnation is more consistent with the supposition that our Lord's
birth took place under the normal conditions of human generation," [22] and Eric Ackroyd, in *The Modern Churchman*
wrote, "If the Virgin Birth is taken literally to mean birth
without sexual intercourse, it is robbed of religious significance." [23] In his valuable book, *Jesus, the Son of God*, Dr.
Frederic Greeves, Principal of a college which trains Methodist ministers, and ex-president of the Methodist Conference,
says, "The writer holds to the position expressed by Dr. H. R.
Mackintosh: 'I should not think of regarding explicit belief
in the Virgin Birth of our Lord as essential to Christian
Faith.'" [24] (See also pp. 347-48.) Says Dr. Fosdick in a recent
book, "I am not telling you what you should think about the
Virgin Birth, I am simply indicating that personally I cannot
believe it." [25]

We must pass on now to the miracles of Christ which for
some laymen are such a formidable barrier to belief.

[22] P. 82, S.P.C.K., 1938. See also p. 12.
[23] *The Modern Churchman*, April, 1964, p. 163.
[24] *Op. cit.*, p. 79 (Epworth Press, 1939)   [25] *Op. cit.*, p. 60

Miracles

Once we accept the view—which is my own belief—that Christ was a divine Being who was not only at home on our plane but on a higher spiritual plane also, authentic miracles become to him normal happenings.

Let us imagine two friendly dogs chatting together, one of which has hurt its paw, which looks as if it is turning septic. All that its friend could suggest by way of therapy would be for the sufferer to lie up, rest the paw and lick the wound. But supposing the owner of the sick dog, a compassionate man, seeing the situation, gave the sufferer an injection of penicillin, bathed the wound in antiseptic, dressed it and bound it up, then the resultant speedy and uncomplicated cure would be a miracle *to both dogs*, if we imaginatively endow them with the power to talk things over! It would involve procedures familiar on the plane on which *men* live, involving activity which is entirely law-abiding and largely understood by men, impinging on to a lower plane where it set up amazement—if dogs can be amazed—among lower beings who could not understand it or repeat it unless they acquired the power to progress on to man's plane.

To my mind, this imaginative parable gives us a clue to miracles. There was no "suspension of the laws of nature." The universe must be law-abiding, and if Christ suspended law it would be a criticism of his Father as one whose laws were inadequate for certain possible situations which might arise. "We say," said St. Augustine profoundly, "that all portents (=miracles) are contrary to nature, but they are not so. For how is that contrary to nature which happens by the will of God, since the will of so mighty a Creator is certainly the nature of each created thing?" [26]

My illustration of the dogs goes further. We can assume that dogs could never discover penicillin. In the same way I would reserve the word "miracle" for those events which

[26] Augustine, *The City of God*, 21:8.

manifest the activity of processes inaccessible to man *at his present stage of development.*

Henry Drummond once asked, "May it not be perfectly normal for a perfect man to rise from the dead as Christ did?" The answer may be "Yes." And as man spiritually develops he may be able to do many things that Jesus did. This seems hinted at by Jesus himself. "Greater things than these shall ye do, . . ." [27] "Our present limitations," said my great teacher, Dr. W. R. Maltby, "are not His bounds, nor even ultimately our bounds." [28] But, at man's *present* stage of development, to rise from the dead in the manner of Jesus is to use laws which are as much—one would think—beyond man as the use of penicillin is beyond a dog.

My definition, then, of a miracle is that it is *a law-abiding event by which God accomplishes his purposes through the release of energies which belong to a plane of being higher than man, at his present stage of development, has reached.*

When we read of the miracles recorded in the New Testament, however, we must be awake to several factors.

1. The fact that a so-called miracle is wonderful does not make it a miracle in the sense just defined. The Arabs with whom I lived in the desert during the First World War thought the electric telegraph a miracle. Quite soon, however, they could operate it themselves. In the field of healing I have seen things happen which in the Bible are labeled miracles—a paralyzed patient, for example, cured through accepting forgiveness[29]—but the marvelous is not the *test* of miracle, though the marvelous is characteristic of miracle. All miracles are marvelous events, but all marvelous events are not miracles.

2. The so-called miracle is not a proof of divinity. My Arab friends thought the electric telegraph a miracle, as I say,

[27] John 14:12.
[28] *Significance of Jesus*, p. 28 (Student Christian Movement Press, 1929).
[29] Mark 2:1-12. See my *Psychology, Religion and Healing*, pp. 69-73.

but they did not suppose that the telegraphists were divine! As Dr. Orchard once facetiously remarked, "If I saw someone walking on the sea I should not say, 'You must be Divine,' I should say, 'Excuse me, do you mind showing me how you did that?'" When Jesus saw a leper, it is incredible that he said to himself, "Now I will work a miracle and prove that I am divine." Surely he had the same feeling as a mother who treats her child's injury. She loves the child and she knows how to make him better, so she gets to work with her superior knowledge without thought of what impression she makes on the child. Christ loved lepers and he knew how to make them well. So he got to work. Readers who think that the test of a miracle is the marvelous element and that it points to divinity should read a book like Father Thurston's, *The Physical Phenomena of Mysticism*[30] in which phenomena like stigmata, levitation, telekinesis and a dozen other marvels are seen to be—certainly paranormal—but not belonging to any higher plane of being than that open to man at his present stage of development.

3. A third fact to remember as we read the miracle stories is that men have an inveterate way of seeking to make a great person appear greater in the eyes of others by embroidering his deeds and adding unhistorical elements; by "writing them up" as we say. So the devout have ever made claims for Christ which he would never have made for himself.

When I was in India, an educated Indian student asked for time off from his studies because he said he had heard that Mr. Gandhi had changed a woman into a man! If this kind of thing can be tied on to the character of a great man *during his lifetime* by an intelligent admirer, what is likely to be added to the deeds of a far greater man than Gandhi, in writings which did not appear until over a quarter of a century after his death?

[30] Published by Burns Oates, 1952.

During the *lifetime* of the great Roman Catholic missionary, St. Francis Xavier, no miracles were claimed for him either by himself or by his missionary companions. But after his death at least a dozen striking miracles were attributed to him, including making salt water fresh, causing an earthquake, burying a town under ashes, inducing a crab to restore a crucifix lost at sea, and even raising the dead.[81] St. Francis himself admitted how difficult he found it to learn the simplest elements of the Japanese language, but in the "lives" of the saint, biographers claimed that he spoke Japanese so fluently that his hearers thought he was a Japanese himself, and other nationalities present heard him miraculously *in their own tongues.*[82]

Many miracles were ascribed to St. Thomas à Becket of Canterbury. The early stories of his power we can accept, but as the gulf of time widened after his death, we find stories like the following: One story involved turning Canterbury water into milk; in others, allegedly amputated members were restored; a baby of eight months sang the Kyrie Eleison; a dead cow which had been skinned and the hide sent to the tanners was restored unharmed to its owners; and so on.[83]

Mohammed distinctly disclaimed all possession of miraculous powers, but his followers sought to increase admiration for him by heightening some stories and inventing others. Thus he was credited with having made the sun stand still, having obtained water from a flinty rock and having fed thousands from a little food.[84]

Are we to suppose a further miracle, namely that in regard to the Gospel stories about Jesus, heightening and invention were excluded?

[81] Andrew D. White, *A History of the Warfare of Science with Theology in Christendom*, Vol. 2, pp. 5-23.
[82] Fosdick, *Modern Use of the Bible*, p. 143 (Macmillan Co., 1924).
[83] Edwin A. Abbott, *St. Thomas of Canterbury, His Death and Miracles.*
[84] George Foot Moore, *History of Religions*, vol. 2, p. 476.

The question which I feel it is so relevant to ask is not, "What deeds lay within Christ's power?" for I wonder if anyone can, or ever will be able to answer that question. The relevant questions to my mind are, "Is this alleged happening like him? Is it the kind of thing he would be likely to do? Is it an expression of his compassion and love for men? Does it fit into the picture of him in one's mind after all the available evidence has made its impact?" Healing a leper seems to me a perfect example of a miracle, desire to make a sick man well being the motive, not desire to do something startling, but whether turning water into 120 gallons of wine (six water pots, each holding twenty gallons) which would keep a small village in wine for some time, a story only recorded in one Gospel, written half a century after the event described, is to be regarded as factual, I feel we may be allowed to doubt, since nothing important hangs on it.[35]

Some other stories I think are in the category of narratives which have been "written up," and it is legitimate for the modern man to seek natural explanations. Indeed, intellectual honesty demands this. It is superstitious to adopt a supernatural explanation of a phenomenon if a natural explanation just as satisfactorily accounts for it. When I crossed the Sea of Galilee myself in a motorboat in 1934 a terrifying storm arose and as quickly subsided. The occurrence is still common. It would have been very easy to ascribe the sudden calm to a wonderful person on board who spoke, not to waves—which do not understand Aramaic!—but to men. As I read the story, Jesus spoke sternly to frightened fishermen, not to unconscious water, saying "Peace, be still," [36] since their infectious fear was spreading panic.

---

[35] I have discussed the Cana story fully in *It Happened in Palestine*, pp. 69 ff (Abingdon Press, 1936).

[36] I have discussed this and other miracles in my book, *When the Lamp Flickers*, pp. 64-72 (Abingdon Press, 1948). The word translated "Be still" is literally, "Be muzzled," or colloquially, "Shut up!" and was spoken to the *men*, though Mark understandably thought Christ was rebuking the alleged storm-demon.

One wonders whether Christ really cursed a fig-tree when it was not even the time of figs.[37] One wonders whether a boy-follower did not offer his lunch to Jesus and whether Jesus did not say to the multitude, estimated at between four and five thousand, "If you all are willing to share as this lad has done there is enough for all." [38] I was told in Palestine that the fish they call "musht," or, more commonly, St. Peter's fish, loves, magpie-like, to pick up bright metals such as a coin, and keep it in a pouch below its jaw. What more likely than that Jesus teased Peter and said, "Go and catch a musht, you may find the temple tax in its mouth." [39] What more likely than that Jesus, standing on the shore, saw a shoal of fish gathering where warm water enters the lake (I have seen the place myself) and directed His disciples to haul in what was later called a *miraculous* draught of fishes (Luke 5:4 ff)? One wonders whether the story of the daughter of Jairus, always quoted as a raising from the dead on the part of Jesus, was not a case of healing a girl who was in a coma. Many believers insist that the girl was dead, which is odd when Jesus so definitely said she was not.[40] None of this is written to belittle Christ but to understand him; to have a reverent agnosticism concerning possible accretions which men love to add to a venerated figure, forgetting that they only make more difficulties. They do nothing to make the modern man love him more or serve him better. They obscure the real Jesus from us and by implication make claims for him which are irrelevant and unnecessary and which he would never have made for himself.

[37] See *When the Lamp Flickers*, pp. 73-80.

[38] See *A Shepherd Remembers*, pp. 51-54 (Hodder and Stoughton).

[39] See Matthew 17:27, and *It Happened in Palestine*, pp. 62-63. This habit is also attributed to another fish, the Coracinus, by Rix in *Tent and Testament*. Dr. H. D. A. Major says, "A fish of such habits might carry a coin in this way." *The Mission and Message of Jesus*, p. 245. Some people think Christ meant, "Sell the fish and, with the price you get, pay the tax."

[40] See Mark 5:39, and *Psychology, Religion and Healing* (rev. edition, pp. 65-69, where every healing miracle of Jesus is discussed). Bishop Gore says, "There is nothing in Mark's story to show that the girl was dead."

Some of the healing miracles may not have been miracles in the sense defined on p. 107. They may have been accomplished by means which we shall understand later, such as the use of odic force or absent healing through prayer.[41] But some seem to me to be as far from our reach as the use of penicillin is from a dog, and to be "miracles" in the sense defined.

So we are left looking in awe and adoration at a Divine Being whose divinity is evidenced more by his *desire* to serve men rather than by his undoubted miraculous ability. The nature of a Divine Being is seen more clearly in deeds which are loving than in deeds which are marvelous. He does not need miracle to make us love him or to prove that he is more than man. The unanswerable argument for his religion is that wherever he is sincerely followed men's lives are changed. When an old drunkard, who had almost sold up his home to get money for more and more drink, was truly converted, he said a very profound thing: "I don't know whether Christ turned water into wine, but for me he did something that was much more use. He turned beer into furniture."

This power to change men's lives whatever their nationality, color, creed, education, century or other differentiation, seems to me the unanswerable argument for Christianity and the greatest miracle of all, a real impact, on our plane, of energies that belong to a higher one. In Christ, God stooped to enter our lowly plane and redeem us with a grace that is never of human achievement but always a divine gift.

The Cross of Christ

I was delighted to find so reputable and well equipped a theologian as my friend the Dean of St. Paul's, Dr. Matthews, writing thus: "We need to get clear on the point that no *doctrine* of the Atonement is part of the Christian Faith and

[41] I have discussed the operation of both these energies in *Wounded Spirits* (Abingdon Press, 1962).

that many different views are possible concerning the manner of the Divine Forgiveness." [42]

Few matters so muddle the thoughtful layman—for whom I am writing this book—than the attempt to link the death of Christ in A.D. 29 with the sins of men today.

Let me set down quite bluntly some of the questions which I have been asked by thoughtful people.

1. "How can the fact that Christ was put to death nearly two thousand years ago have anything to do with my sins? I wasn't born then. Surely it was nothing to do with me. I cannot honestly sing, 'In my place condemned He stood.' "

2. It is suggested that God could only forgive man because Jesus had died and "paid the price of sin," but I forgive my child if he sins and is sorry, without asking that some innocent person should suffer, as if there were a measure of suffering that in some fantastic ledger-account balanced the degree of sin. Dr. Frederic Greeves reminds us that, "There is no recorded saying of Jesus in which He explicitly connects His death with the forgiveness or remission of sins," [43] and Dr. Vincent Taylor, one of our greatest living New Testament scholars, agrees.[44] One line of a terrible hymn says: "Exacted is the legal pain." Surely sin is not a debt which someone else can pay for me. I have to pay at least part of it myself. Besides, did not God forgive the Psalmist who wrote Psalm 51, when he pleaded penitently for forgiveness—"Hide Thy face from my sins and blot out all my iniquities"? [45] The Old Testament is full of petitions for pardon. Were they useless because Christ had not then paid this mythical "price of sin"? Sin is not something which can be "paid for" by the suffering of

[42] The Rev. Dr. W. R. Matthews, K.C.V.O., D.D., *Seven Words*, p. 29 (Hodder and Stoughton, 1933).
[43] *The Meaning of Sin*, p. 104 (Epworth Press, 1956).
[44] *Forgiveness and Reconciliation*, pp. 13-14 (Macmillan, 1941). Both Greeves and Taylor regard Matthew 26:28 as unauthentic. The death of Christ induces man's penitence and forgiveness but is not essential to forgiveness. Clearly, Old Testament penitents were truly forgiven.
[45] Psalm 51:9.

113

another. Both the nature of sin and the nature of God are distorted by this idea. The prodigal, the woman taken in adultery, the boy let down through the roof were all forgiven at once. Frankly it is nonsense to say, "Without the shedding of blood there is no remission of sins" (Hebrews 9:22).

3. In some sermons—says the layman—the Cross is presented to us in the imagery of the law court. God is a stern Judge seated on the Bench and humanity is in the dock and found guilty of sin for which the punishment is hell. One hymn says:

> *And then in pity Jesus said,*
> *He'd bear the punishment instead.*

Another says:

> *For what you have done,*
> *His blood must atone,*
> *The Father hath punished*
> *For you His dear Son.*

But how can what Jesus suffered be called a punishment inflicted by God? Was not the Son obediently doing what he conceived to be his Father's will in the circumstances which evil had set up? Did he not cry in agony in Gethsemane, "Not my will but Thine be done"? What kind of logic is this? We watch a Son, in great mental agony, seeking only his Father's will, and then, when he does it, the church calls it his Father's *punishment* and sings, "The Father has *punished* for you His dear Son." And what good does it do to punish an innocent person for what I am going to do two thousand years later? Besides, though anyone who loves me can share my shame, no one can bear my guilt. It is indubitable that guilt cannot be transferred, for authentic guilt makes me feel blameworthy. If I go and commit adultery, or murder an old woman and steal her life savings, another may feel the deepest sympathy. If he loves me deeply he will feel involved and he will suffer. He may determine to help me to change. But it is unreal to suppose that he feels as guilty as I do. I did it. He did not. He is in no sense to blame.

"And sin, how could He take our sins upon Him?
What does it mean?
To take sin upon one is not the same
As to have sin inside one and feel guilty.
It is horrible to feel guilty,
We *feel* guilty because we *are*.
Was He horrible? Did He feel guilty?" [46]

I cannot with any degree of reality sing, "I lay my sins on Jesus," or the verse which runs:

> *My faith looks back to see*
> *The burden Thou didst bear,*
> *When hanging on the accursed tree,*
> *And knows her* GUILT *was there.*

And although we hear words rendered in the great music of Handel, about "The Lamb of God who *taketh away* the sins of the world," the trouble is that they are not "taken away." Mine and every man's remain, working still their evil entail in the very cells of our bodies and brains, and in the lives of others whom we have hurt.

4. We rightly call Jesus "the Savior of the World," but some of the words used in the Communion service worry many laymen: "Who made there (by his one oblation of himself once offered) a full, perfect, and sufficient sacrifice, oblation, and satisfaction, for the sins of the whole world. . . ."

Every time the Anglican Communion service is used, the word "propitiation" occurs. ("He is the propitiation for our sins.") But "propitiation," to the layman, means an act by which one buys off the anger of another, "expiation" means

---

[46] "How Do You See?" Stevie Smith, *The Guardian,* May 16, 1964.

paying or suffering in a way regarded as somehow the equivalent of the crime, "satisfaction" means an act which makes
reconciliation possible without the offended person losing
face. Do any of these words express a helpful explanation of
the Cross to the modern layman? If Jesus really did use the
word "ransom" about himself,[47] I wonder if he used it in the
sense in which the contemporary Greek used it, namely the
amount paid to purchase the freedom of a slave *in order to
make him the protégé of some particular god*.[48] A ransom is
paid to someone. The fact that the favorite theory in the early
church for no less than nine centuries was that the suffering
and death of Jesus were a ransom paid by God to the Devil on
condition that the latter would then let mankind out of his
clutches, and not keep them in hell, shows how far a theory
can get from any helpfulness to thoughtful men, and how
long absurd theology can bedevil the minds of men.

It is obvious that, in every generation, men are at liberty to
try to make sense of important events by reference to the
thought-forms of their own time. The Jews were familiar
with the age-long idea of obtaining a sense of forgiveness by
sacrificing an animal on an altar. When therefore the early
Christians, steeped in Judaism, were confronted with the exe-
cution of Jesus, it is no wonder that, to make sense of it, to
explain an omnipotent God's non-interference and Christ's
willingness to die (since he could easily have escaped), their
minds hit on the idea of sacrifice, and Jesus, whom John
the Baptist had called the Lamb of God,[49] was thought to be
the climax of the age-long sacrifices in the temple, and it is
probable that Paul thought in this way also. Paul was

---

[47] Matthew 20:28, Mark 10:45. Dr. Hastings Rashdall, in *The Idea
of Atonement in Christian Theology*, rejects this passage as unauthentic.
[48] Deissmann quoted by Vincent Taylor in *Jesus and His Sacrifice*, p.
103 (Macmillan, 1937).
[49] John 1:29. It is only in the Johannine version of the Baptism of
Jesus that John the Baptist is alleged to call Jesus "the Lamb of God."
Early Christians must have tried, by the time the fourth Gospel was
written in about A.D. 100, to make sense of Christ's death and begun to
think of it as in the same category as Jewish sacrifices.

a great theologian as well as a great saint and a heroic missionary, but we are not bound to imprison our minds in his theories. Newton was a great scientist, but it is no disparagement of Newton to realize that even schoolboys today know more than he did about atoms. Thought moves on in every field of inquiry.

So we have the author of the epistle to the Hebrews writing about Christ as one who made "propitiation for the sins of the people (2:17), telling us that, "apart from the shedding of blood there was no remission" of sins (9:22), and putting the point I am making with devastating clarity when he writes, "For if the blood of bulls and of goats, and the ashes of an heifer sprinkling the unclean, sanctifieth to the purifying of the flesh: How much more shall the blood of Christ, who through the eternal Spirit offered Himself without spot to God, purge your conscience from dead works to serve the living God?" (9:12-14).

The writer of the book of Revelation, influenced by the mystery religions, goes further still from modern western thought when he writes of the Christians in heaven who have "washed their robes and made them white in the blood of the Lamb." [50]

Apart from the slip, which any schoolmaster would correct in a boy's essay, that robes washed in blood would be red not white, and overlooking what is to us the revolting horror of the whole idea, we must note that the picture offered is taken direct from the mystery religions.

Let me quote here Dr. William Barclay: "The Mystery Religions were all founded on the story of some suffering and dying and rising god. This story was played out as a passion play. The initiate had a long course of preparation, instruction, asceticism and fasting. The drama was then played out with gorgeous music, marvellous ritual, incense and everything to play upon the emotions. As it was played out the wor-

[50] Revelation 7:14.

shipper's aim was to become one with the god, identified with the god, in such a way that he passed through the god's sufferings and shared the god's triumph and the god's divine life. The Mystery Religions offered mystic union with some god. When that union was achieved the initiate was, in the language of the Mysteries, *a twice-born*. . . . The most famous of all Mystery ceremonies was the *taurobolium*. The candidate was put into a pit. On the top of the pit there was a lattice-work cover. On the cover a bull was slain by having its throat cut. The blood poured down and the initiate lifted up his head and bathed himself in the blood; he was washed in blood; and when he came out of the pit he was *renatus in aeternum*, reborn for all eternity. When Christianity came to the world with a message of rebirth, it came with precisely that for which all the world was seeking." [51]

The idea of rebirth is an essential part of the gospel and was certainly part of the message of Jesus,[52] but the modern layman can well do without Paul's obsession about sin and the imagery of being washed in blood. The latter has come down to us in hymns still sung by some. Can there be a more revolting idea than this of William Cowper?

> *There is a fountain filled with blood,*
> *Drawn from Immanuel's veins;*
> *And sinners plunged beneath that flood,*
> *Lose all their guilty stains.*

One would have thought that by 1800 (when Cowper died), men would have broken away from the imagery of the mystery religions, but some seem still to revel in it. They still cry in the words and tune of a hymn of which a rude version was sung by men in my regiment in the route marches of the First World War.

[51] The Gospel of St. John, Vol. 1, pp. 115-16, *Daily Bible Readings* (Church of Scotland Press, 1955).
[52] John 3:3.

> *Wash me in the blood of the Lamb,*
> *And I shall be whiter than snow.*

Another hymn which is still sung says definitely:

> *Christ the Heavenly Lamb*
> *Takes all our sins away,*
> *A sacrifice of nobler name*
> *And richer blood than they.*

But we are not first-century Jews. The death of an animal on an altar, or ceremonial taken from a mystery religion would not help us to feel forgiven. And in later Judaism even, the Jewish prophets taught that God desired "mercy and not sacrifice" (Hosea 6:6, and Micah 6:8), and the Psalmist cried: "Thou hast no pleasure in burnt offering. The sacrifices of God are a broken spirit" (51:16, cf. 40:6). We must seek another interpretation of the cross, and at the same time we must realize that the generations ahead will discard *our* interpretations. For centuries men will wonder and adore, but as far as understanding goes they will be Christian agnostics and sing:

> *We may not know, we cannot tell*
> *What pains He had to bear,*
> *But we believe it was for us*
> *He hung and suffered there.*

Let me try, however imperfectly and briefly, to offer a way of looking at the cross which provides, for me at any rate, a place where my mind can rest, although, of course, many questions still remain unanswered.[53]

Humanly speaking, of course, Jesus came into conflict with the Jewish and Roman authorities and between them they successfully plotted and carried out his death. What message

---

[53] I have worked out in far greater detail my own view of the significance of the cross in *A Plain Man Looks at the Cross* (Abingdon Press, 1958).

does it hold for the modern man? For myself the message is twofold. His death is a revelation of the nature of God, and a pledge that God will stand by me until I am made one with him. (At-one-ment.)

1. Revelation. Any man, we have said, to the extent to which he is good, reveals the nature of God. When I watch Jesus, then, in any significant action, or hear any word which I can feel sure is his, I get as true a glimpse as is available of the reactions and nature of God.

Jesus could easily have run away. His disciples successfully did. Jesus could easily have conquered his oppressors. A thousand swords would have flashed from their scabbards if he had led a revolt—which is just what many of his friends, especially Judas, wanted him to do. But apart from that, supernatural energies were at his disposal which would have left Herod a maniac and Pilate a drivelling imbecile. "Thinkest thou not," Jesus said, "that I might pray to my Father and He would send me twelve legions of angels?" [54] Twelve legions instead of twelve cowards! One angel would have been enough! But the restraint of love's respect for human personality held back the legions and sent him to the cross willingly. "No man taketh my life from me," he said, "I lay it down of myself." It was "a decease that He *accomplished*." [55] It was the cup which the Father had given him.[56] It was not something that overcame him. It was something he *did*. "Ought not the Christ to suffer these things?" he said,[57] as if it were suitable, and in character with a plan.

The stage was set by evil hands and the circumstances produced by evil men, as Peter said,[58] but Jesus was not the victim but the Master. He *chose* to die. His earliest followers knew this. They never moaned over a murder. They knew the death carried God's message and was only in appearance the murder of an innocent man. It was another illustration of the way God makes the wrath of men to praise him.[59]

[54] Matthew 26:53   [55] Luke 9:30-31   [56] John 18:11
[57] Luke 24:46   [58] Acts 2:23

[59] Psalm 76:10

Now what was the message? It was a revelation of God's reaction to human sin. To be hurt and hindered by it, but to go on loving, and go on loving, and go on loving, without reprisal or answering violence until men see what sin is and what sin does, and turn with loathing from that which has so grievously hurt the greatest Lover of the human soul.

And as Jesus went to the uttermost—for no man while still in the flesh can do more than die to show his love for another —so God will endlessly labor, using all the resources which infinite love possesses, to bring us into harmony with himself. God also will go "to the uttermost."

2. But I think the message of the cross goes further. I think that on the night before his death and in his dying, Jesus pledged himself in an acted parable to an infinite redemptive ministry on man's behalf.

Jesus never called himself the Lamb of God, but he did call himself the Bridegroom[60] and gave men the parable of the ten virgins and the Bridegroom.[61] He spoke of his men as "children of the Bridechamber" and I have often wondered why the church has never made more of his own choice of this title for himself.

The words "Behold the Bridegroom cometh" opened the Jewish ceremony of the Passover long before Jesus was born. And the Passover was regarded as God's marriage to his people. Jesus at the last supper said, "With great eagerness have I desired to eat *this Passover* with you" (Luke 22:15). The idea of God as the Bridegroom and of his people as the Bride was familiar to his men. Hosea makes use of it.[62] Jeremiah does the same.[63]

Were the events of that last evening, when Jesus celebrated "this Passover" with his men, meant to be an acted parable— as was his triumphant entry into Jerusalem? And was this acted parable one of his marriage to the church, which ever afterwards rejoiced to call itself the Bride of Christ? John

[60] Matthew 9:15; Mark 2:19; Luke 5:34   [61] Matthew 25:1-6
[62] Hosea 2:19-20   [63] Jeremiah 2:2; 31:32

saw the redeemed like a bride adorned for her husband (Revelation 21:2). And Paul tells husbands to love their wives "as Christ loved the church *and gave Himself up for it*" (Ephesians 5:25). It is interesting to note the parallel. In a Jewish wedding the bridegroom sought first to bring the bride to his own home. Jesus invited the twelve to supper in the room lent to him, since he then had no home. When the bridegroom got the bride home, he first of all knelt and washed her feet. Jesus washed the disciples' feet. Then at a Jewish wedding the wedding feast followed. Jesus ate roast lamb and unleavened bread with his men. After supper, at a Jewish wedding, came the words of the wedding covenant. Jesus made "a new covenant" with symbols of the broken bread and the poured out wine. I read that four cups of wine were used. The first all drank. This was the cup of blessing. The second none drank. It represented the curse and was "poured out," but at the last supper it is surmised that Jesus drank it alone (cf. "Are ye able to drink the cup that I drink?" Matthew 20:22). The third was an overflowing cup (the cup of salvation, cf. Psalm 116:13), which all drank. The fourth was "the cup of the Kingdom," and at the supper it is supposed that all drank except Jesus (cf. "I will no more drink of the fruit of the vine until the Kingdom of God shall come," Luke 22:18). When he went to the cross to have his body broken and his blood poured out, could they possibly miss the message that he was "married" to them, committed to them forever? This was a "Passover" with a special purpose.

A marriage is a covenant which ideally is never broken, and some words of Dr. W. R. Maltby[64] express just what appeals to me most as the inner meaning of the cross. "On Calvary Christ betrothed Himself for ever to the human race, for better, for worse, for richer, for poorer, in sickness and in health. It is not what God once was, or Christ once did, that can save us, but what Christ once did is the sacrament and

---

[64] *The Meaning of the Cross*, pp. 10, 14-16 (Epworth Press).

visible pledge to us of what He is and does for ever, and shows to us, each one, if we will, the God with whom we have to do. . . . We know what it means to 'wash our hands of a person,' but we have no word for the opposite thing." It was that "opposite thing" to which Jesus committed himself. He committed himself to the task of recovering all humanity to God, however long it might take, however arduous the way, however unrewarding the toil.

I cannot find much help in ideas about Christ's death that see him as a Lamb offered on an altar to appease or propitiate an angry God. I cannot get help from thinking of him in the dock accepting a sentence of death from an outraged Judge, whose will he had sought to do! For sin is not a kind of debt which another can pay, or a burden another can carry. Nor can I think of a God unwilling to forgive me, if I am truly penitent, unless someone's sufferings "paid the price of sin."

But if I am told that this Divine Person, this aptly named "Savior of the World," showed once, by his attitude to sinners, that he is committed by a sacred bond and covenant to stand by me, never to forsake me or give me up as a bad job, and is similarly committed to all men and women, and, from the unseen, is engaged in a ceaseless ministry on my, and all others' behalf, until all are brought into unity with him and thus with the Father; if the cross is at the same time both a revelation and a pledge, then the cross takes its central place in my religious thinking and its appeal and power are irresistible. Here is one whom death does not relieve either of his humanity or his mission, and who committed himself to endless sacrifice and service for the redemption of the world. So the church, with Charles Wesley, will go on singing:

> *The dear tokens of His passion*
> *Still His dazzling body bears.*

There is a wonderful passage in the letter to the Hebrews

(certainly not written by Paul), in which we read,[65] "He is able to save to the uttermost them that draw near unto God through Him, seeing that He ever liveth to make intercession for us." The Greek word translated, "to make intercession," does not, I read,[66] mean imploring his Father to be kind to us. What a horrible idea that would be if God is in any sense a Father! The word used expresses the idea of acting on behalf of another person to whom one is committed. To my mind, which sees things in pictures, Christ does not bow before the Father in supplication that God will have mercy on his own children, but rather that Christ endlessly is at work with and within man, by all the ways open to love—without coercion, or bribing, or favoritism—to effect a unity, an at-one-ment between man and God. He is acting on behalf of us because he has committed himself to us. He who has one hand in the hand of God, his Father, with whom he has so much in common, has his other hand—as it were—in the hand of man, with whom he also has so much in common. He does not bring his hands together in intercession like the "praying hands" we so often see depicted. Rather he brings his hands together by putting the hand of man into the hand of God. He can only end his work when all men are one with God. I think it was his contemplation of an age-long task, just when he thought that he would be able to resume the glory he had with God "before the world was," [67] that made the agony in the Garden of Gethsemane so terrible. Others have suffered equally in terms of bodily pain but he was called upon to retain the limitations of humanity—except the flesh —and for ages to serve men and suffer with them. No wonder "he began to be sorrowful and"—as Dr. David Smith translates—"very homesick." [68] But to be made one with God is

---

[65] Hebrew 7:25.

[66] Bishop Westcott's *Commentary on Hebrews*, p. 191 (Macmillan).

[67] John 17:5.

[68] David Smith, *The Disciples' Commentary on the Gospels*, Vol. 1, pp. 419-20 (Hodder and Stoughton). Dr. Vincent Taylor says, "The verb denotes the distress which follows a great shock," c.f. Professor A. S. Peake, *Century Bible*, p. 162 (T. C. and E. C. Jack).

the whole *raison d'être* of man. This is why man was created. This is the goal to which we move. This is the work of the Savior. As the Indian poet, Rabindranath Tagore put it, "Our Master Himself has joyfully taken upon Him the bonds of creation; He is bound with us all for ever." [69]

The Resurrection

That Jesus survived death and proved his survival to his followers seems to me convincingly proved. Let us leave for the moment the question how he disposed of his fleshly body and ask ourselves how, save by admitting his survival, we can account for the fact that eleven men in hiding, terribly disappointed and disillusioned, suddenly became missionaries who, within six or seven weeks of his death, were preaching his resurrection in the very area where he had been done to death? "God raised Him from the dead," said Peter, preaching within a short time of the crucifixion and within a mile or so from where it took place, and added, *"of that we are witnesses."* If this were not true, why in heaven's name, did not someone come forward and say, "Don't be silly, I can show you his body!" It is quite incredible that with no significant lapse of time the disciples could have got away with a lie and then proceeded to die for its truth.

We believe in our own survival but we do not leave behind us an empty grave. Had that grave continued to contain a corpse, or had the body been found elsewhere, no one in those days would have proclaimed a resurrection, or any special conquest of death.

In modern days Rudolf Bultmann, Professor of New Testament studies at the University of Marburg (1921-51), carries his "demythologizing" process to the point of regarding the resurrection as a kind of myth, with no historical basis, which only means that Christ has influenced men after his

[69] *Gitanjali* (Macmillan).

death. His disciples had a spiritual experience of him after his death and the myth of a "resurrection," for Bultmann, accounts for it.

Acknowledging gladly Bultmann's eminence and the value of much of his "demythologizing," I cannot, for myself, account for the evidence by suspecting the historicity of that empty tomb. Nor can I account for the volte-face in the minds of Christ's followers at that point in history which we call Easter Day. A myth takes longer than three days to grow up and be effective enough to bring, from their hiding place of terror, eleven men who proceed to preach it and to lay down their lives for its truth. One wonders also why a "myth" of resurrection did not prove necessary to account for the influence of other great teachers after their death. In passing, it is interesting to meditate on the fact that if his followers had not been convinced that Jesus was alive not one word of the New Testament would ever have been written.

To account for the empty tomb every possible theory has been put forward without success. Even a writer of the mental stature of Renan suggested that Jesus did not really die on the cross but fainted with the heat and the pain, was taken down from it and placed on a cold stone slab in a cave-like tomb and in the coolness recovered and made his way out. Dr. J. G. Bowine, senior anaesthetist of St. Thomas' Hospital, London, recently repeated the theory, repudiated the following week by a professor of anaesthesia.[70]

But a score of questions leap to the mind. Would the disciples preach the "resurrection of Jesus Christ from the *dead*" if, in fact, he had never died? Would they regard such a recovery from torture as a conquest of death? Such a suggestion asks more of credulity than orthodoxy asks of faith. How could a person too weak *before* his crucifixion to carry his cross, who had been scourged, tortured, nailed to a cross through the hot hours of a whole day, and into whose side a spear had been thrust, drawing not only blood but the water-like serum in the pericardial sac—or else urine from the blad-der—get off a stone slab in the dark, remove his own tightly wound wrappings or bandages, push back from the mouth of the cave-tomb a heavy, grindstone-shaped boulder, like a solid stone wheel, which it took several strong men to move, evade the guards, procure from some unexplained source some clothing, and then appear to his friends not as an invalid needing weeks of nursing back to health, but as a man so fit that, in spite of two terrible wounds in his feet, he could, on the same day, walk seven miles to Emmaus with two disciples, have supper with them, and then travel another seven miles to Jerusalem in time to meet the rest of his friends? Inciden-tally the centurion's very life depended on his being sure that his prisoner was dead. This is desperate skepticism indeed and can safely be discarded.

Those most concerned at the time were either the friends of Jesus or his enemies. If his friends had hidden the body it is incredible that no one ever divulged the secret as to where it lay. The new resting place would have been a venerated shrine, like Lenin's, but it would not have been the basis of a world faith in a risen Lord.

If the Roman or Jewish enemies of Jesus had removed the body, they had only to produce it or indicate its whereabouts in order to crush the faith of the disciples in an hour.

If Jesus had a friend in the Jewish police guard, to whom the risen Lord appeared, as Mr. Frank Morison has suggested, and for which suggestion he has given impressive evidence,[71] then that friend might well have told his officer that he had seen Jesus outside the tomb, and the obvious answer of the officer would have been, "Roll back the stone and let us see."

One is convinced that by the time the heavy stone was rolled back, the grave was empty, *except for the grave-clothes.* Otherwise, why should the priests offer money to the guard

[71] See his thrilling book, *Who Moved the Stone?* (Zondervan, 1956).

to get them to say, "His disciples came by night and stole Him away while we slept." [72]

Students of the resurrection never seem to me to have paid enough attention to the meticulous details about the grave-clothes which the fourth Gospel gives. This narrative —unlike some parts of the Gospel—seems to me to be based on the account of an eye-witness.

It is made clear that the grave-clothes, covering the body up to the armpits, had *collapsed* as if the body had evaporated. We are told how that the turban wound round his head stood on its edge as if the head also had evaporated. If the student will turn to the twentieth chapter of the fourth Gospel and read the first twenty verses, he will realize that it was the way the grave-clothes were lying that convinced Peter and John that Christ had disposed of his physical body in a way which we do not understand, but which suggest words like "evaporation," or "evanescence," or "dematerialization." If the corpse had moved or been moved, then the hundred pounds weight of myrrh and aloes[73] would have made a conspicuous heap on the floor and been remarked upon. We are given the idea that not a fold of the "linen cloths" was out of place and the turban was "wrapped up in a place by itself," its supporting head having evanesced.

Such an evanescence we do not understand and probably we are considering a miracle in the sense defined on page 107, though Dr. Raynor Johnson writes, "The reader may not know that there are accounts given from time to time of meetings with advanced beings who can materialise a physical body when they wish and dematerialise it at will. In this scientific age such reports are naturally treated with reserve, but it is unwise to dismiss them as impossible in the light of the little we know. With some knowledge of psychical research and in the face of all the evidence that He was a very advanced soul, nothing in the resurrection account leaves me

[72] Matthew 28:12-15   [73] John 19:39

128

surprised." [74] Probably we are as little likely to see an event like Christ's resurrection repeated as we are to see other events repeated such as the beginning of life on a planet, or the change from the man-like ape into the ape-like man.

Yet, although such a change in matter from the flesh and bones of a body into gas, which could easily escape through the crevices of the cave-tomb, or indeed into nothingness, or some invisible form of energy, is beyond us, we know enough to make it credible when a mind like the mind of Jesus is at work. He who had such power over other men's bodies that he could heal a leper at a touch—involving immense changes in gross matter—may have been able to set in motion at his death amazing changes in the matter of his own body.[75]

We do know that heat changes matter from solid and liquid to gas, and we know that mental conditions can react on the body as heat does. For example, to quote from my own experiments, one can "burn" the flesh of a hypnotized person and raise a blister by simply telling the patient that one's finger or fountain pen is a red-hot iron.[76] Did Christ, by the immense power of his mind and spirit, dispose of the material of his body?

We do not know, but it should be realized that if we claim that he walked out of the tomb with the same flesh and blood as that which was laid in it, we are faced with many difficult questions, e.g. what eventually happened to his flesh and bones, since presumably they did not go "up" to Heaven at the Ascension? And further, whence did he get the clothes in which he appeared to Mary and the others, since the grave-clothes were left in the tomb, and his ordinary

[74] *A Religious Outlook for Modern Man*, p. 96 (Hodder and Stoughton, 1962).
[75] I have tried to work this out more fully in a booklet called, *The Resurrection of Christ*, published by Hodder and Stoughton in London, and by Abingdon Press in America, where it is called, *The Manner of the Resurrection*.
[76] See my *Psychology, Religion and Healing*, p. 116 (rev. ed., Abingdon Press, 1954).

clothes were stolen by the soldiers at the cross? If his physical life continued, why is there no word of it in the Gospels, and why complete silence about his ultimate death?

I am in no doubt in my own mind that Jesus finished in the tomb with the matter which composed his earthly body by means of a metamorphosis which we cannot yet understand, and that what the disciples saw after Easter Day was technically an apparition.

Frank W. Moyle, in his excellent book *Our Undying Self*, points out the way in which New Testament writers use two different Greek words for "see." They use *"blepo"* or *"theoreo"* for what comes through the optic nerves, and *"horao"* for mental insight or spiritual vision. He illustrates this from John 16:16 (Revised Version): "A little while and ye shall not behold (*'thereo'*) Me, and again a little while and ye shall see (*'horao'*) Me because I go to the Father." Moyle adds, "If this had received the attention which the writer of the fourth Gospel obviously intended it to receive, there would have been much less controversy about the nature of Christ's resurrection. I have no doubt whatever that he intended by using the word 'behold' (*'thereo'*) for Jesus's physical presence and 'see' (*'horao'*) for His spiritual or resurrection presence, to rule out the idea (so deeply imbedded in the Jewish mind) of a physical or bodily resurrection." [77]

Sir Oliver Lodge also supports my view. Speaking of Christ's resurrection he says,[78] "Was His spirit so high that it not only animated the body, but changed it, altered the perceptible material form, so that in a literal sense He became the first fruits of them that slept? [79] . . . It seems to me quite possible that his case was an anticipation of what in time may happen to many, that after a long course of evolution our bodies too may become dematerialized, and that all the repul-

[77] Frank W. Moyle, *Our Undying Self*, p. 67 (Longmans, Green, 1958).
[78] Sir Oliver Lodge, *My Philosophy*, pp. 310-11 (Benn, 1933).
[79] See 1 Corinthians 15:20.

sive paraphernalia of burial or burning, to get rid of the unwholesome residue of de-organizing or disintegrating matter that we leave behind, shall no longer be necessary. Not that our bodies will rejoin the spirit, the spirit will not need them, it will have a spiritual or etheric body of its own. Our present material bodies are formed of earthly particles, and to the earth they will always return; but perhaps they need not always go through the processes of decomposition which to many are so repulsive. The atoms themselves may separate and so spontaneously disappear from our ken; and the body, having served its purpose, may be not only discarded, but may cease to be. I do not know if this will ever be the fate of the higher portions of humanity. It is a long time ahead yet anyhow, but we need not shut our eyes to the possibility. And if we find the evidence good, we may adhere to our faith that our Elder Brother had already attained this high eminence, and that the tomb could not hold the body which had been animated by so lofty a spirit."

At the same time, it must be recognized that the important truth in the resurrection story is that the essential ego of Christ survived death and proved that survival to his followers. We may account, in the way I have suggested, for the disappearance of the fleshly body *from the tomb,* but the particles which formed it, if they became gaseous, were still in the world as truly as if his body had been stolen and laid in another tomb. What matters is not what happened to his body but that his personality survived and was recognizably active in the world. This alone has religious significance, though had his body remained in the tomb in recognizable form, his conquest of death could not, in those early days, have been received by his followers.

In saying that the appearances of Jesus on and after the first Easter Day were those of an apparition it is most important to differentiate between a hallucination and an apparition. My suggestion is that Christ's risen appearances were those of a special kind of apparition. Hallucinations are experienced by individuals not groups, and are usually the fruit of longing or expectation. On the contrary, Jesus appeared again and again to many people together. Paul says, in a narrative written earlier than any of the Gospels, that on one occasion he appeared to five hundred people at once,[80] and those who first saw him were anything but expectant. They were in hiding and in despair. A hallucination is thus ruled out.

On the other hand, an apparition involves the mental activity of at least two people, an initiator and a percipient, even though the mental activity of the latter is sometimes functioning on unconscious levels. A hallucination does not involve mental rapport with another person. It only involves the mental condition of the person who sees it, and—differing again from an apparition—can be induced by hypnotism and by drugs like mescalin, lysergic acid and psilocybin.

Apparitions are of various kinds, but the one to which I wish to draw attention is the kind which is willed by an initiator, can be seen by more than one person, and, most importantly of all, *involves the presence of the initiator*.[81] Here, I believe, serious psychical and perhaps physical research will illuminate this field of phenomena.

In the realm of physics we may subsequently find support for a view that there may be a universe which interpenetrates this one with very little, and very infrequent interaction between the two. In a Third Program talk printed in *The Listener* of July 21, 1960, headed "Matter and Sub-Matter," Denys H. Wilkinson, F.R.S., said, "Perhaps there do indeed exist universes interpenetrating with ours; perhaps of a high complexity; *perhaps containing their own form of awareness* constructed out of other particles and other interactions than those that we now know, but awaiting discovery through some common but elusive interaction that we have yet to spot. It is-

---

[80] 1 Corinthians 15:6.
[81] Illustrations are given in G. N. M. Tyrrell's great book, *Apparitions* (Duckworth, revised ed. 1953).

not the physicist's job to make this sort of speculation, but today, when we are so much less sure of the natural world than we were two decades ago, he can at least license it." (Italics mine.) Can a spirit, using the mechanism we call an "apparition," use something which is partly psychical (etheric) and partly physical, to impinge on the senses of a percipient?

The universe is more than an affair of matter. As Sir Julian Huxley wrote: "Many phenomena are charged with a magical quality of transcendent or even compulsive power over our minds, and introduce us to realms beyond ordinary experience. They merit a special designation: for want of a better one I use the term divine, though this quality of divinity is not supernatural but *transnatural*. The divine is what man finds worthy of adoration, that which compels his awe." [82]

With his permission I quote an illustration from Major Tudor Pole's book, *The Silent Road*:[83]

"During the last war a company commander well known to me was killed by a sniper's bullet at the beginning of an engagement in the Palestine hill country. He was so loved by his men that it was decided not to disclose his death until the battle was over. This officer was killed at seven in the morning and yet throughout that day he was seen leading his men into the attack and on several occasions his speech and guidance saved those under his command from ambush and probable annihilation. At the end of the day when the objective had been successfully reached, this officer went among his men and thanked them for their bravery and endurance. He spoke, and was spoken to in a perfectly natural way. It was only later the same night when the men were told that their commanding officer had been killed early that morning that he ceased to be visible to them and even then there were many who could not be convinced that their leader had 'gone west.' This is an experience which I can vouch for personally as I was there, and I know of others of a similar kind.

[82] *The Observer*, March 31, 1963.
[83] Pp. 40-41, published by Neville Spearman (1960).

"During the present war, for instance, the following account was given me by an airman whose level-headedness I have no reason to doubt.

"He was briefed to pilot a bomber plane for a raid over a German city. I will quote his own words so far as I can remember them: 'This was my first operational flight and I was nervous. My squadron leader, for whom I had a great affection, called me aside before we set out and gave me his final instructions. Having done so, he added: "If you get into trouble, signal me and I will look after you." The outward journey was successful, and I dropped my bombs and turned for home. At that moment a flak splinter entered the cockpit and smashed my instruments. I lost touch with the squadron and found myself alone in a fog circling over the North Sea. I had lost my bearings. Oil and petrol were running low. I got through to X and he replied giving me my right course and suggesting methods for making the best use of my petrol reserves. As a result I landed safely at the base. To my amazement I then heard that X had been shot down and killed during the raid, some time *before* I had heard his voice over the R.T. giving me clear directions which undoubtedly saved the lives of myself and my crew. My observer heard and recognised his voice as clearly as I did.'

"If there is any moral to be drawn from these experiences I think it is this: the bond of love is stronger than the power of death and under certain circumstances can overcome the barrier which is caused by death. Were these isolated incidents they might be explained away, but many more of a similar kind could be quoted to suggest that physical death in itself does not necessarily mean the complete severance of tangible ties between men on earth and their companions who are no longer here." [84]

---

[84] Cf. the interesting communication of Sir Oliver Lodge's son, *Raymond*, via the medium, Mrs. Osborn Leonard, "Those who are killed in battle even go on fighting. . . . They don't believe they have passed on." Sir Oliver Lodge, *Raymond*, p. 127 (Methuen, 1916).

The kind of apparition we are dealing with here is, I repeat, the kind which is initiated by a powerful and loving mind, which can be seen or heard by a number of people at one time, and which involves the presence of the initiator. Experiences of such an apparition, then, are not to be dismissed by saying, "So the disciples only saw a ghost!" Jesus seems to have been eager to guard this point himself.[85]

Apparitional experiences are as "real" and valid and authentic, as experiences which involve the sense organs, and once Jesus finished with his flesh—which I believe he did in the tomb—he had no other way, save the apparitional one, of convincing his men through their senses that he had conquered death and was with them for ever.

Gradually these apparitional experiences ceased, and for very good reasons. Once Christ had established his survival by using the *senses* of his followers, he seemed eager to make them independent of their senses. To Thomas, the unbeliever, he had to allow the astral equivalent of the sensation of touch so that Thomas could be convinced. But when Mary in the Garden was already convinced through sight and hearing, he would not let her touch him. "Touch Me not," he said (John 20:17) as much as to say, "I have had to use two of your sense-centers, sight and hearing, to get through to you. I don't want you to use a third, touch, because I want you to be independent of all your senses and think of me as always present, when you cannot see, or hear, or touch."

It may be that the farther any human spirit gets from the moment of death the harder it is to get through to people on earth. The Proceedings of the Society for Psychical Research are full of well-authenticated accounts of people on earth who see and hear their loved ones *immediately* after the death of the latter, but these appearances seem rarely maintained and

[85] See Luke 24:36-43. Note: "A spirit hath not flesh and bones as ye behold Me having." He was no hallucination of disordered minds, he was real and he was there. His etheric body could make the same impression on their senses as physical matter made. The eyes are not the only gateway to the seeing centers in the brain.

cease to happen. Even Jesus may have found these appearances extremely taxing.

Be that as it may, once he had securely established the fact of his survival and continuing presence—a ministry of forty days after the resurrection in which his appearances and disappearances taught them never to think of him as absent—he "ascended into Heaven" or, in other words, withdrew into the plane of being that is normally unseen, and carried on his endless ministry without further engaging their senses. This withdrawal we call the ascension into heaven, but in effect it brought him *nearer* to men on earth; spirit with spirit. And in what is called the Holy Spirit all his promises of his own continuing ministry and nearness were fulfilled (see Chapter VI).

Without doubt it was "expedient" [86] that, in a sense, he withdrew, for a vision, an appearance that is "seen" tempts some people to travel to the locality where the apparition appeared, and to venerate it there as men have done at Lourdes, Fatima, and other places. This in turn would make it harder for the faithful to think of him as available everywhere and with them wherever they were.

Further, some people seem psychologically unable to see apparitions, and no religion could be universal if some were excluded by their own make-up from what would come to be regarded as its most convincing experiences. What a wealth of insight lies behind the words, "Blessed are they that have not seen and yet have believed." [87] Christ's "ascension" has many valuable meanings,[88] but here we are content to accept the thought that he ceased to manifest his presence through the senses of his followers, because in the ministry of the forty days of post-resurrection appearances he had made the senses superfluous.

However agnostic we may remain about the *manner* of the

---

[86] 1 John 16:7   [87] John 20:29
[88] These are worked out in my book, *His Life and Ours*, pp. 319-34 (Hodder and Stoughton, 17th ed., 1961).

resurrection, the fact that it happened is basic, for without it the infant religion would have died with Christ. Because of what happened on the first Easter Day the main missionary message of the early church was not a reproduction and repetition of Christ's teaching. It was a reiteration that Christ had risen from the dead and thus conquered the final power of evil and of death.[89] "If Christ be not risen," Paul said, "then is our preaching vain and your faith is also vain." [90]

It seems to me illogical to argue that because Christ rose from the dead we shall do the same. Because a unique Person had a certain experience, it does not follow that we shall do the same. What are to me convincing arguments for man's survival I shall deal with later.

But Christ's resurrection does most powerfully support our *hope* of survival. It proves that there does exist another plane of being, and his reported promise, "I go to prepare a place for you," [91] is better evidence of *our* survival than is his own resurrection. It is right and fitting that at every funeral we should be comforted by hearing that great triumphant declaration of the fourth Gospel, "I am the Resurrection and the Life: He that believeth on Me, though he die, yet shall he live. And whosoever liveth and believeth in me shall never die." [92] But the earliest Christians, I think, did not concentrate on the relevance of Christ's resurrection to their own survival of death. To them it proved that in spite of all appearances, and though evil still had immense power, it had no final power, and things like persecution and tyranny, cruelty and torture, were defeated. Love, which so often looked feeble, and was met by the worldly with derision, was allied with omnipotence and had the final word, both for the individual and in the life of a world, which at last would own the crucified and risen Redeemer as its Lord and King.

[89] Cf. Acts 1:22; 4:2; 4:33; 17:18; Romans 1:4; Philippians 3:10; 1 Peter 1:3, etc.
[90] 1 Corinthians 15:14.
[91] John 14:2   [92] John 11:25

God may have other words for other worlds,
But for this world, the Word of God is Christ.

This quotation, from a poem by Harriet Eleanor Hamilton King, sums up part of my thought about Jesus. That he was the *only* Son of God, no one can prove. Christ may have visited other planets himself, or other incarnations of God—if incarnation is the word—may have been made in other parts of the universe. His equality with God was the idea of Paul, but we are no more committed to Paul's theology than to Newton's physics. Christ's reported word, "I and the Father are one," a statement only found in the fourth Gospel, may only have meant that he had attained a unity of spirit and purpose with God.

It is hard to suppose that the evolutionary scale moves from the amoeba to man and that then there is a complete break until we arrive in thought at God. There may be not only "angels and archangels," but a hierarchy of beings as superior to man as man is superior to the animals; beings who partake of the nature of God to a degree which makes them as far advanced from us as, say, the intellect of an Einstein is advanced beyond that of a child of five. These beings may have achieved this spiritual eminence not only through one life but through a thousand incarnations. Who can say? I find myself more and more attracted to the thought that Christ, who, through endowment, moral achievement, and perhaps the discipline of many earlier incarnations, had reached a high level of spiritual attainment, was willing for love's sake to become incarnate in our lowly flesh in order to win us to unity with God. He may be one of many other "sons of God," and they may be at work in other parts of the vast universe, but God's word for this world is Christ, and Christ is rightly called the "Savior of the World," though his work has only begun.

After this chapter had been typed, I came across a passage in a book called *Beyond Life's Sunset*, by the Rev. C. Drayton Thomas,[93] who had the psychic sensitiveness of a medium. He recorded some alleged communications with his deceased father, who had been a Methodist minister.

Mr. Thomas asked his father, "Does God bear the same relation to worlds in the farthest part of the universe as He does to this world?"

His father is reported as making this answer: "Yes, He is the Supreme and Only Being. The question must have come to some minds, 'Are there different Gods in the different systems of worlds?' No, only one God. But there may be, from what I have heard, in each system and possibly to each planet, some holy one of His creating who is Master and Saviour of that system."

So for myself I would accept for Christ the label "avatar." He was an incarnation of God. Through him we learn as much about God as we are able to gather without guessing. There may be other avatars for other worlds.

If I equate Christ with God I say more about Christ than the evidence warrants. God does not pray to God as Jesus did, and agonize to know God's will. He would be praying to himself! God does not use language like, "If it be possible. . . ." Christ's saying, recorded in the earliest Gospel, "Why callest thou me good? There is none good but God," [94] is a denial by Christ himself that he is to be equated with God. And the fact that words like these were kept in the Gospel text when the tendency must have been to ignore or omit them is strong evidence of their authenticity. Further, would a being on an equality with God use words like these: "I ascend to *my* God and your God." [95]

Yet if I equate Christ with man I say less about him than the evidence warrants as I have shown in another place.[96]

For myself, therefore, I take the view that Christ was a Divine Being, an avatar or incarnation of God, Man to the

[93] Psychic Press Ltd. (1949).
[94] Mark 10:18   [95] John 20:17
[96] *His Life and Ours*, pp. 22 ff. (Hodder and Stoughton, 17th ed. 1961).

*n*th degree, who, perhaps through many previous incarnations had reached in the unseen an august place in a Divine Society and who, for man's sake, had volunteered to take on our flesh and our circumstances and had committed himself, as God's utterly devoted servant and intermediary, to our redemption.

I entirely agree with the Bishop of Woolwich when he writes,[97] "Popular preaching and teaching presents a supranaturalistic view of Christ which cannot be substantiated from the New Testament. It [the preaching] says simply that Jesus was God, in such a way that the terms 'Christ' and 'God' are interchangeable. But *nowhere in Biblical usage is this so*. The New Testament says that Jesus was the Word of God, it says that God was in Christ, it says that Jesus was the Son of God; but it does not say that Jesus was God, simply like that, or rather, not in any passages that certainly require to be interpreted in this way. Passages that *may* be so interpreted are Romans 9:5 and Hebrews 1:8. But see the alternative translations in the *Revised Standard Version* and the *New English Bible*." . . . "It is indeed an open question whether Jesus ever claimed to be the Son of God, let alone God" (p. 72). "Jesus never claims to be God, personally: yet He always claims to bring God completely" (p. 73).

The famous passage in the opening of John's Gospel, "And the Word was God" which suggests that Christ could be equated with God is discussed by the Bishop, who applauds the *New English Bible* translation, "And what God was, the Word was" (p. 71). In other words, if one looked at Jesus one saw God. The Bishop adds: "Here was more than just a man."

If, then, Christ is not to be equated with God, and yet we are compelled to say, "Here was more than just a man," it seems reasonable to place Christ in a unique category of avatar, truly man but more God-like than man has ever at-

[97] *Honest to God*, pp. 70 ff. (Westminster Press, 1963). Italics mine.

tained on earth. As the centurion said, "Truly this man was *a* Son of God." [98]

None of these speculations takes Jesus from us. For this world he is the Word of God in whom we see God's nature and purpose. He is committed to our humanity, and each one of us is precious in his sight. He is the Savior of our world and man can follow no higher way than to commit himself in return, to obey and to follow.

As Albert Schweitzer said, in those tremendous sentences which close his book, *The Quest of the Historical Jesus*, "He comes to us as One unknown, without a name, as of old by the lakeside He came to those who knew Him not. He speaks to us the same word, 'Follow thou Me,' and sets us to the task which He has to fulfil for our time. He commands. And to those who obey Him, whether they be wise or simple, He will reveal Himself in the toils, the conflicts, the sufferings which they shall pass through in His fellowship, and, as an ineffable mystery, they shall learn in their own experience Who He is."

[98] Mark 15:39, *New English Bible.*

CHAPTER VI

THE HOLY SPIRIT AND THE SPIRIT OF GOD

"What is impenetrable really exists, manifesting itself as the highest wisdom and the most radiant beauty."

Albert Einstein (born 1879)

"My religion consists of a humble admiration for the Superior Spirit who reveals Himself in the slight details we are able to perceive with our frail and feeble minds."

Albert Einstein

VI

THE HOLY SPIRIT AND THE SPIRIT OF GOD

I STILL believe in the Holy Spirit, but more and more, I have come to regard the phrase as a symbol of God's activity in the world and in the hearts of men, and to spell the word "spirit" with a small "s." In writing this book for the thoughtful layman I do feel that in this matter we are in an area of thought in which a measure of Christian agnosticism should be allowed.

Let us be realistic and acknowledge that thousands of truly devout and sincere Christian people find little or no place for the Holy Spirit in their thinking. Between one Whit Sunday and the next, apart from conventional words in church, in the Benediction, in the ascription before the sermon and the odd references in hymns and lessons, they never think of him. The phrase, the Holy Spirit, let alone "the Holy Ghost" does not cut into their consciousness, make any image in their minds, or play any part in their devotions. In all this the layman would find some strong support among the teachers of the church. In the Rev. Dr. Marcus Dods's letters, he writes to a friend, "I doubt if we can make much of a personal Spirit interposed between God and us." No one could accuse the late Rev. Dr. Garvie of being a modernist. "The life in the spirit," he wrote, "is indistinguishable from fellowship with the living Christ. . . . Christian experience does not, and cannot distinguish between Christ and the Spirit as Christian

145

doctrine has tried to do." [1] The Father, all Christians love and worship. The Son, they love, adore and seek to follow, but, if they think of the Holy Spirit at all, they think of an influence, almost a vapor, and if they knew that the common word for him in the New Testament is *"pneuma"*—the word from which we get "pneumatic," as in "pneumatic tyre"—then, more than ever, they would think of him as an impersonal kind of force. Indeed, the words of Christ himself, as recorded in the fourth Gospel, suggest an impersonal influence. "He then *breathed* on them, saying, 'Receive the Holy Spirit.' " (20:22). The phrase the "Holy Ghost" is equally vague to the modern mind. "The idea of God in three persons is difficult enough," writes Dr. Harry Emerson Fosdick, "without compounding the difficulty by calling one of them a 'Ghost.' " [2]

Layfolk often think of God as indwelling men, as inspiring men, as expressing himself in beauty and truth, in goodness and love. They think of God's spirit as they think of a man's spirit when they say, "What a fine spirit he showed!" or , "I wish he had more of his father's spirit!" A third person in a hypothetical Trinity seems superfluous, and most of the texts that are dear to them, such as, "I will pour out my spirit upon all flesh," fit in either with that concept or else seems a synonym of God's presence. The sentence, "Whither shall I go from thy spirit? or *whither shall I flee from thy presence?*" (Psalm 139:7) indicates that "spirit" and "presence" mean the same thing.

We can state with entire confidence the fact that *in experience* there can be no distinction between an experience of God the Father, God the Son, or God the Holy Spirit. Dr. Denney in the Cunningham Lectures published after his death wrote: "To be a believer in Christ and to have the Spirit are identically the same. . . . The doctrine of the Holy

---

[1] *Christian Certainty and Modern Perplexity*, p. 179. See also Mackintosh, *The Person of Christ*, p. 374.

[2] Rev. Dr. H. E. Fosdick, *Dear Mr. Brown; Letters to a Person Perplexed about Religion*, p. 119 (Harper & Row, 1961).

Spirit, as an element in the ecclesiastical doctrine of the Trinity, goes far beyond this, and far beyond anything which the New Testament defines. But," he continues, "we can think of no presence of the Spirit except the spiritual presence of Christ Himself." [8]

This identity in experience seems borne out in the New Testament. When Jesus promises the Comforter (John 14: 26), he adds, "I will not leave you desolate, I will come to you." When he promises that the Spirit will abide in men (John 14:17), He adds, "Abide in Me and I in you" (15:4). So unless the abiding in men of the Father (John 17:23), the Son and the Holy Spirit involves three gods, then the same experience is being referred to in each case.

Paul seems to regard the experience as one. The Holy Spirit bids him and his companions to speak the word in Asia. In the very next verse it is "the Spirit of Jesus" that "suffered them not" (Acts 16:7). In one verse Paul writes, "The Spirit of God dwelleth in you," and then says to the same people, "Know ye not that Jesus Christ is in you?" (1 Corinthians 3:13; 2 Corinthians 13:5). In Romans 8:9-11, we have in the same sentence, "The Spirit of God dwelleth in you," followed by the phrase, "If any man have not the spirit of Christ he is none of His." The subsequent language deepens the idea of identity. There can be, so to speak, no rivalry of experience. In 2 Corinthians 3:17, Paul writes explicitly, "The Lord is the Spirit." Who can blame the puzzled layman if he ceases from any effort to distinguish between them or to suppose that two separate *persons* are at work?

Paul Tillich, a German scholar now serving the Union Theological Seminary, New York, wrote: "This eighth chapter of his [Paul in Romans] is like a hymn praising in ecstatic words the new reality which has appeared to him, which was revealed in history and had transformed his whole existence. Paul calls this new being 'Christ' in so far as it has first be-

---

[8] I owe this quotation to *Our Common Faith,* edited by Canon Dorrity (Hodder and Stoughton, 1921).

come visible in Jesus the Christ. And he calls it 'Spirit' in so far as it is a reality in the spirit of every Christian. . . . *Both names designate the same reality.* Christ is the Spirit and the Spirit is the Spirit of Christ." [4]

I know that other passages suggest the opposite of identification, but they seem to me vague. I agree with Dr. George Jackson when, in this connection, he says: "It is by the way of practical identification that we shall most adequately interpret the experience of Christian men, whether in the first days or in our own, and that we shall best deliver ourselves from that web of unreal words which vulgar and learned alike have in the past so often woven about our feet." [5]

I quoted earlier (p. 41) some words of one of our greatest astronomers, Sir Bernard Lovell, to the effect that he believed "there were many communities of other beings in different parts of the universe." [6] I should like to add other words of the same writer,[7] "Most of us who have been brought up in the traditional manner of the first half of this century, and have absorbed the conventional interpretation of theological doctrine and of astronomical theory, have usually accepted as axiomatic that human life on earth was unique. Now we are faced with an entirely different situation. We believe that the solar system, far from being the sole example of its kind in the cosmos, is probably paralleled by planetary systems around stars which are of extremely frequent occurrence in space. This conclusion is very generally accepted today". . . . "The net result is that probably only a few per cent of all stars are in a condition where one of their planets is able to sustain some form of organic evolution. In the solar neighbourhood, where our detailed knowledge of stars is greatest, the number in this category has been estimated to be about

---

[4] *The Shaking of the Foundations*, p. 134. Italics mine (Pelican Books, 1963).
[5] *Our Common Faith*, p. 76 (Hodder and Stoughton, 1921).
[6] Speech in Moscow reported in *The Times*, July 16, 1963.
[7] *The Sunday Times*, December 3, 1961.

5 per cent. In order to obtain a probable lower estimate of the numbers involved in the Milky Way we will reduce this figure to 1 per cent. Since there are about 100,000 million stars in the Milky Way system this means that some 1,000 million stars must have planets in the appropriate condition to support long-term organic evolution.

"When we consider the cosmos as a whole the situation becomes even more dramatic. The structure of the Milky Way is typical in size and form of the spiral nebulae which are known to populate extra-galactic space as far as our telescopes penetrate.

"Within this observable part of the universe there must be at least 1,000 million galaxies with a size structure and stellar content not dissimilar from that of our local galaxy or Milky Way system. Our estimates therefore lead us to conclude that in the observable universe there are probably some trillion stars possessing planets in a suitable condition for the support of organic evolution."

It is possible, then, that sentient life has reached or passed human levels on other planets. It is possible that "sin" spoiled life there. It is possible that Christ visited other planets and was incarnate—if that is the word—there. It is equally possible that God shared the life on other planets by other "sons of God," other incarnations, other embodied revelations of his glory.

This being so, how presumptuous it is of us mere men, of insect stature on this unimportant speck of dust amid all God's glittering worlds, to imagine that with human words, like those about the Trinity, we can express the being and the doings of that awe-ful and majestic Being in whose unfathomable mind this vast universe was once an idea!

It is easy to understand why such words were set down. Men knew of God the Father. They knew and loved Jesus Christ. He had spoken of the Spirit. Their Trinitarian doctrine was their answer to the charge of worshiping three gods. Even the complicated theory of the Trinity, which took

149

four centuries to formulate and therefore can hardly be an essential of early Christianity, does not really get us out of the difficulty, for it is insisted that there are three *persons* in the Trinity. To worship three *persons* is, to all intents and purposes, to worship three gods. The fact that the three are held to be only one nature—an impossible demand on the modern mind—does not, in practical devotion, insure one God. Even if the word *"persona"* is used in its original sense of an actor's mask, our difficulties remain. God and Jesus existed at the same time. How could they be the same person wearing different masks?

As Dr. Nathaniel Micklem says, "In Trinitarianism the number three is quite secondary. . . . If the early theologians had thought fit to say that God is manifested first as the Ground of Being, second as the divine Wisdom, 'sweetly ordering all things in heaven and on earth,' third, in the Incarnate Word, and fourth, as the Holy Spirit known in the communion of the church, their apprehension of God would have been in no way different from that expressed in the Trinitarian formula . . . the number three is not important or significant." Dr. Micklem goes on to say that where the formula is not made intelligible, "It serves as a hindrance to the understanding and acceptance of the Christian Faith. It is not a divinely revealed 'mystery' but a doctrine worked out in various ways after centuries of Christian speculation." [8] So, in this matter, the Christian may be agnostic, and in spite of St. Athanasius he can be a Christian without believing in the Trinity. Time, and understanding of the universe, may make us want to add a score of other Divine Beings who exist in the unity of God.

I feel that the church of today must not imprison the modern man in the thought-forms of three hundred years ago, and since the personality of *man* baffles the wisest psychologists of our day, man can hardly hope to do more than make

[8] Nathaniel Micklem, *Faith and Reason*, pp. 103-4 (Duckworth, 1963).

guesses at the personality, or supra-personality of God. "Dr. Cyril Richardson, professor of Church History in New York's Union Theological Seminary, has forthrightly said what many of us long have felt," writes Dr. Harry Emerson Fosdick.[9] "My conclusion, then, about the doctrine of the Trinity is that it is an artificial construction. It tries to relate differential problems and to fit them into an arbitrary and traditional threeness. It produces confusion rather than clarification; and while the problems with which it deals are real ones, the solutions it offers are not illuminating. It has posed, for many Christians, dark and mysterious statements which are ultimately meaningless . . . We are confronted in the New Testament with three dominant symbols of God. These we can and should use to express deep Christian concerns. But we should avoid supposing that they do not overlap or that they imply three distinct Persons in the Trinity."

It is important to remember that for many years after Christ's death, converts were baptized into Christ's name alone. The idea of baptism into "the Triune Name" came much later.[10]

I find it impossible to believe that on the first Whit Sunday the gathered apostles were possessed by some stranger whom they recognized as a separate person called the Holy Spirit. Surely they felt that their beloved Master was back in their midst once more as he had promised, and back with the power he had promised.

Let us turn to some of his own words. "I will not leave you desolate; I will come to you." [11] And again, "There be some of them that stand here which shall in no wise taste of death till they see the Son of man coming in His kingdom." [12] He told them that they should not have gone through the cities of Israel until the Son of man be come.[13] He told them that

---

[9] *Op. cit.*, p. 121.
[10] See p. 350, and Dr. H. D. A. Major in, *The Mission and Message of Jesus*, pp. 227-50 (Nicholson and Watson, 1927).
[11] John 14:18   [12] Matthew 16:28; Luke 9:27
[13] Matthew 10:23.

they should *see* the Son of man coming with great power and glory.[14] No distant "coming" could fulfill those words. Pentecost meant their fulfillment. They had only made a beginning on the cities of Israel, and not one of them had tasted of death save Judas, and here, in the familiar upper room, Jesus was with them in power and glory, as he said.[15]

I think we shall not get the best out of our meditation on Pentecost if we concentrate our minds too much on the phenomena, on the fire and the wind and the supposedly foreign tongues. I sometimes wonder if the wind and the fire do not illustrate the impossibility of conveying to others a great experience.[16] I may be quite wrong in this and perhaps psychic research will one day interpret for us the two words, "wind" and "fire," for certainly the blowing of a strong wind is the concomitant of many psychic experiences. But there may be a much simpler solution. Men have said, "I felt on fire with the Presence of God," or, "I felt as if a great wind were sweeping through the place and cleansing us all."

As for the tongues, I find it difficult to believe that simple Galilean peasants suddenly began to speak in foreign languages. For one thing, there was no necessity for them to do so, since Hellenistic Greek was the world language, understood and spoken by all those whose countries are mentioned in the second chapter of Acts. This was their own language in which they were born (Acts 2:8). Peter could not even speak his own language without a brogue that gave him away.[17] Did he suddenly start talking some other language without understanding himself what he was talking about? It doesn't sound like him to me, nor does it sound like evidence that God was with him, for Babel, where there was a confusion of tongues, represented to the Jews the *disapproval*

[14] Mark 13:26.
[15] Matthew 24:29-31; Mark 13:24-27; Luke 21:25-28.
[16] Cf. the earthquake, wind and fire in Elijah's experience (1 Kings 19:11-12).
[17] Matthew 26:73. "Your accent gives you away" (*New English Bible*).

of God.[18] It would thus be difficult for Jews to regard foreign tongues as a symbol of the Divine favor. Further still, there *was* no specific language belonging, for example, to the Cretans.[19] Paul's crushing reply to those who spoke in "tongues" is very clear in Moffatt's translation of 1 Corinthians 14:2-18 finishing with the sentence, "I would rather say five words with my own mind for the instruction of other people than ten thousand words in a 'tongue.'"

I am in no doubt myself that what happened, and what so surprised the multitude, was that Galilean peasants, who normally spoke with a strong accent and in dialects as different from one another as Scottish is from Cornish, were all found to be speaking clearly in eloquent Hellenistic Greek.

This point is illustrated for me by an experience that happened to a friend of mine, the late Professor J. Alexander Findlay. He tells us[20] that when he began his ministry, after taking his degree at Cambridge, he was sent direct to a colliery village in Durham. He found it difficult to understand a word of the dialect spoken by his flock. But he tells us of a Durham miner, *whom normally he could not understand,* who, when he prayed at a prayer meeting, "poured forth a flood of beautiful language without a trace of dialect." Dr. Findlay writes: "If I could have copied down his prayers in shorthand and published them, I am sure they would have been recognised as classics of devotion. They were not simply a patchwork of verses taken from the Bible or the hymn book. They were his own and yet not his own. I asked him once to let me write them down, but he could not reproduce them. I have always thought this a supernatural gift and have met no psychologist who could explain it to my satisfaction. There was no evidence that he had ever met anyone capable of teaching him such prayers, or that he had ever read them. Incidentally, he was the greatest saint I have ever known ... and when I try to visualise the face of Jesus, that

[18] See Genesis 11:1-9   [19] Acts 2:11
[20] *The British Weekly,* November 26, 1942.

of Isaac Hewitson at prayer comes to my mind: he was lit from within." Dr. Findlay continues, "The secret of power is to be possessed by the spirit of God; this involves no mere enchancement of a man's own faculties; it is a supernatural endowment."

So we have the story of a sense of the power of the risen Christ which *intoxicated* these men. I use the word carefully, for they were charged with being drunk, and I can never escape the feeling that Peter had a great sense of humor in the answer he gave to the charge. When those in the crowd said disgustedly, "They are filled with new wine," Peter did not seem at all offended by this attack on their respectability. He merely pointed out that being only nine o'clock in the morning, the pubs had not yet opened! "These are not drunk as ye suppose, seeing it is but the third hour of the day." [21] When we chant or say the General Confession we pray that hereafter we may live "a godly, righteous and *sober* life." But I wonder sometimes if we are too sober. The impression made by the apostles was that they were drunk; intoxicated with God.

To read the book of Acts is to read a book which is at once thrilling and depressing. It is thrilling to read the story of these men full of power and full of joy. They were like Jesus of whom the present Dean of St. Paul's, Dr. Matthews, wrote a golden sentence, "Men knew where He had been because of the trail of gladness that He left behind Him." They went out through the known world, preaching, teaching, healing, inspiring, and, in spite of opposition, hostility and persecution, they won men and women everywhere to the new way. Nothing could stop them, not even the might of Imperial Rome, and is there in literature a more thrilling story than the story of that radiant Christian witness, of that infectious Christian living, of that unquenchable enthusiasm?

[21] Acts 2:15.

It is depressing to find so rarely that exuberant living in the modern church.

So far as Christian discipleship is concerned, then, there is really no need to import a third person of a mysterious Trinity into the Pentecost situation. The risen Christ is sufficient. They could hardly want more. The great trouble is that we may never know in this world what exactly Christ *did* say. Most of the words about the Comforter occur in the fourth Gospel and everyone knows that it was not written down until scores of years after the time when, it is alleged, the words were spoken. It is true that Scripture teaching presents a strong case for belief in the Holy Spirit and Paul alone refers to him one hundred and twenty times, but I do feel that a measure of agnosticism is allowable concerning him, and that no layman should feel outside the fellowship of the church if thought of the Holy Spirit but rarely enters his consciousness. After all, in one of the very greatest hymns of the church, the *Te Deum Laudamus,* the Holy Spirit is, as it were, tucked into a single phrase, the wording of which almost suggests an afterthought—"Also the Holy Ghost, the Comforter." Even in the Apostles' Creed, six words sum up the matter: "I believe in the Holy Ghost." If the modern layman were wholly honest and outspoken he would add, "But I don't know who he or it is, or how he is related to God the Father, or to Christ, or to me, and to be honest I scarcely ever think of him. If I did I should lose my sense of the majestic unity of God, I can't worship three persons however closely related without worshiping three gods." The late Canon Streeter put the matter bluntly: "Popular Christianity," he wrote, "is Tritheism with reservations."

Many ministers, if honest, would admit the same kind of confusion. It is the correct pose, in phrasing pious sentences, to make reference to the Trinity and men speak of God acting through Christ *by the Spirit,* but they have no clear idea themselves what the last three words mean. They drag in the Holy Spirit just as the author of the *Te Deum* did.

It is true that the Athanasian Creed has more to say: "The Holy Ghost is of the Father and of the Son: neither made nor created nor begotten but proceeding," but like the late Dr. George Jackson who taught me to be mentally honest in my theology, "I can find nothing in Scripture or experience to tell me what the words mean." [22]

After I had written this chapter, Geoffrey Bles and Co. published the posthumous volume by C. S. Lewis called, *Letters to Malcolm, Chiefly on Prayer.* Speaking of a friend, Lewis wrote, "He trusts in the continued guidance of the Holy Spirit. A noble faith, *provided, of course, there is any such being as the Holy Spirit.* But I suppose His existence is itself one of the 'traditional doctrines' which . . . we might any day find we had outgrown." [23]

The baffled layman should not be cast out if he spells the word spirit with a small "s" and rests his mind in the less ambiguous lines of Charles Wesley:

> *Thou O Christ art all I want,*
> *More than all in Thee I find.*

[22] Rev. George Jackson, B.A., D.D., Professor of English and the English Bible, Didsbury Theological College, Manchester, in *Our Common Faith*, p. 61 (Hodder and Stoughton, 1922).
[23] *Letters to Malcolm*, p. 48. Italics mine.

CHAPTER VII

THE CHURCH AND THE CHURCHES

"Dr. Percy Dearmer, a great authority on Christian worship, said long ago that we ought 'to go back to the older liturgical tradition and not make the Creeds a necessary feature of all our services.' Until the Reformation the Apostles' Creed was only said privately at Divine Service, and there was no Creed at Matins or Evensong. The Roman Church got on very well without a creed at all in the Mass for a thousand years, and only inserts one now on Sundays and other special occasions. The so-called Athanasian Creed is dropping out of use, for few can say today, 'which faith except everyone do keep whole and undefiled without doubt he shall perish everlastingly.' Even in the revised form of the 1928 Prayer Book it is hard enough: 'which faith except a man keep whole and undefiled, without doubt he will perish eternally.' Bonhoeffer in his outline for a book, never completed, proposed a revision of the Apostles' Creed, to bring it more in line with Biblical teaching and emphasis.

"The Free Churches have given up using creeds in normal services, and they will no doubt beware lest they are imposed on them again in schemes for church union. The Quakers have thrown them over entirely, and even the more traditional Methodists only profess to hold 'the fundamental principles' of the historic creeds and do not use them in most services. Yet the World Council of Churches in its agreed Basis has formulated and imposed a new statement of faith, of debatable orthodoxy."

Dr. Geoffrey Parrinder
(*The Christian Debate: Light from the East*)

"In 1816 John Keats said [about the churches] 'They are dying like an outburnt lamp.' He forgot something. As another put it, 'The first essential of a quiet funeral is a willing corpse,' and the churches are certainly not that."

Rev. Dr. Harry Emerson Fosdick
(*Dear Mr. Brown*)

"Within the strange, sprawling, quarreling mass of the churches, within their stifling narrowness, their ignorance, their insensitivity, their stupidity, their fear of the senses and of truth, I perceive another Church, one which really is Christ at work in the world. To this Church men seem to be admitted as much by a baptism of the heart as of the body, and they know more of intellectual charity, of vulnerability, of love, of joy, of peace, than most of the rest of us. They have learned to live with few defences and so conquered the isolation which torments me. They do not judge, especially morally; their own relationships make it possible for others to grow. It does not matter what their circumstances are, what their physical and mental limitations are. They really are free men, the prisoners who have been released and who in turn can release others."

Monica Furlong
(*With Love to the Church*)

VII

THE CHURCH AND THE CHURCHES

IN our earliest Gospel, Mark's, written about A.D. 65, it is thought at the dictation of Peter, or at any rate based on Peter's memories, we read that Jesus appointed a band of twelve men to be his companions.[1] It is interesting that he gave them nicknames as we do when a bond of special affection is established. Simon he called "Peter" (the rockman) and James and John he called "Boanerges" (sons of thunder) and so on.

Thus the church on earth began. It began with men who were friends of Jesus, and in my opinion that ought still to be the test of membership. They all believed different things and had different points of view. Jesus, with his immense respect for personality, did not try to make any intellectual demands on them. It is interesting, in view of some present-day attitudes, that not one of them had ever heard of the Virgin Birth, and the last thing a Jewish monotheist was likely to believe was that a man was God. Gradually some of the great facts about him, which we still treasure, became true for them, but they were more interested in carrying out his wishes than in arguing about creeds, as the end of the verse quoted shows. "He appointed twelve as His companions *whom He would send out to proclaim His Gospel,* with a commission to cast out devils."

[1] Mark 3:14. Both J. B. Phillips and the *New English Bible* use the word "companion."

159

So the early church, without creeds or elaborate organization, without any buildings or financial, social, educational or political backing, went out to change and to conquer the world. Its first members were his friends. They cherished fellowship with him. His was a way of life not based on intellectual agreement. They sought to meet the challenges of life by reacting as he would react, and they preached his Gospel by word and by life. His Gospel, as the fourteenth verse of the first chapter of the earliest Gospel tells us, was as follows: "The time has come at last. The Kingdom of God has arrived. Change your way of looking at life and believe the good news." And what good news it was! Everyone was dear to God and precious to him. His love was unending, and men must love one another because all were brothers. In every relationship of life this spirit must be acted upon, and by this means the whole life of the world would be revolutionized. Though later this love was exemplified in his death, this power in his resurrection, yet still, I hold, the church's central message stands as the Gospel, the good news which Jesus declared in Galilee. As the minister of a church, I would accept anyone into church membership who declared that forthwith he would seek to follow Christ's way of life as it applied within his own circumstances, and that he would try to show Christ's spirit in any situation that might arise and in any challenge he had to meet. I would later on put before him what I believe *about* Christ and God and man, hoping that I could so set out what for me is true, that his mind would stretch out and grasp it, make it his own, and have his faith strengthened and reinforced.

If this be the basis of membership—as it was at my beloved City Temple for nearly a quarter of a century—I would press all those who believed in Christ to join. The word "in" there is important. I believe *in* many of my friends and they *in* me. This does not mean that we are in close intellectual agreement. One of my dearest friends disagrees with me about both politics and theology, but this does nothing to harm our friendship. All lovers of Christ can believe *in* him without believing the same things about him.

I have long ago come to the conclusion that the human mind works very differently in different people. When, as a registered pilgrim, I traveled to Lourdes in the same compartment with Bishop Beck, the Roman Catholic bishop in charge of the pilgrimage, we spent the greater part of twenty-seven hours in fierce debate, and continued in the hotel and on the homeward journey. At the end of the trip, when we got back to London, I had an immense reverence and affection for him, but I was an even more convinced Protestant, just as he, I am sure, was a completely convinced Catholic. I just could not have made my mind believe the things which he regarded as incontrovertible. I realized that two thoughtful men, both trying to be intellectually honest, and both trying to think straight, could passionately believe things which, at our present state of knowledge, are completely irreconcilable. If church unity means that all must believe the same things in the same sense, it can never be achieved. I should regard it as undesirable, and I should feel that any pressure brought to bear to achieve it, unwarranted. To my mind, the way to unity is not by endless discussions aimed at making men believe the same thing or worship in the same way.

What then *is* the way forward? I am convinced, after years of attending conferences on church union, that it is by getting to know, love, respect and tolerate one another, and then *by showing a united front against every form of evil*. I doubt if there is one evil in our beloved land, or even in the world, which could survive for a generation the onslaught of all the followers of Christ united against it. Think of some small town—because that is easier for the imagination—in which Anglicans, Presbyterians, Methodists, Quakers, Baptists, Congregationalists, Roman Catholics and Salvationists concentrated in one tremendous campaign against, say, unspeakable slums, the introduction of some brothel, political graft and the unscrupulous greed sometimes practiced in big business.

In uniting against evil we should get to know one another. Knowledge leads to understanding, understanding to loving, and loving ends intolerance. *It is the intolerance in disunity that is evil*, not the difference in belief and worship. To love is far more important than to be orthodox. No one minds a man saying, "I like the use of the creeds," as long as he does not add, "If you don't believe them you are no true Christian." No one minds a man saying, "I believe in episcopal ordination," as long as he does not add, "And no Scottish Presbyterian or Methodist minister is a true minister of Christ's Church."

My favorite illustration is that of a man's hand. Let the fingers and thumb have a certain separateness. They have grown out of, and belong to, something larger than any one of them alone, namely, the palm of the hand. The same pulse in the wrist brings the life blood to each of them. Let the fingers not twitch in nervous disease and rub one against the other. Let them close in one fist and hit out at that which opposes them all. So the churches can have a great usefulness in their partial separation. The basic truth which unites them is far bigger and more important that the things which separate them, and love for Christ pulses through them all and gives life, power and unity to them all. This, in my opinion, is the only kind of church unity which is at present possible, but it may well lead, as we love one another more, to a more closely knit organization, and this is desirable as long as no one is forced into it or made to surrender something he holds precious.

I would, however, plead that in every denomination there should be a far greater effort to make the activities of the church relevant to the needs of ordinary men and women. "The Church is her true self," said Bonhoeffer, "only when she exists for humanity."

Some years ago, at a service in an Anglican church, I sat just across the aisle from a working man who fumbled with his Prayer Book, unable to track down a Psalm. So I went across the aisle and told him the page. When it came to the collect, no one told him the page or that it was the twenty-first Sunday after Trinity, or whatever it was, so I tried to help him again. He thanked me, but finally gave it up, closed his Prayer Book, muttered to me that he "couldn't make sense of it" and walked out. I thought that Christ must have felt angry that a man, braving perhaps the sneers of his mates and hungry for a word of God to help him face life, should have been starved by the formality of the unfamiliar service and robbed of the bread of life.[2]

Frankly, I often wonder why so many people *do* go to church. Christianity must have a marvelous inherent power, or the churches would have killed it long ago. Now I am at the listening end of services I sometimes come away feeling frustrated and angry that a vital, glorious, joyous thing like the Christian religion should have been made so dull, boring, irrelevant and meaningless. Many a church service just gives one the hump. "The churches," wrote Maurice Wiggin lately, "are largely monuments to the piety of the past; spiritual power-houses that have suffered a power cut which no one seems able to put right." [3]

Where people get a service which touches life where they touch it, which deals with the problems which they have to face, and which is not a demand but an offer, not a burden imposed but an energy imparted, not luggage but wings, not gloomy disapproval but the healing touch of a loving fellowship, then people will crowd the churches, and I could give examples, irrespective of denomination, where this happens.

[2] When I related this incident in a talk, broadcast by the B.B.C., a lady wrote indignantly and said, "Surely you don't want us to scale down our services to the level of an ignorant visitor"! But Christ made his message one which ignorant people could receive. "The common people heard him gladly."

[3] In *The Sunday Times*, August 30, 1964.

People are very interested in non-sectarian religion, and the religious broadcaster may get a thousand letters after a single broadcast service.

In my opinion, dull church services, using archaic, ambiguous and meaningless words, sometimes accompanied by incomprehensible ritual are killing church-going, helped, of course, by our accursed materialism and the change from a set-up in which God counted, to one from which he is being politely bowed out as if he were a heavenly Santa Claus whom we had seen through and could do without, now that we were grown up.

What would the Communists give, if, in every village in Britain, they had an educated, full-time agent with adequate premises at his disposal? Britain would be red in ten years. The Church of England has had those assets for *four hundred years*, and in that time the services it offers its hungry worshipers have hardly altered. Tradition has seemed far more important than adaptation. Attempts have been made, but a Member of Parliament, who may scorn religion in his heart, has a voice and a vote concerning the way the Church of England says its prayers and runs its services. The Revised Prayer Book was thrown out by the House of Commons.

Honestly, how can modern man cling to the Prayer Book without his tongue in his cheek? No one today believes in "the resurrection of the body," though the creed, recited every Sunday, asserts it. And to turn to earlier expressions of the creed makes matters worse, for *"anastasis sarkos"* in Greek, and *"resurrectio carnis"* in Latin both mean the resurrection of the *"flesh."* Until 1543 this sentence read, even in English, "I believe in the resurrection of the flesh." The Prayer Book even today, in the service of the Baptism of Infants, includes the question to the parents, "Dost thou believe in the Resurrection of the FLESH," though this phrase never occurs in the Bible. No one believes that Christ took to heaven "His body with flesh and bones," though every Anglican clergyman signs his belief in the absurdity.[4] What nonsense is the prayer for fine weather which begins, "O Almighty Lord God, Who for the sin of man didst once drown all the world except eight persons . . ." Every Sunday Anglicans pray, "O Thou Who alone workest great marvels, send down upon our Bishops and Curates . . . the healthful spirit of Thy grace . . ." as if it would indeed be a marvel if the Bishops and Curates woke up; the Vicars and Rectors being past praying for! And what are we to make of the petition, "Give peace in our time O Lord because there is none other that fighteth for us but only Thou O God"? In other words, "Let's have peace, because if war comes we've only got You!" As H. A. Williams says, "The General Confession with its repeated and elaborate protestations of guilt looks like a desperate attempt to persuade God to accept us on the score of our eating the maximum dust possible. Even after the Absolution we are uncertain whether we have succeeded in our project. . . . It is inevitable that what looks like Cranmer's deep lack of faith in God's mercy should communicate itself to many who use his liturgy. . . . Unless, to the very last we assure God of our unworthiness, so much as to gather up the crumbs under His table, He may lock the dining room door in our face."[5]

Cranmer's childhood, dominated by fear—he had a sadistic schoolmaster—has infected the whole Prayer Book. Typical is the obsequious: "We beseech Thee favourably to hear the prayers of Thy people, that we who are justly punished for our offences may be mercifully delivered by Thy goodness."

---

[4] Canon Pearce-Higgins, having swallowed the Thirty-nine Articles, laid down four hundred years ago, to which every Anglican clergyman must give assent, before being installed as Vice-Provost of Southwark Cathedral, was honest enough to regurgitate and admit he did not believe them. (*The Times,* October 7, 1963.) According to the *Daily Mail,* May 27, 1963, the Canon called the assent of the clergy to the articles, "scandalous dishonesty and humbug." See also *The Observer,* May 26, 1963.

[5] H. A. Williams, M.A., Fellow and Dean of Trinity College, Cambridge, in *Soundings,* p. 79 (Cambridge University Press, 1962), and in "Unchristian Liturgy" in *Theology,* October 1958, pp. 401-4.

I always feel sorry for a devout couple who marry in an Anglican church. At their marriage they are told that marriage is ordained as "a remedy against sin and to avoid fornication." But when, having done what the church tells them in order to avoid sin, they ask for their child to be baptized at home, the priest tells them that their child was *"born in original sin and in the wrath of God."* Evidently the remedy doesn't work! If they take the innocent baby to church, the very first prayer asks that he may be "delivered from God's wrath"; the second prayer asks that he "may receive remission of his sins" and the faithful are exhorted to pray "that our Lord Jesus Christ would vouchsafe to receive him and release him of his sins." What sins? Why wrath? What a lot of nonsense about an innocent baby only a few weeks old!

Many Anglicans only attend church for marriages, baptisms and funerals. At their third visit they are told that man is "cut down like a flower," and those present pray that they may be delivered from "the bitter pains of eternal death"—whatever that means. Finally, tremblingly, they pray, "Suffer us not, at our last hour, for any pains of death to fall from Thee," and as they commit their dear one to the ground they pretend that "it pleased Almighty God *of His great mercy"* to take their beloved from them! Presumably they have been trying to defeat this merciful God all through the illness of the patient! What kind of God will those three visits to church conjure up in an untaught mind? I would not worship a god like that for five minutes!

Equally far from realism are some of the hymns. It would take many pages to quote all the absurdities, the unreality and the hypocrisy which they express. Even the well worn, "O God our help in ages past," is sung at almost all Armistice services. With the armed forces standing round on parade we sing:

> *Sufficient is Thine arm alone,*
> *And our defense is sure.*

An obvious lie, or what are the troops there for? Standing before a war memorial on which are engraved the words, "We will remember them," we proceed to sing:

> *Time, like an ever rolling stream*
> *Bears all its sons away,*
> *They fly forgotten, as a dream*
> Dies at the opening day.

Nor, of course, is the Church of England alone in this childish unreality. In churches of all denominations lessons are read because they are "set," and we have the stories of bloody massacres (Joshua 8:25), battering babies against the rocks (Psalm 137:9), rape and incest, and the glorification of the completely unjustifiable rape of Palestine by the Jews because these stories are "in the Bible" and God was supposed to approve.

The chanting of the Psalms is equally dangerous unless they are carefully chosen. Recently a dear old lady in the row in front of me at an Anglican church was lustily singing, "Whoso privily slandereth his neighbour: him will I destroy" (Psalm 101:5), when, though no doubt candidates for extinction were all around her, she appeared to have brought only her umbrella!

At another service which I attended the choir chanted this from Psalm 68, verses 21-23:

> "But God shall wound the head of His enemies, and the hairy scalp of such an one as goeth on still in his trespasses.
> The Lord said, I will bring again from Bashan, I will bring my people again from the depths of the sea:
> That thy foot may be dipped in the blood of thine enemies, and the tongue of thy dogs in the same."

I could only mutter, "How long, O Lord, how long?"

One Sunday, in the freezing cold of an apparently unwarmed church, and having left behind us frozen pipes, we listened to the choir singing, "O ye Frost . . . bless ye the Lord:" and, later still, we, intelligent people in 1963, heard the words, "O ye Whales, and all that move in the Waters, bless ye the Lord." And yet we wonder why, on a wet Sunday evening, people seem reluctant to leave the fireside and the television, take bus or subway, pay the ever increasing fares, give to a collection and get their feet wet!

In the Free churches we too frequently offer a slovenly service. Few things are more depressing than a huge, ugly chapel, badly attended, badly lighted, scarcely warmed, horribly decorated, where extempore prayers are offered which wander round the world and are almost entirely unexpectant, and where there is not a beautiful line which pleases the eye, a beautiful phrase of music which delights the ear, or, in a platitudinous sermon, one strengthening, comforting or challenging idea on which the mind can bite and the soul be sustained. The line from Amos, "Let me have no more of your noisy hymns" [6] might have been written for those who arrange Methodist Circuit rallies! But at any rate, what is said and done does usually, in the Free churches, make sense. In the Church of England this is often not so, even in a great cathedral with so many advantages over the ugly chapel. Recently, hungry of soul, I attended a service in one of our great and glorious cathedrals. The architecture was grand, and the music superb. But to the fifty or sixty of us, in a building which could have accommodated well over a thousand people, there could be seen a distant figure in wonderful robes, with his back to us making curious noises at the altar. No one could possibly hear what was going on. Another priest, standing between two candle-bearers in the aisle *intoned* the gospel, though the cathedral was adequately lit with electric light and loud speakers would have rendered even a poor speaking voice audible. A third announced that he was going to preach about "alterations about to be made in the liturgical practices

* Amos 5:23 (J. B. Phillips' translation).

of this cathedral." What a message for a hungry soul in the distracted world of today!

"There are only too many men and women who think that, if they have scrupulously repeated the prescribed phrases, made the proper gestures and observed the traditional tabus, they are excused from bothering about anything else. For these people, the performance of traditional custom has become a substitute for moral effort and intelligence. They fly from the problems of real life into symbolical ceremonial; they neglect their duties towards themselves, their neighbors and their God in order to give idolatrous worship to some traditionally hallowed object, to play liturgical charades or go through some piece of ancient mummery." [7]

As the Bishop of Woolwich wrote: "We must be ready to be stripped down and ask how much of the baggage which the Christian church now carries around with it is really necessary?" [8]

Yet the possibilities of the church are immense. Ideally it is the Christ-centered, loving community drawn together in fellowship to worship God, to learn of his ways with men, and to care and pray for one another and for all those "who, in this transitory life are in trouble, sorrow, need, sickness or any other adversity."

Far more people are in distress of mind and body because they are starved of love than because their religious beliefs are in a muddle, or because these have largely been given up. I feel sad when I pass some of the Free Churches and realize that their main doors are open only for a few hours on Sundays, and that if one penetrated through the back or side doors to various meetings one would only be offered devotional succor: prayer, hymns and exhortation.

People must sometimes pass those doors on the way to com-

[7] Aldous Huxley, *Ends and Means*, p. 229-30 (Chatto and Windus, 1938).
[8] *The Honest to God Debate*, pp. 247-48. Ed. by David L. Edwards (Westminster Press, 1963).

mit suicide,[9] or on their way to ask their doctor questions
which he is not trained to answer. Suicide, so-called nervous
breakdown and insanity increase, and below that level of
despair, thousands feel frustrated and unhappy because life
has become meaningless. Far more people are ill because they
are unhappy, than are unhappy because they are ill.

In a sense, the various healing movements, the existence
of the marriage guidance councils, the Freemasons and the
Rotary Clubs—all excellent organizations—are a rebuke to
the churches in that men have not found in them an answer
to their questions, the satisfaction of their need of fellowship,
or adequate scope for their service to others. All this and
much, much more they should have found in the churches,
and the need for many organizations would not have arisen if
the churches had cared more for men and less for creed and
ceremony.

I know churches which are "counselling centers," never
closed to the needy, where a wider use of dedicated laymen
is made than is possible when they are only used to hold
office or to conduct services as lay-readers or local preachers.
There are Christian mothers, lawyers, teachers, marriage
guidance counsellors, psychiatrists, medical men and women
and businessmen and women ready to give advice, who
would willingly give time each week to skilled counselling
which the minister alone cannot hope to offer. Of more than
one such church I can speak from experience, and concerning
them, it would be true to say that there is scarcely any trouble
into which a person could fall but the minister could say,
"We have just the person you need to advise you." [10]

---

[9] Five thousand people commit suicide in Great Britain every year;
about a hundred a week. "How many people try and fail cannot be known,
but it is probably about eight times as many as succeed; that is forty thousand people a year throughout the country—the population of a sizeable
town." (Mental Health Research Fund Pamphlet, No. 2.) How many are
miserable who never come near suicide we cannot conjecture, but the
church exists to help them.

[10] See *Healing Through Counselling*, ed. William H. Kyle (Epworth
Press, 1964).

It may be said that other social services meet people's needs, the National Health Service for instance, but few N.H. doctors have time to sit down and listen to a problem that is a real and frantic worry to someone, but which, in the telling and the advice, may take an hour, and many such problems are nothing to do with medicine or even psychiatry. As one indignant minister of religion said to me, "Am I to send people to a psychiatrist because they are lonely?"

In the matter of marriage, how often the announcement is made, the ceremony performed and the couple exhorted to attend church. In how few churches is there any preliminary teaching concerning such problems as pre-marital intercourse, birth control, family planning, frigidity and sexual anxiety, and the way to bring up children.

Yet skilled help on these points is available, and, by following the example given, the church could use her laymen and laywomen more, and at the same time open her arms to all in trouble whatever their creed, color or nationality. Is not this what the church exists to do?

I know that many are so disappointed in the churches as at present organized that they rarely, if ever, attend services. I hate to sound disloyal to the brave and devoted souls who seek to maintain them, but the position of the hearers must be sympathetically considered. And one sometimes wonders whether a useless thing should be supported, even for worthy motives, or whether its abandonment might not awaken its promoters to the fact of its uselessness. Many wonder how the elaborate ritual and ceremony of some services can possibly have developed from the teaching of a young man in a boat on the Sea of Galilee who talked so simply and yet so profoundly and relevantly to very simple people. Others find so much meaningless drivel preached in sermons that they feel it is a waste of time to listen to them and a crime to encourage them. Thousands feel that church services are no longer relevant to the modern outlook and the modern need.

We sometimes tell people they should go to church to worship God, but some services make that impossible. They offend the mind, or the aesthetic sense, so deeply that they get in God's way. We *know* we could worship better alone among the hills or by a lonely shore, and get just as good fellowship on the golf course.

We sometimes tell people they should go, not just to get but to give. It is a heavy demand and hard to carry out, for many people feel indignant that the glorious gospel has been made to sound so dull, or that a message which has revolutionized so many lives in so many countries in the world should be stated in a way that makes it seem dull, conventional, irrelevant, unadventurous, boring and misleading, not to say false.

Yet I often think of the words written of Jesus, "He went, as His custom was, into the synagogue on the Sabbath day." [11] He could have worshiped much better in the hills. He can scarcely have profited much from the dry and ponderous sermons of some desiccated rabbi. But I sometimes imagine myself there, waiting for the service to begin, spiritually hungry, longing for some message from God, some assurance that man is not left alone. Then Jesus enters. I see his quiet, yet radiant face. I note the serenity of his whole bearing. He kneels and then sits, relaxed and happy to be with God's people on God's day. I find myself wishing he were nearer to me. Yet his entry has made a difference to us all. The whole spiritual temperature has risen. A strange sense of quiet joy and well-being seems to seep into my heart. I become sure of God and sure that I am forgiven, loved, understood, accepted. So I think that if I go to church in these modern days, lovingly, prayerfully, not self-consciously being "an example to others" but praying with them, I may be a tiny power-center which lifts the spiritual potential of the service and is of use to God who is seeking to reach us all. I may make it easier for others to pray, easier for others to believe in God and to

[11] Luke 4:16.

find him, easier for troubled minds to find peace and the heavyladen rest.

When we were children, if someone had asked us what we meant by "the church," we should probably have told them about the building at the corner of the road in which we worshiped with our parents. When we got older we should have defined the word in terms of our denomination. Later still, our views would have widened to include all men and women everywhere, of all races and creeds, who loved and believed in the Lord Jesus Christ and tried to follow his way of life.

That last would pass as a description of the church on earth, but it is of very great importance, in my judgment, to realize that even that wide vision is not big enough.

The church is not something that began on earth, and then, as men and women passed away, existed also in heaven. THE CHURCH CAME DOWN OUT OF HEAVEN FROM GOD. That sentence seems to me the most important thing that can be said about the church, though it sounds strange and even repellent to modern ears which dislike any reference to the supernatural.

In John's lovely vision in the last book of the Bible, we find that the Holy City has no temple. The community and the church are one and the same. He saw "no temple therein," [12] but he saw the Holy City "coming down out of Heaven from God." [13]

The church *on earth* began, as we have seen, when Jesus, in Mark's lovely phrase, chose twelve men "that they might be with him," and every denomination has developed from that fellowship. But there is no denomination that is not a mere reflection of that fellowship in the unseen and eternal world which existed before this little insignificant planet began its course; a fellowship which will go on when the earth hangs, a frozen planet in the sky, or is burnt up in our sun or some other star.

[12] Revelation 21:22   [13] Revelation 21:10

We realize this awesome truth in the Communion service when we adore God, saying, "Therefore with angels and archangels and all the company of heaven, we laud and magnify Thy glorious name, evermore praising Thee and saying, 'Holy, holy, holy, Lord of Hosts. Heaven and earth are full of Thy glory. Glory be to Thee, O Lord Most High.'"

If I could make every church member see that vision of the church, he would say in a hushed voice to himself, "I, even I, am allowed to belong to that august communion." To see such a vision is to realize that being a church member is the most wonderful privilege life can offer, and one of the most powerful ways of maintaining faith during days of stress and storm.

Illustrations are not easy to find, but there is one to hand as we think of the life of Christ. It was not the life of a man who became so good that he was dubbed divine. Achievement had its necessary part in his nature, but we most truly understand the incarnation, not when we regard it as a man climbing up into divinity, but as a Divine Being coming down from the eternal, unseen world and expressing himself in the life of man. The life of Jesus was a translation into humanity, of the life of God, as far as man is capable of discerning the latter. In the same way, the church is not something born on earth which grew to divine proportions and significance, but a translation into terms of space and time of the divine community eternally existent in heaven. What a privilege to belong to *that!*

Therefore, as I think ideally of the churches, I see them stretching their hands outward and touching all communions of Christians, whatever their denominational label, in all lands, on all shores, under all skies. I see them stretching their hands forward to hand on Christ's message to those who come after, until, perhaps, they cover the earth. I see them stretching their hands backward, touching those of the generation before us, and so, back and back, until the last man slips his hand into the hand of Christ. But also I see the hands of men and women in the earth-bound church stretched upward to link not only with those who have gone into the unseen, but with "angels and archangels and all the company of heaven" who worship God in the Eternal Beauty on a higher plane of being than we have yet known.

My faith in the church is not faith in the drab and unbeautiful building at the corner of the road, where Mrs. Smith won't speak to Mrs. Brown because she was snubbed twenty years ago, or where Mr. Jones resigns once a month in the hope of getting his own way and blackmailing his minister, or where Mr. Robinson sings lustily that he is "washed in the blood of the Lamb," but would not tolerate a stranger in his pew and has not paid his milkman's bills, where Mrs. Jackson attends every service and every meeting and "adores the dear Vicar," but makes a hell of her own home by her temper, tears and tantrums, or where committees wrangle and fight about trivialities, gossip behind one another's backs, and show less goodwill and good fellowship than one finds in a golf club committee or in an Army mess where nothing is professed save decency and gentlemanliness. It is not easy to keep a vision bright and faith strong in a church where the minister is submerged in such an endless effort to raise money and attend committees that the *raison d'être* of the church is lost sight of completely, where bazaars, whist-drives, dances, bingo evenings and dramatic performances are given much more prominence than changing men's lives, and where every new enterprise—floated usually on tea—aims at money rather than men.

From the conception of the eternal church many truths about the church on earth emerge, with which there is no space to deal adequately, though I will state some of them:

1. How foolish it is of the critics to speak of the church failing! Whenever men really grasp an eternal idea they never let it go. They express it in various ways, and the *expressions* are imperfect, and sometimes fail. The idea may be lost sight of for years, but, once grasped, it leaps out again in this form

175

and in that, and never disappears. The idea of the brotherhood of man has been seen. It is in danger of being lost sight of, and one form of it—the League of Nations—broke, but already another is born, the United Nations, and the *idea* will never die. One day there will be one world in which all nations function in peace. The same is true of the church. I hope its denominations *will* fail, that their purpose will exhaust their form but the *idea* will never die, for it is of spiritual birth and essence. All its *expressions* may break down, but its message is part of eternal truth, and we shall be driven to accept it and live by it. No foolishness or devilry of ours can make or destroy truth. Every denomination may be seen to be a passing phase, but the eternal fellowship of God with men is part of invulnerable reality. The church is eternal. Faith in the future is justified by this truth alone.

2. How foolish it is to make the church's threshold low and beseech men to cross it by offering them inducements! "Come and join our church—you will find billiards, dances, whist-drives, bingo evenings, tennis parties. . . ." These things may have a place as expressions of the fellowship of men and women *already committed to God* themselves and desirous of showing forth his power and love, but the inducements and "stunts," should they fill our churches, would do only the greater harm, for people are made immeasurably to misunderstand the whole nature of the church by such methods. Further, the best human response is evoked not by making entrance easy, but difficult; not by inducements, but by the call to sacrificial service. How utterly degrading it is for the church to have people in it who come because they thus do a favor to those who invite them, or come for what they can get in terms of a cheap social club!

One of the hindrances in the church at present is that it is cluttered up with well-meaning, spiritually anemic people who have never taken Christ seriously, and do not even intend to do so, and who, through years of church-going, have developed such a thick armor against the shafts of Jesus that his most searching and scathing words neither challenge nor touch them. The trouble is that, not entering his Kingdom themselves, they stop others, for assuredly no one wants to be like *them*. There is no rich quality about their lives or their mastery of its problems that makes others long to share their secret. Actually the church can count on very few of its members really showing forth the way of Christ in the world. A high percentage of its members are not changed themselves. Therefore, of course, they have no burning message or witness for others. Many are willing to work in order to "fill the church." They have no vision of what the church exists to offer to those who fill it. They don't see that they are bluffing themselves, and trying to bluff God and evade his challenge to them, by pressing others to accept what they themselves have refused. "Come and be like us," they cry. But the man in the street says in his heart, "From ever being like you may your God deliver me!"

3. A third point I would make is that there are many outside the churches who ought to be in. They may feel excluded, and some exclude themselves, but Christ, I feel, would welcome them. They criticize from outside. If they would criticize *from within* with positive suggestions, their words would not be so resented and would be more likely to effect the changes they desire. This would be to the benefit of all. Criticism hurled across a gulf of hostility or indifference is of far less value, and widens the gap between the church and the people.

Let us try to see the Galilean standing on the beach, with the blue sky above him and the green hills behind him, the waves rippling to his feet, with the sorrows of the whole world on his spirit, but with the unquenchable joy of God in his eyes, calling to men to show the world a new way of life and reveal the beauty and glory of God. For *that* is what the church exists to offer—to offer men Christ, to bring them into the eternal fellowship of this holy, supernatural, august thing which men called the "body of Christ," and to teach

177

them how to worship God. This is the highest activity of which man is capable, and no man can cut it right out of his life without serious loss. Nature gives us no ground for believing that life can go on indefinitely in an organism completely and finally cut off from its environment. Without light, the eyes perish. Without air, the lungs die. The environment of the soul is God and God is ideally contacted through men. Worshiping man finds his fullest spiritual life in the worshiping community called the church. In her fellowship he finds communion with God, and through that fellowship he finds ways of serving God. For although God *can* be worshiped in solitude, he can only be *served* as we serve our fellows.

THE SACRAMENTS OF THE CHURCH

Most denominations practice the sacraments of infant baptism and Holy Communion, and I only want to append to this chapter a brief note about them for the sake of the bewildered laymen for whom this book is intended. Neither sacrament, in my opinion, is *essential* to the living of the Christian life. The Quakers are among the best Christians in our society and they do not practice either. Further, as Dr. D. M. Baillie says, "It has been widely questioned by modern scholarship whether the words of command and institution of baptism and the Lord's Supper are really authentic utterances of Jesus Himself in the days of His flesh." [14]

1. Infant Baptism

It must seem odd to many thoughtful laymen that the baptism of little babies who are often, and indeed, from the minister's point of view, desirably, fast asleep at the time,

---

[14] Donald M. Baillie, D.D., late Professor of Systematic Theology in the University of St. Andrews, *The Theology of the Sacraments*, p. 42 (Charles Scribner's Sons, 1957). All scholars agree that the end of Mark's Gospel is no part of the original, and Matthew 28:19, is a later addition. See Baillie, *op. cit.*, p. 73.

should have become elevated to the dignity of a sacrament of the church, only, in some denominations, to be conducted by an ordained priest.

The practice is based presumably on our Lord's lovely gesture in pleading that a group of little children should not be driven from him but brought to him. He said, "Suffer the little children to come unto Me and forbid them not, for of such is the Kingdom of God . . . and He took them in His arms and blessed them, laying His hands upon them" [15]

Further, the early church needed some ceremony of initiation into membership, to supersede the rite of circumcision practiced among the Jews, and one which was applicable to females as well as males. So, in some areas, infant baptism began to be practiced as early as the first century.

The whole case for baptism, as it is set forth in the New Testament, is expounded brilliantly by W. F. Flemington, Principal of Wesley House, Cambridge, in his scholarly volume, *The New Testament Doctrine of Baptism*,[16] and the interested reader is referred to this book.

The older I get and the more I study and meditate, the more logical and meaningful seems to me to be the ceremony which is followed by the Baptist denomination, in which an adult person after training and preparation, being fully conscious of the solemn step he is taking, carries out a rite which clearly goes back to Christ's own day; and to which he himself submitted.[17] "No less an authority than the Church of England Liturgical Commission, set up by the Archbishops of Canterbury and York, states in its report, *Baptism and Confirmation*, 'In the New Testament, adult baptism is the norm, and it is only in the light of this fact that the doctrine and practice of Baptism can be understood.'" [18]

Flemington says frankly, "There is no direct evidence in

[15] Mark 10:14-16 [16] S.P.C.K. (1957)
[17] Mark 1:9-11; Matthew 3:13-17; Luke 3:21-23.
[18] Letter from the Vicar of Holy Trinity, Twickenham, *Church Times*, January 1, 1965.

the New Testament for the baptism of infants." [19] He adds, "It can hardly be denied that many Christians at the present time have an uneasy feeling that all the good arguments really support the Baptist position. . . . We must frankly recognize that much harm has been done, and a superstitious attitude to baptism too often encouraged, because New Testament language, used originally of believers' baptism, has been applied indiscriminately, as it stands, to the baptism of infants." [20] Professor G. M. Carstairs, in the Reith Lecture for 1962, wrote, "The rituals of the Church persist, some of them, such as the practice of infant baptism, with remarkable tenacity—but one suspects that they are often mere forms, as empty of significance as the habit of touching wood for luck." [21]

The only authority in Scripture for the baptism of infants which can be pressed into use is the statement that whole families were sometimes baptized,[22] and presumably such families sometimes contained infants, but the Roman Catholic attitude that unbaptized infants who die lose something important, or are in any way barred from the grace and love of God because this particular ceremony has not been carried out, is just a relic of silly superstition without a shred of justification in Scripture or in church tradition. Yet some Roman Catholics teach that the omission of baptism determines a child's destiny for all eternity. What a lot of cruel nonsense can still cling to Christ's Gospel of love!

At the same time, I sincerely believe the words I have so often spoken in taking a service of infant baptism, "Doubt ye not, therefore, but earnestly believe, that [Christ] will favourably receive this little child." There is a value in some service of dedication on the part of parents and of the acceptance of the child "into the congregation of Christ's flock." It is said that all his life Luther would repeat, in hours of de-

[19] P. 131   [20] P. 135
[21] *This Island Now*, p. 83 (Hogarth Press, 1963).
[22] Acts 16:14, 15, 33; 1 Corinthians 1:16.

pression about his spiritual life, *"Baptizatus sum,"* I was baptized. The affirmation seemed an anchor for his soul. Calvin called the church the "Mother of all who have God as their Father."

During the Methodist service, the parents declare that they will provide a Christian home for their child, bring him up in the faith of Christ, and surround him with what is "pure, true, lovely and of good report." They promise that they will "so order their lives that no stumbling block is put in their child's way. They promise to give him "access to the worship and teaching of the church, that so he may come to the knowledge of Christ his Saviour."

The church on its part promises to maintain a fellowship of worship and service and to surround the child and his family from the first with loving prayer.[23]

All this, I hold, is splendid. The child can be told later what was done in his infancy, in the hope that in adult life he will conform voluntarily to that which was done on his behalf when he was a baby, and who knows enough to assert that the prayers of a loving community for a tiny sleeping baby can have no actual effect on him? My contention for years has been that prayers for a child are more potent than those for an adult, on the ground that a child's deep mind is less walled up by unbelief, doubt and prejudice against the percolations of spiritual energies.

I do not see why infant baptism should be called a "sacrament," any more than laying hands on the sick for healing is thus labeled. Such a rite could be much more powerfully supported from the New Testament. I cannot see why infant baptism is any more a sacrament—an outward and visible sign of an inward spiritual grace—than Christian marriage.

But I would retain the service where parents wanted it, because for them it is an hour of solemn dedication, and for the child an added grace. It seems fitting that a child should

[23] I quote from the official Methodist Order for the Baptism of Infants.

later be told that as he had the privilege of entering a human family when he was tiny, so he had been received into Christ's family, and that he must try not to let down either. But I would never make any form of baptism compulsory for the Christian. Paul seems quite proud of the fact that he baptized no Corinthians—he says bluntly, "I thank God that I baptized none of you save Crispus and Gaius!" [24]

In the Methodist Church, to which I belong, there is a baptism service for adults. They are not usually immersed, but this is only a matter of convenience. So those who feel that adult baptism is more meaningful can have that if they so desire.

Both services end with words which I think are beyond criticism: "We receive this person or child into the congregation of Christ's church and trust that he will be Christ's faithful soldier and servant unto his life's end."

2. *The Holy Communion*

I want to write about the sacrament of Holy Communion with special restraint and with deep reverence because I realize that for many of my fellow Christians this service is the very heart and essence of their worship. Dr. Donald Baillie writes, "I once heard a highly intellectual and deeply devout Anglo-Catholic say: 'To me Christianity simply *means*—the blessed sacrament.' I once heard a young woman student, again a deeply Christian Anglo-Catholic, say that she simply *lived* on her weekly Communion, and could not get on without it." [25]

I was brought up in a Presbyterian home and we attended a church where "The Lord's Supper" was celebrated only once or twice a year. On the other hand, many of my Anglican friends partake at least once a week, and my friends who are

---

[24] 1 Corinthians 1:14. He apparently baptized Lydia and her household (Acts 16:15) and Stephanas and his (1 Corinthians 1:16).

[25] Professor Donald M. Baillie, *op. cit.*, p. 92.

of the men in the room when he said, "Do this in remembrance of Me." When the woman anointed his feet we are told that he said, "Wherever in the world my gospel is preached, this that this woman hath done shall be told as a memorial of her," [29] but he made no such comment about the bread and the wine, and it was quite foreign to his methods to institute ritual and ask for it to be perpetuated.

I am not suggesting that we should not hold Communion services. They have been of immeasurable help to millions, but no layman should feel excluded from Christian discipleship or that his allegiance to Christ is of a lower order, if frankly this particular service makes little appeal to him.

I note that some scholars, including even Westcott and Hort, believe that the words, "Do this in remembrance of Me," are an interpolation in Luke's account, and that none of the other Gospel writers mentions this sentence. Dr. Hastings Rashdall said, "There is nothing to suggest that our Lord had the intention of founding an institution or permanent rite of any kind. Whatever actually happened at the Last Supper, the idea of perpetually commemorating that supper or investing with a new significance the Jewish offering of cup and bread at the table, was the work of the church, not of its Founder." [30] Dr. Barnes says, "There is but a frail foundation in our Lord's words and actions at the Last Supper for the elaborate sacrament and teaching of developed catholicism." [31] Dr. Glover hints at the same point of view in his book, *The Pilgrim*, and elsewhere says, "There is a growing consensus of opinion among independent scholars that Jesus instituted no sacraments." [32]

My own view, in brief, is this: that whether or not it was the purpose of Jesus to institute a ceremony which he desired all his followers to carry out, we do not know. About this we

[29] Matthew 26:13.
[30] *The Idea of Atonement in Christian Theology*, p. 59 (Hodder and Stoughton).
[31] *Should Such a Faith Offend?* p. 214 (Hodder and Stoughton).
[32] *The Conflict of Religions in the Early Roman Empire*, p. 158.

must remain agnostic. At the same time I feel that he is not displeased by our reproduction of that last sacred meal. Those who partake of it are not bound to any particular view of the sacrament and its meaning and importance. If they like to accept the words of Jesus as recorded by Luke and Paul, "Do this in remembrance of Me," and if they come to carry out an act of remembrance in accordance with what they believe to be the command of Jesus, then their coming in that spirit is, I am sure, not displeasing to him. If they think of the bread and the wine, given in the simplest sense, as means by which he may be remembered, then they are entitled to take that view and to come in that spirit. If they feel that the service is a symbol of community, and that they sit down with Christ, sharing bread and wine, as a common meal, with all that that implies, then let them come. At the same time, for myself, I believe that as the meal proceeded the bread and the wine became to Jesus himself symbols of that uttermost self-giving which he contemplated so soon, and I think that those who come with the simplest of thoughts about the theology of the sacrament will find mysterious things happening to them. First of all they will find a sense of presence, and secondly, they will link the partaking of the bread and wine with Calvary, and their devotion to Christ will be quickened. I could not possibly hold that the bread became his body, or that the wine became his blood, and indeed, if Jesus had wanted to say, "This bread *represents* my body," and "This wine *symbolizes* my blood," the words in which such statements would have been reported are the same words which are translated, "This *is* my body," "This *is* my blood." [33] And if some people have allowed superstition and magic to make them interpret this rite in a certain way, we must not swing to the other extreme and suppose that there is no value in it.

I suggest we should partake of it and let it come to mean

[33] Cf. Moffatt's translation of 1 Corinthians 11:24 ff.: "This *means* My body broken for you," etc.

to us whatever God can make it mean to people constituted as we are. To some, as I say, it is merely an act of remembrance. To others it is a *sacramentum*, an oath of allegiance. To another it symbolizes his death. Another argues that as bread and wine nourish our physical body, so it is the very being of Christ himself, received into the soul, that nourishes it and makes it live and grow, and that the elements symbolizes this fact. They think of him as the Bread of Life. Most of us find that material things can be channels by which a reality is reached greater than the means which produce it. A great poem gives us something not explained by our understanding of the meaning of the words of which it is made. Lovely music induces a certain state of soul, an end far greater than the means which produce it. Surely we must come to the sacramental service and allow it to mean for us whatever our faith can make it mean.[34]

Love is the food of the spirit of man and it is love also which God asks from us. The broken bread and the poured out wine are symbols of the uttermost self-giving love which God mediates through Christ. In "taking the holy sacrament to our comfort" we make in response our *sacramentum*, our oath of allegiance to Christ, and offer him our love in response to his.

Many feel, as I said, that to take communion is central, vital and essential, but no Christian, I hold, should feel excluded from the fellowship of Christ's church because for him this is not a very valuable way into an experience of the divine presence.

---

[34] I have quoted here some paragraphs from an earlier book, *His Life and Ours*, pp. 235-37 (Hodder and Stoughton).

CHAPTER VIII

THE BIBLE AND ITS INSPIRATION

"The Lord hath more light and truth yet to break forth out of His Holy word."

Parting words of Pastor John Robinson
to the Pilgrim Fathers, 1620.

"As to the Bible, 'the message is . . . so inextricably human and divine in one, that no single sentence can be quoted as having the authority of an authentic utterance of the All-Holy God.'"

Prof. John Baillie quoting Archbishop Temple
(The Idea of Revelation in Recent Thought, and
Nature, Man and God)

"Nothing is the vehicle of revelation for me unless I hear God speaking to me through it. But there is no Christian who hears God speaking to him through every passage in the Bible, so that for each of us there are some passages that are not revelatory at all. Nevertheless it is always our duty to ask ourselves whether the defect may not be in ourselves rather than in the text; whether even here it is not we who are not willing to listen rather than that nothing significant is being said."

Rev. Dr. John Baillie
(The Idea of Revelation in Recent Thought)

VIII

THE BIBLE AND ITS INSPIRATION

WHAT is the modern Christian layman to think about the Bible? He is told he ought to read it, some advisers say daily. He knows that it is a best seller and has sold better than most popular novels. The British and Foreign Bible Society tells us that twenty-three million copies are sold every year and their translations in foreign tongues are snapped up as soon as they are printed. The Chairman of the Northern Ireland branch of the B.F.B.S. said that in two months, four hundred thousand Gospels were sent to Brazil alone, and "almost immediately sold out." [1] In this country fortunes have been made by translating the Bible into popular language, and the *New English Bible* was a best seller from its birth.

Yet few people read it. Most of us have our favorite passages. Many of us could recite some favorite passages by heart. J. M. Barrie answered the stupid allegation of one narrow-minded verbal-inspirationist, who claimed that all parts of the Bible were equally inspired, by remarking that his mother's Bible opened of itself at John 14.

But while all Christians feel the beauty and inspiration of some passages both from the Old Testament—notably the Psalms—and the New—notably the Gospels—it must be admitted by all honest readers that much of the Old Testament is dull, meaningless, irrelevant and hopelessly sub-Christian in its sentiments, and that in the New, though an immense

[1] *Irish Christian Advocate,* November 6, 1953.

respect for Paul's courage is evoked, and his hymn to love in 1 Corinthians 13 makes us ready to forgive him almost anything, yet we find some of his arguments in "Romans" either difficult, irrelevant or unconvincing, and we wonder why our teachers set such store by "reading the Bible" when we get so much more spiritual help from other books. As for the matter of the equal inspiration of all parts of the Bible, I defy any honest reader to allege that he has gained spiritual help from the verses in the last book of the Bible which describe "the judgment of the great harlot that sitteth upon many waters, with whom the kings of the earth committed fornication," or that we feel uplifted in spirit by being told that "they that dwell in the earth were made drunken with the wine of her fornication." Nor are we thrilled to learn that "he carried me away in the Spirit into wilderness and I saw a woman sitting upon a scarlet-coloured beast, full of names of blasphemy having seven heads and ten horns and the woman was arrayed in purple and scarlet and decked with gold and precious stones and pearls having in her hand a golden cup full of abominations even the unclean things of her fornication" (Revelation 17:1-4). The rest of the chapter is given up to an explanation which doesn't get us much further, and one cannot help feeling that if this is the "inspired word of God," we can do better without it, for we can find far better food for the soul's hunger elsewhere. True there are some great passages in Revelation, but the book on the whole is like boarding-school plum pudding, where the plums are scarce and far apart.[2]

Do let us be honest about the Bible! Politeness and convention and deeply sincere appreciation make us reverence it. The Old Testament was, after all, a book dear to Christ, and

---

[2] The book of Revelation yields its maximum value, of course, to those who study it with an adequate commentary. I would recommend to the layman, Austin Farrer's *The Revelation of St. John the Divine* (Clarendon Press, 1964), a commentary on the English text. Martin Kiddle's volume in the Moffatt Commentaries (Harper & Row, 1940) is a first-rate verse by verse exposition.

the New contains a revelation of him and the best news in the world. But we should not just leave it on our bedside table unread, where it remains to impress, but also to hinder the housework of those who care for us but have to dust it! We should one day take a blue pencil and cross out whole chunks of it like the violent imprecatory Psalms, and other passages which contradict the Christian spirit,[3] the long genealogies, the incomprehensible parts of Isaiah and Ezekiel and Jeremiah, the worries of Paul about circumcision, his obsession with sin and guilt, and his Jewish emphasis on animal sacrifice—meaningless to a modern westerner—and the parts of Revelation written in code to members of an underground movement in danger of persecution, a code to which we have largely lost the key.

If this sounds shocking to some, I would remind them that John Wesley issued on September 9, 1784, as part of his own edition of the Prayer Book, an expurgated Psalter, and in the Preface to it he wrote: "Many Psalms are left out and many parts of others as highly improper for the mouths of a Christian Congregation." How right he was![4]

A writer in the *Church Times* (November 22, 1963) tells us that the church excluded the reading of the Old Testament from her public worship in the fifth century and it was only dragged back by Cranmer when he ransacked the monasteries for his Matins and Evensong. The writer (Rev. Christopher Wansey, Rector of Woodford) asks, "Did he make a big mistake?" Billy Graham endlessly reiterates, "The Bible says . . . ," but "The Bible says that the flesh of swine is not

[3] The Rev. Bryan H. Reed, writing to *The Methodist Recorder* (August 8, 1964), rightly complained that the Methodist Lectionary for July 26, suggested for public reading, 1 Samuel 15. "This passage," said the writer, "telling of Samuel's rebuke of Saul for failing to carry out a total massacre of the Amalekites, and saying that by showing mercy Saul had incurred the displeasure of God, is totally unfit for use in Christian worship."

[4] E.g. Psalm 137:8-9, "O daughter of Babylon . . . happy shall he be that rewardeth thee as thou hast served us. Happy shall he be that taketh and dasheth thy little ones against the rock." This complete antithesis of Christian teaching Wesley omitted, as he did Psalm 139:19-22.

to be eaten, that usury is wrong, that wages earned one day are not to be kept back till the next morning, that blasphemers are to be stoned, that it was right for little children to be torn by bears because they had mocked at the prophet of God. People are encouraged to read the Bible but they need to be taught to read it intelligently so that when they come up against such things as these and a thousand others they will not be fogged and confused by them." [5]

One of my own ambitions is to write a book called *The Busy Man's Bible*. In it I should preface each book with a short essay on the purpose which the author or editor had in mind, the time it was written and a brief background of the setting. Then would follow those parts of the book which were still worth reading, with copious footnotes to make the meaning clear. For instance, we read, "she hath received at the Lord's hand double for all her sins" (Isaiah 40:2). This obscures a thrilling meaning. I have read that in Isaiah's day if a man became insolvent the list of all his liabilities was written on a parchment and nailed up, with a nail at the top and another at the bottom, in some public place. If a rich friend saw this humiliating document he would sometimes take out the bottom nail, double the parchment in two, write his name across the folded document and drive the bottom nail in again next to the top nail, securing the parchment in this folded form. His signature meant that he would be responsible for his friend's debts. I have wondered whether this practice is referred to in this passage. The grim account of our sins is doubled up and God's name written across it. One is reminded of the book which recorded the taxes to be extracted from each town and village in France. The page headed Domremy, where Joan of Arc lived, is said to be doubled back, and across the folded portion one finds the words written—"Free for the Maid's sake."

I used to wonder why, on the first Whitsunday, Peter

[5] Rev. Dr. Roderic Dunkerley in *The British Weekly*, April 2, 1964.

quoted the quaint prophecy of Joel about "blood and fire and vapour of smoke," "The sun shall be turned into darkness and the moon into blood before the day of the Lord shall come (Joel 2:28 ff. and Acts 2:19 ff.).

Then I read Velikovsky's great book, *Worlds in Collision*,[6] and realized that it is thought that at the time of the plagues (Exodus 7 ff.) the earth passed through the tail of a comet, or actually collided with some heavenly body and that masses of red dust settled on the earth. The boils suffered by men and cattle, the rivers that seemed "turned into blood," and the very color of the sea, called for this reason, "the Red Sea," had their origin in this all pervading red dust. As one watched, the sun seemed dark and, as the dust cleared, the moon could be seen through it, but it was the color of blood. Since the Israelites believed that God sent these signs and plagues to deliver *them*, it was popularly believed that a Divine deliverance would again be accompanied by similar wonders in the heaven above and signs in the earth beneath.

There are scores of passages which could be turned from meaninglessness into spiritual food and mental understanding by a simple footnote. "Cast thy bread upon the waters: for thou shalt find it after many days," we read in Ecclesiastes 11:1. My picture used to be that of half an old loaf floating about in a Thames backwater, and I wondered why anyone would want to "find it after many days," since it looked uneatable already! Light broke when someone explained that the reference was to rice apparently cast away on the waters of a rice field but taking root in the ooze underneath and coming up again "after many days" in the green beauty and promise of a harvest. Immediately we see its true meaning, the verse becomes a living and relevant parable.

By some such method, then, the rich treasures of the Bible could be made available quickly and easily for the busy man,

[6] Victor Gollancz, 1960. Velikovsky gives evidence of ancient observers in other parts of the earth who noted the same phenomena in Rome, Mexico, Egypt and Finland. All record the red dust and the darkness.

who too often now makes a great resolution to "read the Bible through" since it has been praised so often by so many. He starts valiantly at Genesis, flags a bit in Exodus and perishes in Leviticus, wondering why people praise it so highly, and why missionaries bother to translate into Chinese and Urdu and Somali the rules for a Levitical priest in 700 years B.C., and what an Ashanti schoolgirl makes of the passage quoted above from Revelation. Indeed, our own young people are hindered rather than helped by having the Bible thrust at them with the advice to read it. Sir Richard Acland well says, "By pushing the Bible at them when, for want of a basically religious outlook, they cannot understand its message, we are in most cases strengthening the armour plating that stands between them and God." [7]

But there are two guiding principles which may be of help to the layman as he looks for the undoubted treasure within the covers of his Bible:

1. We must always remember that the Bible is not one book, but a library of books written by a hundred fallible men over a period of a thousand years. It is no good saying, as Billy Graham so repeatedly does, "The Bible says . . ." I agree with Blumhardt when he says, "It may say what it likes in the Bible—on this point I am greater than the Bible. I admit it is in the Bible, but in the end I must know what is true of God, and not what a man once put into such and such words two thousand years ago. In Christ something total must have come true for the world, and my faith must be such that it can comprehend this totality." [8]

The Bible is made up of myth, poetry, legend, history, prophecy, biography, mystical writing, allegory, parable, drama—indeed, almost every way of writing that exists except that of the scientific text-book.

[7] Sir Richard Acland, *We Teach Them Wrong*, p. 115 (Gollancz, 1963).

[8] C. Blumhardt, Predigten Vol. 3, p. 248, quoted by Theodor Bovet, *That They May Have Life*, p. 216, translated by J. A. Baker (Darton, Longman and Todd, 1964).

It is quite true that the Bible is inspired, but so are many other literary treasures of the world. One of the things that makes this library "different" is that each book in it has as its motive the dynamic idea that "God matters." The biblical historian is not nearly so eager to be accurate as to show God at work in history. The Psalmist is not nearly so eager to write good poetry as to proclaim the glory of God. Shelley would have been horrified to be accused of such a moral motive. "Didactic poetry," he said in the Preface to "Prometheus Unbound," "is my abhorrence." And Keats agreed with him. "A poet," he said, "should have no opinions, no principles, no morality. To be tied to these things spoils true art which should be entirely unfettered." No one could deny inspiration to both poets, but the psalmist is different. He is out to justify *God* and acclaim the importance of righteousness as he assesses it, and this motive outweighs the aesthetic one.

We need not press for the Bible a different *kind* of inspiration than that which we claim for the great poets or prose writers of the world. There is only one *kind* of inspiration, and all work is inspired which makes us respond to truth, beauty, or goodness and makes us feel the appeal of those ultimates. But there is certainly a great difference in *degree* —at times so great that it seems to some a difference in kind —between the inspiration of a picture, poem or sonata, written to express beauty and win an aesthetic response, and a psalm written to win a moral response and express the joy in, and praise of God, or a prophecy which reveals the character of God; a prophecy bursting from a passionate heart too full to contain it any longer, scorching the petty, evil desires of men as with a flame of fire, and rousing dormant consciences to right action; a prophecy which will mean to the prophet loss of popularity, possibly torture and death, yet a prophecy bravely spoken in the name of the God of Truth.

Much was said about the reliability of the Gospels in the chapter on Christ (pp. 95-97) so we may leave the point by summarizing that the Bible is a library of almost every kind of literary form, written or edited by fallible men whose inspiration did not exclude their looking through colored spectacles, or the limitations of the knowledge and outlook of the day in which they lived, or the party to which they belonged.

2. A second guiding thought for the layman to keep in mind is that the idea of God is a developing idea throughout the Bible. It is a pity in a way that the list of the books of the Bible was closed in about A.D. 365.[9] For I regard William Temple, formerly Archbishop of Canterbury, as just as inspired as Paul. Canon J. D. Pearce-Higgins, who repudiated the Thirty-nine Articles, which every Anglican clergyman swears he believes, said recently,[10] "St. Paul was completely wrong in his idea of a second coming and the sudden transformation of the bodies of the still living into etheric or spirit bodies of those who had already died and were expected to return on the clouds of heaven with Christ."

Earlier, Canon Pearce-Higgins told the conference that he considered the present use of the Bible made by the average Christian teacher to be one of the greatest obstacles to human brotherhood and inter-racial understanding which existed. He added: "But what can you expect from a church whose ministers are under a strong moral pressure to repeat parrot-wise their own least valuable heritage in unselective fashion, and day by day spend their time reciting ancient poems often enshrining a sub-Christian and, in many ways, purely a parochial view of the universe, and of reading and rereading uncritically

[9] On Easter Day, A.D. 365, the Pastoral Letter of Archbishop Athanasius was read from all the pulpits in Alexandria. It contained the following: "It seemed good to me . . . to publish the books which are admitted in the Canon, and have been delivered unto us, and are believed to be divine. . . ." Then follows a list of the books of the Old and New Testaments with those of the Apocrypha in an Appendix just as we have them today. This was the first imprimatur of the early church on the Authorized Bible. See *Our Bible in the Making*, Dr. J. Paterson-Smyth. (Sampson Low, 1914).

[10] Reported in *The Guardian*, August 10, 1963.

and often *ad nauseam* stories of old unhappy days and battles of long ago.

"I have come to the painful conclusion that for a very large number of the supporters of religion, their religious views are infantile psychological systems which have been acquired under the stress of the early years of life which give emotional satisfaction to the particular psychological make-up of the individual concerned and which have never been tested by the touchstone of intellectual objectivity and also of emotional reality." I regard the late T. S. Eliot as much more inspired than the author of the Song of Solomon. The late C. S. Lewis' *Screwtape Letters* would willingly be given a place in the sacred library had the list of books not been closed, and *Honest to God* would have been as useful and intelligible as the book of Revelation!

Taking the Bible as we have it, it begins with a local storm god who lives on the top of Mt. Sinai, and when the Israelites get too far from the mountain he has to be carried with them. The smoke of the burning censer, symbolizing the Divine Presence, is seen in daylight as a pillar of cloud, and at night the smoke is lit up by the burning wood and looks like a pillar of fire. Only so can the people be made to believe that their God has not been left behind like the gods of Egypt!

Even when he gets them to Canaan, by a method of invasion on the same moral level as the rape of Ethiopia by the Italians, or of Hungary by the Russians (save that the latter, in both cases, did not pretend it was the will of God!), he remains a jealous, vindictive tyrant, punishing the children for their father's sins and thinking nothing of turning a terrified woman into a pillar of salt,[11] ordering massacres,[12] having a helpless old man hacked in pieces before him,[13] or visiting his devoted servant Job with disease and pain until he longed for death.[14]

[11] Genesis 19:26   [12] Joshua 8:26
[13] 1 Samuel 15:33   [14] Job 2:7-10.

When we *close* the Bible we are left with a loving Father who longs to welcome all men of whatever race or color as his dear sons, to whom everyone is precious and in whose lives he is working out an undefeatable purpose. If we still ask questions about his nature, we find the answer in Jesus who said, "He that hath seen Me hath seen the Father," and we must resolutely tell ourselves that everything is false about God, even if it be found within the covers of the Bible, if it is out of harmony with our total mental picture of Christ made by the unbiased contemplation of all the evidence, including the changed lives of Christ's followers.

But what is the value of reading the Bible? What may we hope to gain by it? When I asked a friend of mine this question she replied that she wanted to find out more about God, to get to know him, and to get help in the business of living. I can hardly think of a better answer. This is a library of books about men's experiences with God, and if we use a blue pencil freely, follow the guiding principles suggested, and turn continually to modern translations, and, if possible, commentaries like the cheap but first-rate paperbacks by Dr. William Barclay [15] we shall find treasure indeed.

For, although our day and circumstances are so very different, God is the same and so is man's need. A sensible modern doesn't expect to find science or accurate history in the Bible, but he does find that the human hearts which are laid bare in the Bible have passed through temptation and loneliness, sorrow and sickness, frustration and despair, depression and worry, victory and defeat, bereavement and treachery, anxiety and guilt. Through the comfort, sympathy, power and help of God, men and women have emerged into sunshine and peace with songs of thanksgiving and gratitude on their lips, even when outward circumstances are still difficult and even dangerous.

Above all, of course, Jesus himself so often steps out of

[15] Published by the Church of Scotland, George Street, Edinburgh.

these sacred pages, human but something more, lovable and compassionate and intensely knowable, and we justifiably comfort ourselves with the thought that if God is really like that, we can trustfully commit ourselves unreservedly into his hands, for life and death and whatever comes afterward. "Jesus Christ seemed to come right out of the Bible," said one of the teenagers from down-town New York, saved from drug-addiction and crime through the magnificent ministry of the Rev. David Wilkerson. "He became a living person who wanted to stand with me through my problems." [16]

When, at an observatory, I was shown the stars, I did not find myself criticizing the telescope. And in those moments when God's loving purposes shine with splendor, and the figure of Christ comes suddenly into focus, I am content to accept the criticisms which are perfectly valid about the Bible, and to make allowance for the human fallibility of those whose words have come down to me, and to secure which so many brave men, have been willing to die. Criticisms of the Bible fall away as unimportant in those moments when, for all its fallibility and early crudity, some eternal truth blazes into vision and I catch a glimpse of God. I find repeatedly that I want to pray a very simple prayer:

> *Teach me to love Thy sacred word,*
> *And view my Saviour there.*

[16] David Wilkerson, *The Cross and Switchblade*, p. 161 (Fleming H. Revell, Co. 5th edition, 1964).

CHAPTER IX

PROVIDENCE AND CARE

"We discover that the universe shows evidence of a designing or controlling power that has something in common with our own individual minds. . . . We are not so much intruders in the universe as we first thought."

Sir James Jeans
(*The Mysterious Universe*)

PROVIDENCE AND CARE

ARE our lives at the mercy of vast impersonal forces in the universe, some of them beneficent but so many of them destructive? Are we the victims of unforeseeable accident? Can chance or ill-luck ruin one person and make another? Are temperament, education, the accident of birth, environment and breeding—factors over which few have any control—decisive in what we make of life?

My own belief is that each one of us is loved by God and precious in his sight. I believe that in each of our lives God is working out a loving purpose, far too vast for our present understanding, which finally will know no defeat. I believe that ignorance, folly and sin, personal and collective, can hinder, and temporarily defeat that purpose, but that *finally* —a word that can postpone success for centuries—God will fulfill his plan, weaving into its wonder all that has happened to us, whatever its source, so that finally, from the perspective of the next world we see nothing as loss, nothing as *mere* accident, or bad luck, or ill-fortune, or as inescapable limitation imposed on us by a fortuitous lack of education, culture or possession. For the thoughtful Christian I can see no escape from some such view. It is incredible that, considering our own power of loving and our tender compassion for others, we ourselves are stranded on a lonely planet, amid the glittering galaxies and the terrifying immensities, doomed to carry out on earth a meaningless round of insect activities determined by blind chance and impersonal forces, material and psychological, and at last condemned to perish finally in the dust of the cosmos, in spite of all our dreams, with no advantage gained from all our sufferings; with both heroism and cowardice, sacrifice and selfishness, lust and love, greed and generosity all brought down to one level of meaninglessness. Nor can I believe that our sense of the numinous—of having *some* link with the glories of a supernatural plane of being, peopled by the beloved dead, and by "angels and archangels and all the company of heaven," can be denied by extinction. No, we have seen:

Visions too beautiful to be untrue

and it requires more from credulity to suppose that *all* the world's greatest teachers, mystics, prophets, seers and saints have been liars, idiots or self-deluded dreamers, and that our deepest sense of values is mistaken—for instance, that murdering a million Jews is no better nor worse than feeding a million starving children—than to believe in a "divinity that shapes our ends," even though our understanding of the workings of that Providence is so often baffling and obscure.

I have written so much on the theme of human suffering, for the problem has teased my mind into activity for fifty years, that what follows may reflect thought already expressed in earlier books.[1] But in this chapter I would like to outline a skeleton argument about Providence, which the modern layman can fill in or reject after further thought and wider reading.

First, however, I would make it clear that I have no faith in what is sometimes called a "special Providence." When a

---

[1] I published a pamphlet, now happily out of print, on *The Mystery of Pain* over forty years ago. In the "Fellowship of the Kingdom" series of pamphlets another appeared in 1932 called *Pain and Providence*. Later, more serious efforts were, *Why Do Men Suffer?* (Abingdon Press, 1935), *Psychology, Religion and Healing* (Abingdon, 1951), and *Salute to a Sufferer* (Abingdon, 1962), and finally, *Wounded Spirits* (Abingdon, 1962).

famous Methodist minister of earlier days was asked by someone whether it was not a special Providence that had guided his aunt to miss a train which met with disaster, the minister replied incisively, "I don't know, I didn't know your aunt." One would rather promote the most crude belief in luck, both good and bad, than encourage the attitude of special protection. As the late Dr. Griffith Jones wrote: "The piety that sees a sign of divine favour in escape from a sudden danger which destroys other lives, is a spurious and egotistic travesty of the faith that knows that 'God spared not His own Son, but freely gave Him up for us all.' The true Christian will ask for no immunity from the common lot, for no freedom from the hardships of experience, for no miraculous deliverance from impending calamity, but he will ask for the power to overcome the world in a spirit that is courageous as well as meek, militant against all forms of evil while profoundly thankful for what seems good in his life." [2]

To that wise word I would add another from a writer who has immensely helped my thought by his books, the late Dr. John Oman. "To trust in anything working for our own good in the way of mere possession and material security is to make a god of this world: and no other delusion so shuts us off from real trust in God or from any need of learning His mind. . . . To build our hopes on the promise [of the world so conceived] is to prove ourselves fools, because it does not work even imperfectly, and much less all of it together for good. Faith is not blindness to life's uncertainties and miseries. *Until faith in Providence as mere beneficence breaks down, the faith which reconciles us to God in face of every conceivable evil cannot arise.* But then, nothing whatsoever in the world is omitted from what works together for good." [3]

We must at the outset give up the idea that the providen-

[2] Dr. E. Griffith Jones, *Providence, Divine and Human*, p. 107 (Hodder and Stoughton, 1925).
[3] Dr. John Oman, *The Paradox of the World*, p. 112 (Cambridge University Press, 1921). Italics mine.

tial care of God is limited to his activity in giving us the things we call good, like health, success, freedom from physical frustration in terms of food, power and sex; the thing we lump together and call "all the blessings of this life." His Providence is rather in providing for us possibilities of reaction with which we must, with all the power and insight which his grace affords, proceed to build character and develop insight, remembering that *his* aims can be reached just as surely by a right use of the things we call evil—like bereavement, pain, suffering, sorrow, frustration and so on—as by a right use of the things we call good.

Any idea of Providence which is based only on God's gifts of ease, plenty, success, wealth and health is soon bound to come to grief, for no one in a long life escapes loss, distress and calamity. I write on a day when news has reached Britain of the fire on a passenger vessel—the *Lakonia*—resulting in horror, terror, the separation of loved ones, the injury of many, and the death of over a hundred people, and for all, the loss of all their personal possessions. No one supposes that such a disaster is God's will in any meaningful use of that word. I have myself seen the incredible stupidity of some passengers on a liner. When I was traveling to Australia, a woman, in spite of large warning notices, started a fire by leaving an electric iron turned on in a cubicle while she went to have her tea. Reverting to the loss of the *Lakonia,* no Christian can believe that God's providential care for a thousand passengers was finally defeated by one person's carelessness, or by an electrical fault or whatever started the fire. With the stones provided by an incident God did not will, all those who suffered may yet erect a splendid structure to his glory. Events caused by human stupidity, ignorance or sin cannot finally defeat a divine, omnipotent and loving Being.

The idea that God's Providence means that he looks after those who serve him by a special use of his power in terms of favoritism is an immoral idea and insulting to both man and God. No true Christian wants to opt out of the trials that beset others, and no worthy idea of God could include his establishment of a kind of insurance scheme by which, if God be worshiped, cancer, for example, could be avoided. Jesus himself who spoke so eloquently of God's providential care, quoting the lilies and the birds, never promised a "special Providence" to his own. Rather he promised that they would face persecution beyond the normal trials of others. But he did promise that he would see them through everything and be with them to the end.

"The very secret of all profitable use of life is just to abandon the expectation that it ever was designed to forward persons devoted to material and merely worldly purposes with no higher ends than gain, or pleasure or pride of place, and to discern that naturally the only ends it could have been designed to serve are God's." [4]

When all this is said, I am sure in my heart that although God wills that effects shall follow causes, and the results of folly, ignorance and sin, personal or communal, must fall upon us, yet his will, in the sense of what he ideally desires, is the health and happiness of all his children. He does not *will* the causes—folly, ignorance and sin—which bring those effects which so often we call evil. He wills their opposites: wisdom, knowledge and goodness. If he does not will the causes, he cannot will the effects which flow from those causes in any sensible use of the word "will." [5]

Yet frequently we foolishly torture ourselves by saying about our troubles, "What have I done to deserve this?" when the only answer must be that it is because we belong to the human family. Because of this we gain what we do not merit and we suffer what we do not deserve. We all gain when one member of the human family discovers penicillin. We may be an unlucky one who suffers because another member

[4] John Oman, *op. cit.*, p. 119.
[5] In *The Will of God*, a pamphlet published by Abingdon Press, I have tried to clear this up by differentiating between the ideal will of God, the circumstantial will of God and the ultimate will of God.

of the human family recommends thalidomide. It is wise for us to ask ourselves whether any disaster derives from our own personal sin, folly or ignorance, but often we shall find that the disaster has no more personal reference to us than the tumble of the football field which—even if it brings to a player a broken leg—has to be accepted as part of the game. No footballer has been known to lie down on the field and say, "Why should this happen to me?"

We must be exceedingly careful, whether our own or another's trouble is being considered, not to call the will of God what Jesus and his servant Paul called the will of Satan,[*] remembering that God *allows* what he does not *will*. He *allows* sin, but his will is holiness. And as he ever strives with man to replace sin with holiness, he strives also to overcome ignorance with knowledge, and folly with wisdom, thus cutting out the causes of much of what we endure as suffering, namely folly, ignorance and sin.

To make the point that God allows what he does not will should be followed immediately by the insistence that the *measure* of what he allows is the *measure* of his purpose in bringing good out of evil. He would not allow anything to happen which could finally defeat his plans. A mother might allow a child to stumble on a thick carpet as he learned to walk, but she would not *allow* him to stumble on a railway line when an express train was due. The first stumble could be built into his training, even though she did not will it (or she would have pushed him over). The second stumble could finally defeat her training altogether.

Having lost three of my dearest with cancer, and been concerned in the agonies of hundreds of my people as their minister, I know that God must have a complete answer to a problem which I do not expect to solve in this life, and I tell myself that the answer that is going to satisfy us, his children, and allow all the terrible agonies of men to fall into

[*] See Luke 13:16 and 2 Corinthians 12:7.

place and be accepted as within the planning of a loving, omnipotent God to deal with, must be a wonderful answer indeed. But faith cannot rest in any affirmation other than this, that "eye hath not seen, nor ear heard, nor hath it ever entered into the heart of man to conceive the things that God hath prepared for them that love Him," [7] and that the sufferings of our present pilgrimage cannot be "worthy to be compared with the glory that shall be revealed." [8]

Part of our difficulty in this problem of God's Providence is that we cannot escape anthropomorphism—of thinking of God as a big man. Many cannot really believe in their hearts that God can be concerned in the troubles of an insignificant individual on one of the minor planets which itself is only a speck of cosmic dust in an immense universe the size of which no brain can really conceive. Many other planets may contain persons dear to God—a thought which makes the problem even greater—but there are enough people on this planet to make *my* little worries and illnesses appear trifling in perspective.

There is some escape from this paralyzing thought by realizing that there are more cells in one human brain than there are people on the whole earth, and yet, presumably, each has its function, its use and its value.[9] Can it be that men and women, even on a million planets, bear a relation to God in some sense comparable to the relation which the cells of my brain and body bear to me? Can it be that in a very intimate sense, "*in* Him we live and move and have our being"? [10] Can it be that he does not watch our lives from outside us, as a hiker might sit on a stile and watch ants in an ant-heap on the ground below him; that he is not like the old woman "who lived in a shoe and had so many children that she didn't

---

[7] 1 Corinthians 2:9   [8] Romans 8:18
[9] W. R. Russell in *The Listener* of October 29, 1959, estimates the number of these highly complex units as 10,000 million, "which have a special capacity either to stimulate each other to action or to stop activity."
[10] Acts 17:28.

know what to do," but that he knows all that happens to us because, in some sense, *it happens to him?*

Jesus stressed repeatedly God's care for the individual. "Not a sparrow falls to the ground," he said, "but God is concerned." [11] How does a sparrow's fall contrast with all that goes on amid the galaxies? And Jesus added, "Ye are of more value than many sparrows." If Jesus really is the best clue to the nature of God, we must humbly learn to sit at his feet here. Christ's concern for men's illnesses, troubles and despair must surely mean that God cares too, for "he that hath seen Me hath seen the Father." We can almost hear imaginatively the compassion in Christ's voice as he says: "If God *so* clothes the grass of the field which blooms today and is thrown tomorrow into the furnace, will not He much more clothe you? O men, how little you trust Him!" [12]

There is very much in the life of men which I cannot yet square with the Providence of an omnipotent and good God, but I cannot escape the certainty that he must CARE. Caring is a higher activity of a personality than not caring, and even I care about what my loved ones suffer and, indeed, what animals that I love suffer. [13] A God, then, who did not care, is lower in any moral estimate than a man who cares.

I believe that the affirmation of God's omnipotence does not mean that everything that happens is his will, for clearly in a world where men have free will, where men are ignorant, foolish and wicked; in a world where we are so closely bound to one another that the bond can mean disaster as well as benefit—in such a world, ten thousand things can happen which a loving God does not want to happen. Omnipotence means to me that nothing can possibly happen which defeats him, nothing is allowed to happen which *finally* frustrates his plans, or from which he cannot achieve a good greater in measure than what looks to me like sheer evil. If those plans

---

[11] Matthew 10:29-31   [12] Matthew 6:30 (Moffatt)
[13] I have tried to deal with the suffering of animals, and with disasters through earthquake, volcano and storm in *Why Do Men Suffer?* pp. 48 ff. and 89 ff. (Abingdon Press, 1936).

were not even defeated by the crucifixion of the dearest and purest of all the sons of men, who in all things sought only his Father's will, then surely nothing that evil can do to me, nothing that I call disaster, can have the last word, but at last—even though it be at long last—it will be woven into a mighty and satisfying plan.

Meanwhile, many of the things that happen to us must in all sincerity be called accidents. By an accident I mean an event which God did not intend to happen and which man could not foresee. All of us could give a hundred instances. One has just happened under my nose. My next door neighbor, an elderly man, took his little dog on a leash for a walk. It was attacked by another dog. The leash tripped up the dog's owner and he fell heavily to the ground, breaking his shoulder and putting him in the hospital. Since I wrote these words he has developed pneumonia and died. This was not something God willed. This was not due to human folly, ignorance or sin. There is no fault to be found anywhere. Yet weeks of pain and misery in a hospital resulted, and finally death. No one supposes that Divine intervention ought to have been available. All we can say is that it was an accident. But the Christian believes that nothing *can* happen to him which God cannot weave into a pattern of beauty and value, and that even if the experience—to change the figure—remains a frozen asset, it will turn out to be gain rather than loss in the final balance-sheet of the soul. Austin Farrer wisely wrote, "We must believe that God has acted in all for the best. How could we possibly think otherwise? It was for the best, therefore, that He made a half-chaos of self-moving, brainless forces to be the bottom and soil of His creation, out of which higher forms should arise. But then a semi-chaos, if it is to be itself, must be a field of limitless accident; and accident is by definition an uncalculated effect. It may be foreseen [by God,] provided against, discounted, or profited by; it cannot be intended or arranged. It would be meaningless to say that God Himself planned the detail

213

of a chaos, or of a semi-chaos either, in its chaotic aspect. His infinite contrivance draws some good out of every cross-accident, and, as we have argued, a unique good. But He has not calculated the accident with a view to the resultant good. If He had, it would not be an accident, it would only seem to be one." [14]

Looking for evidence of God's providential dealing with us is often abortive during a time of trouble. I believe intensely in the loving guidance of God but it is usually only when I look *back* that I can see convincing evidence of it. Reaching various cross-roads in my life I have often been uncertain which way to take, and I have just had to follow what light I had from common sense, good advice and careful thought, and then make a decision and hope for the best. It is only as I look *back* that I feel there was a "Hand that guided and a Heart that planned." I suppose if more direction had been given, less faith would have been required, though at times I could have done with a greater sense of certainty. But again I agree with Austin Farrer when he writes, "*Looking back* over a tract of time, we can see how circumstances have shaped us, even in spite of ourselves, and regret that we have put so many obstacles in the path of a mercy we failed to discern." [15] And, while I maintain that much that happens must be labeled "accident," I think I know what the late William Temple meant when he said, "When I say my prayers I find that coincidences begin to happen."

The comfortable thought in all this to me is that I believe that I am in the hands of a loving, wise, finally undefeatable Power whom I can call Father, and that, like every other human being, I am dear to him and cannot fall out of his hands. God is only at the beginning of his work with this planet. "My Father," said Jesus, "has never yet ceased His

---

[14] Austin Farrer, *Love Almighty and Ills Unlimited*, p. 164 (Collins, 1962).
[15] Austin Farrer, *op. cit.*, p. 171. Italics mine.

work." [16] Man has only just arrived. God's human family is at school but only in the infant class. The seventh day of creation has only just dawned. A great drama has just begun and since the curtain has only just gone up for the beginning of Act I, who can judge the whole drama? All I can do is to play my part, do my best, and try to react to every circumstance in the spirit of Christ. Nothing like crucifixion, the seeming defeat of all I came to do and the defection of all my friends, is likely to descend upon me. If, in face of all that, he could say, "Father, into Thy hands I TRUST my spirit," I must try to say the same. The last word cannot be Calvary. It must be Easter. It is no good pretending there is no darkness. Mystery, horror, pain and frustration darken almost everyone's sky at some time or other. But after that there will come a blessed dawn for every human soul and for the whole human family of God. Let us dare, here, to think the best. The very fact that we can thus conceive of God's providence and care is, to me, evidence of it. For where God is concerned man cannot think better than the truth.

Paul has an interesting phrase, in 2 Corinthians 7:10, about the kind of "godly sorrow which worketh repentance into a salvation which bringeth no regret" (RSV margin), and he contrasts it with "the sorrow of the world which worketh death." Dr. Moffatt lights up the phrase, "godly sorrow" by translating it thus: "the pain God is allowed to guide," and the *New English Bible* is equally suggestive in translating the phrase, "the wound which is borne in God's way." There must always be a difference between the suffering, whatever may be its cause, which is met by resentment and rebellion, hatred or envy, and the suffering that is accepted with cheerfulness and courage and which makes the sufferer ask, "What is God trying to say to me in all this?" "How can I help him use this part of my life for his glory?" When our wounds are "borne in God's way," and our pain is guided by him, it can,

[16] John 5:17 (*New English Bible*).

like the pain of Calvary, be swept into the stream of God's purposes, the fulfillment of which, one day, we shall see without regret. "You bore your hurt in God's way," said Paul to his Corinthian friends, "and see what its results have been!" (2 Corinthians 7:11. *New English Bible*).

After I had written this chapter and had it typed, I came across two sentences of Paul Tillich's which, better than any words of mine, summarize much of my own thought: "Providence means that there is a creating and saving possibility implied in every situation, which cannot be destroyed by any event. Providence means that the daemonic and destructive forces within ourselves and our world can never have an unbreakable grasp upon us, and that the bond which connects us with the fulfilling love can never be disrupted." [17]

CHAPTER X

PRAYER AND FAITH

"At times, in the silence of the night and in rare, lonely moments, I experience a sort of communion of myself with Something Great that is not myself."

H. G. Wells

"There are times when we can never meet the future with sufficient elasticity of mind, especially if we are locked in the contemporary systems of thought. We can do worse than remember a principle which both gives us a firm Rock and leaves us the maximum elasticity for our minds: the principle: 'Hold to Christ, and for the rest be totally uncommitted.'"

Professor Herbert Butterfield
(Christianity and History)

X

PRAYER AND FAITH

IT would be absurd to attempt, in one chapter, to write adequately or exhaustively on either of these vast subjects. Hundreds of books have been written on each. I repeat, however, that in this book I have in mind the thoughtful layman, especially the kind of semi-agnostic whom I have described in the preface. So much time has been wasted in so-called prayer, and so much misleading nonsense has been talked and written about "faith," that many laymen misunderstand both and therefore practice neither. A lot of dead wood needs to be cut away before the shining values behind both these words are revealed and their riches appropriated.

First, in regard to private prayer, if we are entirely honest most of us would agree that it is a most unrewarding one-way conversation which we tend to give up. Some practice it— even using the words of childhood [1]—as a kind of habit that carries as little thoughtfulness with it as washing one's neck in the morning. Others only pray with sincerity at times of great need in their own lives or in the lives of those dear to them.

Surely it is a good thing to give up anything that is plainly a farce or a bit of superstition. Prayer is not instinctive like eating. I wish it were, and that one really hungered for God.

[1] A lady of sixty-nine confided to me years ago that she still knelt at her bedside nightly and said, "Bless Thy little lamb tonight," and finished with, "Make me a good girl"!

If I give up food, I am driven to eat; the less I eat the more I want to, but the less I pray the less I want to.

Knowing that, for me, praying tends to cease altogether unless I have some scheme to help me, and, to help myself rather than others, I first drew up for private use what has since been published as some sort of prayer guide.[2]

I hold that it is better really to pray once a week than maintain a daily farce, and better for the layman, as he passes some point on his way to work, even momentarily, to commit the day to God, and, as he goes to sleep, to run his hand over the day that is past and seek pardon for anything wrong, than to give up prayer altogether. The eyes would soon grow dim if they had no correspondence with light. The lungs would soon perish without any correspondence with air. The mind that has no relation with truth is said to be in a state of unbalance, and the spirit too must have some traffic with God, its relevant Environment, if it is to maintain its fullest health. And since man is a unity of body, mind and spirit, dis-ease at any one level is liable to cause or exacerbate dis-ease at any other. All I am suggesting here is that we should examine our prayer life, cut out anything unreal and meaningless, but keep open—if it be only once a week—some thoroughfare of traffic with God. Although we ought to pray because we love God, it is silly to pretend that it is only for his sake we pray. Our full health depends on prayer.

How my heart responds to Florence Allshorn's simple phrase of prayer, "O God, here am I and here are You!" She writes, "Just as lying in the sun doing nothing, surrendering your body to it, with the sun blazing down on you, affects your body and your senses, so this surrendering of the soul to that transforming Power affects the soul, and I believe that as truly as the sun changes the color of your skin so that Power changes you at the centre." [3]

[2] *A Private House of Prayer* (Abingdon Press, 1958).
[3] J. H. Oldham, *Florence Allshorn* (Student Christian Movement Press, 5th edition, 1955).

I find that hardly ever do I pray for myself. This is not humility, it is just that he knows already. What I want to do is to strain my desires as through a sieve, the sieve being what he sees is best or wise or possible. (Many of my early desires were inherently impossible.) This is what *I* mean by the phrase, "Through Jesus Christ our Lord"; not that a lofty, remote God will not listen unless I persuade Christ to carry my wishes to a higher court, but that I want to cleanse my own desires by passing them through the mesh of the Master's mind, lest, to use a phrase of John Burnaby, I am enmeshed in a "sham of professing desires which are not really mine." [4] Again and again, a quiet, solitary, wordless walk by the seashore with my heart deeply grateful for all his love and mercy; a heart opened to him in adoration and quietly receptive to the impact of his spirit, has meant far more than any prayer meeting or list of petitions, or any verbal confession, or any wordy prayer, for in such an experience the relationship with God is restored and freshened, and this, not being "let off," is the whole meaning of forgiveness.

I believe sincerely in the value of prayer for others as long as I can make the prayer personal and focus it on individual rather than causes. Since, in these days, people take more notice of the *British Medical Journal* than the biographies of the saints, let me quote from it: "It is unquestionable that prayer, inspired by a living faith, is a force acting within the patient, which places him in the most favorable condition for the stirring of the pool of hope that lies, still and hidden, it may be in the depths of human nature." [5] But surely it must be personal and focused. In my opinion, it would be better for a missionary society to ask individual churches to concentrate on specified bits of work abroad, with the exchange of photographs, letters and the like, making personal relationships real, rather than to depend on a prayer like, "God bless the London Missionary Society, or the Methodist or Baptist Mis-

[4] *Soundings*, p. 235 (Cambridge University Press, 1962).
[5] *British Medical Journal*, June 18, 1910.

sionary Society." Recently, I heard a minister pray, "God bless Africa, India, China and the islands of the sea." And another said, "O God bless all the towns and villages of England." Many prayers of this kind I regard as wasting the time of the congregation. One thinks of the old lady who nightly prayed for nearly every nation under heaven. She was not quite sure of Australians, so, after including Indians, Africans, Americans, Chinese and Japanese, she added, "And bless those dear Australians as they swing from tree to tree!"

Similarly, surely it would be better to ask a congregation to pray for a known and especially, if possible, a loved individual, rather than, as I heard a minister do, offer a prayer like, "O Lord, bless all who are sick and make them well." Such a sentence is too full of unexpectancy to be valuable, save that it might conceivably have a subjective effect on some member of the congregation and remind him that there were many people in the world who are ill and starving, ill-treated and neglected, and that he ought to do something about it.

"Doing something about it" makes me want to include here an experience of my own. After a motor accident in which I sustained severe head injuries, two of my friends, both very busy men, reacted in two different ways. The first came to see me and cheered me immensely by his infectious gaiety. The second wrote to say that the hospital was a long way away and he knew I should have many visitors, so he thought the right thing for him to do was to pray for me, which no doubt he did.

But I found the first reaction much more helpful, and, when I meditated on the two reactions, much more religious as well as costly. In fact the first reaction I now think of as a kind of prayer and, like the Bishop of Woolwich, I feel I am praying for a man when I meet him and we both open our hearts to one another on what I want to call "the God level." "To open oneself to another *unconditionally* in love is to be with him in the presence of God, and that is the heart of intercession. To pray for another is to expose both oneself and him to the common ground of our being; it is to see one's concern for him in terms of *ultimate* concern, to let God into the relationship. Intercession is to *be with* another at that depth, whether in silence or compassion or action. It may consist simply in listening, when we take the otherness of the other person most seriously. It may not be talking *to* God, as though to a third person, about him at all. The *Thou* addressed may be his own *Thou*, but it may be addressed and responded to at such a level that we can only speak of knowing him in God and God in him. It may not be specifically religious, it may not be consciously Christian: but it may be a meeting of Christ in that man, because his humanity is accepted 'without any reservation.' The way through to the vision of the Son of Man and the knowledge of God, which is the heart of contemplative prayer, is by unconditional love of the neighbor, of 'the nearest *Thou* to hand.' " [6]

At the same time, in cases where loving prayer is intelligently offered for individuals, especially young children whose deep minds are not walled up against subconscious influences, I have grounds for saying that good is often done.[7] In a lovely phrase of Browning:

> God uses us to help each other so,
> Lending our minds out.[8]

And it seems to me as reasonable to suppose that God can use my prayer for another—my positive outgoing love linking itself with the Divine love—as that he can use the skill of a surgeon, doctor, psychiatrist or nurse. All are forms of cooperation with God, some are material, some are psychical and some spiritual.

[6] *Honest to God*, pp. 99-100.
[7] See my *Psychology, Religion and Healing*, pp. 232 ff., 508 ff., and *Wounded Spirits*, pp. 161 ff.
[8] "Fra Lippo Lippi."

Even so, we have a lot of research to do into the laws which govern intercession. To be honest, it is rarely that prayer can be claimed as responsible for curing illness. Even when the claim is made, the critic can retort that cure would have happened anyway, or that other measures, medical, for instance, could have been the therapeutic factors. I often think of the prayers offered daily and weekly by millions of loyal subjects for the Queen—"grant her in health and wealth long to live"—but members of the Royal Family do not live any longer than anyone else or enjoy better health. If I have a toothache I do not pray, or ask for prayer. I go to the dentist. Is it logical to pray just because I do not know who can make me well? Sometimes I overhear the angels saying to one another, "If only they would spend on medical research what they spend on trying to land on the moon, they could prevent cancer as they have prevented plague, and then they would no more pray about a sick body than they pray about a decayed tooth." We must go on praying, for sometimes prayer seems so to alter mental attitudes and reinforce mental energies as to strengthen the patient's resistance to disease and even overcome it, and in any case to sustain him in the bearing of it. But we must not lose faith when God does not answer prayer in the way we think we should if we had his power.

It is so very important to remember that, while all healing is of God, we must find the answer to the question, "Which is the most relevant way of cooperating with God in the case of *this* particular patient?" It may be surgery, or medicine, or psychiatry, or prayer. Prayer is not relevant in many cases, save as an aid to the patient's mental condition, and God is not going to make of prayer an easy magic, just because we have not used our human resources of money and men in wiser ways.

When we come to faith, it clears my own mind to distinguish between what I call the faith of the intellect and the faith of the will. It is confusing that men speak of having "faith" when they mean believing a lot of intellectual propo-

Prayer and Faith

sitions, some of which, as we have seen, seem to the layman highly improbable, and some of which he cannot accept without doing violence to the integrity of a mind which God made to work in the way it does. We are told to believe "by faith" that Jesus is the Son of God. But when Jesus praised faith [9] and asked for faith [10] he did not mean anything of the kind; he meant *trust*. One man who was healed by faith did not even know who it was who had healed him, far less did the patient believe a whole lot of theological ideas about Christ.[11] And when Jesus told the woman healed of menorrhagia that her faith had saved her, he meant her "trustful expectancy," a risk which her will power enabled her to take, and which made her fling herself before Christ in an abandonment of committal. "If I touch but His clothes I shall be made whole." [12]

Let me write a little on this important difference because I think it may help us to cut out some dead wood and silly superstition from our thinking.

God has given us our minds and we are to use them. Jesus said that the very first commandment was that we must love God with our minds. No honest mind can exclude doubt, or ignore criticism, or shut its ears against reason. And if we could do these things we should be left, not with faith but with a head-in-the-sand superstition. So, in the field of religion, I would define the faith of the intellect as an attitude of complete sincerity, and loyalty to the trend of all the available evidence, plus a leap in the direction of that trend, beyond the hard road of reason but not beyond the kind of speculation which the nature of God suggests.

This kind of faith welcomes, nay demands, the open mind and complete sincerity; complete readiness to part with what we wish were true, if the evidence points otherwise, and com-

---

[9] Matthew 8:10, 15:28; Luke 7:50.
[10] Matthew 17:20; Mark 4:40, 11:22; Luke 17:6.
[11] John 5:1-15, note verse 13, "the cripple who had been cured did not know."
[12] Mark 5:23 ff.; Matthew 9:20 ff.; Luke 8:43 ff.

225

plete readiness to break with convention, prejudice and the pressure of those around us who think differently, and the bias produced by our upbringing and early training. This bias is an extremely difficult thing to overcome as every psychologist knows.

I suppose it would be true to say that Cranmer practically wrote the Prayer Book, which was used for the first time on Whit Sunday, 1549. He incorporated in it collects a thousand years older, gathered from the Sacramentary of Pope Gelasius (fifth century) and of Gregory (sixth century). He used the old Sarum Missal, the Orthodox Greek Liturgy and other ancient manuals of worship. Many of these we can still use sincerely and intelligently.

But some prayers Cranmer wrote himself, and I think it is not unfair to say that he has left the mark of his own mental distortions unforgettably upon some of them, just as Paul did on his Epistles. We know that Cranmer was terrified of his schoolmaster. So, inevitably, Cranmer's God was like Cranmer's schoolmaster. Therefore, some of the prayers in the Prayer Book are the cringing of a terrified child before a sadistic master. Look in passing at just one prayer which appears in the Prayer Book, and which provides exactly the evidence for what I have written. It is the prayer that it would stop raining, a prayer, still in the Prayer Book, which no intelligent person could now use.

"O Almighty Lord God, Who for the sin of man didst once drown all the world, except eight persons, and afterward of Thy great mercy didst promise never to destroy it so again; we humbly beseech Thee that although we for our iniquities have worthily deserved a plague of rain and waters, yet upon our true repentance Thou wilt send us such weather as that we may receive the fruits of the earth in due season; and learn both by Thy punishment to amend our lives, and for Thy clemency to give Thee praise and glory, through Jesus Christ our Lord. Amen."

226

Some laymen feel that, out of loyalty, they ought to cling to ancient ways of expressing the Christian faith and that to doubt is to sin. But doubt is not the enemy of faith. It is the growing edge of faith, and we do not need Tennyson to assure us that,

> *There lives more faith in honest doubt,*
> *Believe me, than in half the creeds.*

or to accord praise to the man who,

> *. . . would not make his judgment blind;*
> *He faced the spectres of the mind,*
> *And laid them: thus he came . . .*
> *To find a stronger faith his own.*[13]

Unbelief is frowned on by some of the elect as though it were a sin, but no one can make another believe until he can so exhibit the truth that the mind of the would-be believer cannot do other than leap out and grasp it and make it his own.

What is sinful is a man's assertion that he does not believe, *after truth has authenticated itself in his own mind,* or if he refuses to contemplate all the evidence, which one is so prone to do if it is offered by someone who is disliked on other grounds. How wisely Dr. John Oman, late Principal of Westminster College, Cambridge, to whom I owe so much, writes:

"In the strict sense, we should not even try to believe; for we have no right to believe anything we can avoid believing, granting we have given it entire freedom to convince us. Strictly speaking, also, we have no right to exhort people to believe, and much of that very common type of exhortation is mere distrust of truth and disregard of veracity. . . . There is only one right way of asking men to believe, and that is to put before them what they ought to believe because it is

[13] *In Memoriam,* xcvi.

true; and there is only one right way of persuading, and that is to present what is true in such a way that nothing will prevent it from being seen except the desire to abide in darkness; and there is only one further way of helping them, which is to point out what they are cherishing that is opposed to faith. When all this has been done, it is still necessary to recognize that faith is God's gift, not our handiwork; of His manifestation of the truth by life, not of our demonstration by argument or of our impressing by eloquence; and that even *He* is willing to fail till He can have the only success love could value—personal acceptance of the truth simply because it is seen to be true."

"Faith," said the writer in *The Times*,[14] "is not concerned with believing historical or other propositions on inadequate evidence. *It is reason grown courageous,* the spirit which inspires martyrs, the confidence that right must eventually triumph, that all things work together for good to those who love God."

From what I have described as the faith of the intellect, I turn to what I call the faith of the will. "Faith is the willingness to act as if the completely unprovable (that God receives men who are 'in Christ') were true." [15] This really means the committal of one's life with trustful hope to the person in whom one has faith. This attitude—which has little to do with the intellect—was the state of the will for which Jesus asked.

But here again we must be careful not to confuse such faith with suggestibility. Few things make me more angry than the absurd and hurtful nonsense of some so-called faith-healers. If, under their treatment, a patient recovers, they frequently rush off into newspaper headlines with a report of "miraculous cures." If the patient is no better, it is implied, and sometimes stated, that the patient had no "faith."

[14] February 8, 1964. Italics mine.
[15] Rev. Dr. John J. Vincent, *Christ and Methodism* (Abingdon Press, 1965).

This is intolerable. Heads the healer wins. Tails the patient loses. The whole treatment is often as ill-founded and little understood as the toss of a coin. I took a notorious and much publicized "healer" to see a member of the City Temple who had a glorious faith and a radiant experience of Christ, but who had been ill with an incurable disease for fourteen years. When nothing happened except an increase of pain and disability, after treatment that was agonizing because the healer insisted on the patient being moved, I invited the healer to comment. She said of the patient, "Oh, she has no faith." I could hardly curb my anger. My own mother and both my sisters died of cancer, but they had a far finer faith than the loud-mouthed "healer." Theirs was a faith in Christ *whether they recovered or not.* Again and again some hysterical patient, with a suggestibility that makes anything "believable," is relieved of symptoms, temporarily at least, but long enough to get into the headlines, while a real saint, with a critical mind but far finer faith, remains as he or she was. It is essential to remember that one can have healing without faith. One can also have a grand faith without healing, because faith, like prayer, is certainly no cure-all.

Perhaps in a parable I can unite my two complementary concepts of faith concepts of both intellect and will.

Imagine then a bit of the south coast to which I could take the reader. It has become separated from the main cliff by wind and wave and weather. There is a good road running toward it, but, of course, the road ends at the cliff edge, firm though that edge now is. From the beach one could not get to the top of the separated portion. The sides are vertical. But an athletic youngster, by running along the road on the cliff top and taking a leap in the air, could land on the separated islet and find, by making that leap, whatever treasure the islet holds.

Faith is like moving along the firm road of demonstrable, accepted fact—of science, if you like—but then making a leap in the same direction as the evidence so as to bring oneself further than the evidence alone will carry one. This kind of leap is not unknown in science. Many discoveries have been made thus. Indeed, it is silly to talk of the conflict between science and faith. The tension is really between two kinds of faith, and in some ways they are not very different, though admittedly not in the same category. The young student, Marconi, was thus rebuked by his teachers. "Stop experimenting with wireless telegraphy! All our scientists have been working on it for twenty years and they will reach a solution before you do. They cannot overcome the resistance of the air. That is the problem." But young Marconi dared to dream that for wireless waves there might not be such resistance. It wasn't in any book. No one had told him, or hinted as such a thing. It was a leap of faith. Again, it was noted that the planet Uranus, in its track through space, swung out at one point from the normal curve of its orbit. What drew Uranus from its course? Independently two astronomers made what could be called a leap of faith, but it was not a wild or superstitious leap. It was rather a leap which was based on the trend of the evidence, evidence provided by careful calculation, along which road they traveled as far as it would take them. Then they made a leap of faith. They swung their telescopes toward what some thought to be an empty space in the sky and they discovered the planet Neptune. Faith was rewarded by sight, as ours one day will be.

The story of Neptune's discovery and of wireless waves does not seem to me so very different from the most important discovery I have ever made. As a child I watched the way in which an influence unknown to me affected the orbit of our family life at home. I heard of Jesus Christ, and when I turned my life in his direction I found him for myself. If now I denied his existence or his influence, I should not know how to account for the loveliest thing in the lives of the men and women I most admire. Since childhood I have seen so much, read so much, noted the orbit of lives all over the world in which, be it noted, more people love him, follow him and are influenced by him than ever before in the world's history, that I could not make sense of the phenomena without reference to him, any more than astronomers could account for the orbit of Uranus without Neptune. So my faith in him, so different from faith in any other of the world's dead leaders, shared as it is by so many millions of every race under heaven, does not seem to me wild guessing, or superstition, or wishful thinking, but a projection from reason and an invitation to an act of commitment.

Let us never think of faith—as the schoolboy defined it—as "believing what you know to be untrue." Let us be content to leave many things in the box of the mind, labeled, "awaiting further light." Let us never imagine that faith can ever be furthered by suppressing doubt, let alone by suppressing evidence. All truth is one, and religion must be as eager as science to know the truth as far as man can perceive it. If something we have treasured as truth is really contradicted by unanswerable evidence, then in the name of the God of truth we must part with it however venerable it may be. Let us never suppose that we can take over faith from our parents without examination, or believe anything merely because another says it is true. But let us not be content with a static agnosticism which never rouses itself to make inquiry. Let us examine the evidence and then in complete loyalty to its trend make a leap both of intellect and will, and, committing ourselves, *acting* as if all were established, try out in life the faith that carries us on wings after the hard road of fact and reason stops. There is a whisper in my heart that tells me there is much treasure to be found. But I know it lies beyond the point where the road of reason ends, and beyond any mountain ranges which my will has conquered. I must leave it to Kipling to explain what I mean! In *The Explorer* he wrote:

> "There's no sense in going further—it's the edge of cultivation,"
> So they said, and I believed it—broke my land and sowed my
> crop—

The Christian Agnostic

Built my barns and strung my fences in the little border station
Tucked away below the foothills where the trails run out and
stop:

Till a voice, as bad as Conscience, rang interminable changes
On one everlasting Whisper day and night repeated—so:
"Something hidden. Go and find it. Go and look behind the
Ranges—
Something lost behind the Ranges. Lost and waiting for you.
Go!"

Yes, your "Never-never country"—yes, your "edge of cultivation"
And "no sense in going further"—till I crossed the range to see.
God forgive me! No, I didn't. It's God's present to our nation.
Anybody might have found it but—His Whisper came to me!

CHAPTER XI

EVIL AND SIN

"Men torture and kill other men in order to satisfy their animal instincts, and to gratify the urges of matter in them. The spark of light, which ought to illumine their road towards their Maker, burns dim, and the voice of their conscience, which is the voice of their Maker speaking through them, cannot always be heard. When it is heard, it helps them to master their instincts and to behave as individuations all born from the same source; whenever they hear it too late, it shows them the extent of their betrayal of the brotherhood or oneness to which they belong, and the loss which their inhuman behaviour imposes upon the one who created them. But all these failings, all the hatred which men have for other men, together with their blindness to truth, their selfishness, and the pride, which leads some of them to believe that they alone know the truth, and that therefore they can dispose of their fellow beings' lives, as if they were worthless insects, cannot be ascribed to any imaginary original fall. These failings are part of their finitude, and therefore part of the human condition. Yet man, like the rest of creation, is not static, he is part of the continuous creativity which informs the Universe. In fact, although very young on this earth, he has already accomplished immense strides, which consist in having become aware of the direction in which he is going, and of the possibilities of his brief, yet precious, life."

J. Chiari
(*Religion and Modern Society*)

XI

EVIL AND SIN

FIRST of all I would distinguish between evil and sin, as I use those words in this chapter. It seems to me to make for clearer thinking if we keep the word "sin" to describe a conscious, responsible act of the will, by which, recognizing the existence of a moral choice, one chooses wrong, knowing it to be wrong, because, for the moment, at any rate, it is desired more than its alternative. Clearly, if that definition be accepted, "many men," as Lord Russell once wrote, "who do not believe in God nevertheless have a sense of sin," [1] though the Christian has a more acute sense, since he perceives that his sin hurts and hinders a loving God whom he is pledged to serve. "Sin," said St. Augustine, "is so much voluntary evil that it is not sin at all unless it is voluntary." [2] "Sins" said Dr. Hadfield, the famous Harley Street psychiatrist, "result from a deliberate and conscious choice of the self and depend upon the acceptance of a low ideal." [3]

I therefore deny the existence of what has been called "unconscious sin." If a person is honestly unconscious that he is choosing to follow an evil course, I could not charge him with sin. He may be morally obtuse like those Christians who kept slaves. He may have anaesthetized his conscience and need waking up. He may have repressed a sense of sin into the unconscious part of his mind and be doing evil and harm. He

---

[1] Bertrand Russell, *Human Society in Ethics and Politics*, p. 89 (1954).
[2] St. Augustine, *De Vera Religione*, XIV, 27. I owe both quotations to Dr. Frederic Greeves, *The Meaning of Sin*, p. 32 (Epworth Press, 1956).
[3] J. A. Hadfield, *Psychology and Morals*, p. 44 (Methuen, 5th edition, 1925).

may be suffering from what can only be called moral disease —of which more later. He may be morally blind like the gypsy boy brought up to steal in order to help the family, and doing it without any sense of guilt, but I would keep the word "sins" to describe those things we choose to do because we want to do them, although we know they are wrong; things which later, in a moment of insight, we shall regret.

Similarly I can no longer use the phrase "original sin." It is true that we are born with trends in our nature which make "sin" easier and more alluring than goodness. The origin of these I shall discuss. These trends deceptively seem to offer quicker returns than the "better way." It is also true that we are all born into a community in which all men and women commit sin, so that we are at a greater disadvantage than we should have been if we had been born into a perfect society. Together these conditions form a bias toward sin from the beginning of our lives. But to talk of a baby "born with original sin," as Augustine did in *De Peccato Originali,* and as the Prayer Book still does in the service for the Baptism of Infants,[4] is in my opinion nonsense, because it is years before the baby can recognize that a moral choice exists.

Further, in my own thought, I have excluded the idea of the Fall of Man. As I try to show in this chapter, man has made a long climb from the status of the animal until the time when he could recognize right and wrong. That recognition, at first, was based on behavior that paid, that avoided

---

[4] This seems to me a terrible service. It opens with the assertion that all men are "conceived and born in sin." In the first prayer the baby is prayed for "that he being delivered from Thy *wrath* . . ."! Later, it is prayed that "he may receive remission of his sins by spiritual regeneration" and that our Lord Jesus Christ will "release him of his sins" though often he is only a few weeks old. Those who bring him swear that they will renounce, "the carnal desires of the flesh," without which the baby would never have been born! The prayer is also offered, "Grant that all carnal affections may die in him." What a bleak outlook for his wife-to-be! If the prayer were answered, his marriage would be wrecked from the start, and he would be a neurotic patient needing psychiatric treatment to restore his "carnal affections." What a lot of nonsense a church can retain in its services for the sake of age-long tradition!

the retribution of the tribe and the gods, and that enabled the primitive society to function. Yet, however lowly in origin —and I am referring to a period centuries before right seemed to be worth following simply because it was right, or because man's dignity and status were sustained by doing right; centuries before right was conceived as pleasing to God because *he* was holy and righteous—that earliest *recognition* of a difference between right and wrong was an immense advance, even though wrong was chosen. As someone has said, "If this was a 'fall,' it was a fall upwards." As Dr. John Whale wrote, "Man's tragic apostasy from God is not something which happened once for all, a long time ago. It is true in every moment of existence. . . . It involves no scientific description of absolute beginnings. Eden is on no map, and Adam's fall fits no historical calendar. Moses is not nearer to the Fall than we are, because he lived three thousand years before our time. The Fall refers not to some datable, aboriginal calamity in the historical past of humanity, but to a dimension of human experience which is always present—namely, that we who have been created for fellowship with God repudiate it continually; and that the whole of mankind does this along with us. Every man is his own 'Adam,' and all men are solidarily 'Adam.' Thus, Paradise before the Fall, the *status perfectionis*, is not a period of history, but our 'memory' of a divinely intended quality of life, given to us along with our consciousness of guilt." [5]

This being so, it only confuses the layman to write as if a historical "Fall" were still believed in, and that because of the choice of our mythical ancestors, Adam and Eve, we were all born with "original sin" before we were capable of "sin" at all. Paul's words that "through one man sin entered into the world, and death by sin". [6] can be dismissed as nonsense. Sin entered into the world through the fault of millions of men

---

[5] John S. Whale, *Christian Doctrine*, p. 52 (Cambridge University Press, 1941).
[6] Romans 5:12.

and women emerging from animal, and therefore amoral situations, and death was in the world long before man arrived. Dr. Temple and his colleagues who completed the volume *Doctrine in the Church of England*, were honest enough to write: "We agree that there is no guilt attaching to the individual in respect of original sin. . . . In our view the doctrine of a universal tendency to evil in man is not bound up with the historical truth of any story of a 'fall.' " [7]

In this chapter I mean by "evil" things like war, slums, poverty, injustice, the exploitation of others by the rich and powerful, disease, hunger, many, but not all of which were brought upon humanity by the sins of individuals and the corporate sins of communities including that of indifference, dilatoriness and carelessness.[8] I mean by "evil" those things, however caused, which an ideal community would seek to end.

Many have puzzled about the origin of the sin and the evil in the world.

It may be that there are evil entities in the universe who have mysterious access to the lives of men. Our ancestors conveniently ascribed the evils which beset mankind to the devil and his assistants. It was alleged that man "fell" because he was tempted by Satan. It has been the fashion for years to regard the Devil as a symbolic name for the ignorance, folly and sin of man, and to regard belief in "evil spirits" as old-fashioned, outmoded and disproved by science. I am not so easily persuaded to dismiss these ancient beliefs, and I was glad to read that so profound a thinker as the late Archbishop Temple wrote: "I believe that he [Satan] exists and that a large share of responsibility [for sin and evil] belongs to him and to subordinate evil spirits." [9] C. S. Lewis wrote, "It seems to me a reasonable supposition that some mighty created

[7] Pp. 64 and 69 (S.P.C.K., 1938).

[8] Disease indubitably existed among animals before man arrived on the earth, and the idea that it is due to man's individual sin cannot be sustained, but to spend millions on reaching the moon, when disease could be largely excluded by uninhibited research for which funds are not available, is an evil built up by our corporate sins.

[9] *Nature, Man and God*, p. 503 (Macmillan, 1934).

238

power had already been at work for ill on the material universe or the solar system, or at least the planet earth, before ever man came on the scene. . . . If there is such a power, *as I myself believe*, it may well have corrupted the animal creation before man appeared." [10] And Professor David Smith, to whom, years ago, I owed much, wrote, "There remains no theoretical obstacle to believing in an order of evil spirits." [11]

We ourselves turn evil emotion like hate into angry action. We do not yet know the real nature of emotion. I suspect that it is not merely a subjective thing, wholly without objective reality. I can tell at once if I enter a room where there has been a violent quarrel, and I spent a sleepless night in a perfectly comfortable bed and bedroom sensing unhappy emotion, only to learn for the first time next morning that the mother of my hostess had recently committed suicide there. Similarly, an old church, where people have prayed and worshiped for a century, has an "aura" as real as the walls and windows. May it be that evil entities can use the evil emotion lying about in the universe through man's sins and selfishness, and turn it into forces which hinder and divert God's loving purposes.

In other books of mine I have collected what I think is strong evidence for the existence of evil spirits,[12] and this I will not repeat here, but more and more thinkers are disposed to regard evil entities as the creators of things like some of the germs, bacilli and viruses of disease, the poisonous snakes and other organisms which seem the inveterate enemies of human well-being. It may be so. The Christian believes in angels, spirits kindly disposed to men. It is not illogical for him to believe in evil spirits hostile to men. If the former can do good, the latter may be able to do evil.

Christ's own attitude is very interesting. It would seem that

[10] *Problem of Pain*, p. 122 (Macmillan Co., 1943). Italics mine.
[11] *The British Weekly*, March 5, 1914.
[12] *Psychology, Religion and Healing*, pp. 89-101, and *Wounded Spirits*, pp. 124-38 (Abingdon, 1962).

he believed in angels.[18] He appears to have believed in evil spirits also. Demon possession, if it exists, may now be called epilepsy, or dementia, or schizophrenia, or paranoia, but while possession by evil spirits is the last diagnosis to which one would be driven, and further knowledge will increase one's reluctance to accept such a diagnosis, I find it hard, in the light of Christ's language and of other evidence, especially some from the mission field and from psychic sources, to exclude the demonology of the New Testament as nonsense. But let us turn to other factors.

I get some light on the problem of the origin of evil, when, in imagination, I think of the long story of the development of life on this planet millions of years ago.

When the earth had cooled sufficiently, warm seas washed the hot rocks of the world, and, at last, so we are told, in the warm sea something moved of itself for the first time and not merely in response to wind or wave and tide. Life began on the earth, Sir Julian Huxley tells us, about two and a half billion years ago.[14] Some very simple form of life was produced by unknown means, some think by the effect of cosmic rays from the depths of space. This early organism sought and found food, lived and mated and propagated its kind, and life began on the earth.

Take now an imaginative leap of centuries. Some forms of life have crept on to the shore. Some have developed wings. Some are huge of carcass though small of brain. All are driven on by innate, inherent energies. The fight for life begins. The urge to establish its own kind and win security dominates every species. The instincts of self-preservation, of sex and of the herd are clearly the driving forces of every living thing.

[18] Matthew 13:41, 16:27, 22:30; Luke 12:8, 15:10, etc.
[14] Article entitled, "Evolution Becomes Self-conscious," in *The New Scientist*, June 20, 1963. In *The Observer* of March 31, 1963, Sir Julian wrote, "Man is a product of nearly three billion years of evolution, in whose person the evolutionary process has at last become conscious of itself and its possibilities. Whether he likes it or not, he is responsible for the whole further evolution of our planet."

The passion to preserve life, to propagate its own species and to find strength by membership of a community, all these instincts are the most important assets throughout the whole gamut of creation from the insect to the dinosaur. It is as though Nature is trying experiments to see who will win the battle for survival.

It certainly looks now as though man will win. He has conquered many enemies of his well-being. Some by the use of sticks and stones, some by means of bows and arrows, some with explosives, some with DDT, some with antibiotics. Let us not forget that, as our forefathers fought back the wolves that threatened them in their winters, we still have to fight the flu germs that threaten us in ours. The enemy now is smaller, and the weapons are different. But the battle is the same; man's ceaseless battle to have dominion in the earth.[15]

But let us imaginatively go back to the time before man appeared on the earth, and jungle rules alone prevailed. The fierce, hungry tiger seeks to end his hunger by attacking the gazelle for whom speed, touched off by fear, is the only hope of escape. No one can rightly use the word "cruel" about the tiger. Moral values do not exist. A strong tiger finds another feasting on a deer and drives the weaker tiger off the prey. This is not "stealing." Moral values are unknown. The tiger feels the urge of sex and seeks a mate. If he is strong enough, he may take a tigress, sought after, and already possessed by, another, and he copulates with her. At this stage of development "adultery," "lust" and "promiscuity" have no meaning.

Along one evolutionary path let us now imagine the arrival of very primitive man. The manlike ape becomes, through millions of years, the apelike man. As Dr. Eric Waterhouse said, "None knows when the frontier that separates zoology from anthropology was crossed by our earliest ancestors."[16] But MAN has arrived. One of his early efforts is to master all

---

[15] Cf. the promise in Genesis 1:26, and the affirmation in Psalm 8:6.
[16] Eric S. Waterhouse, Professor of the Philosophy of Religion in the University of London, *The Dawn of Religion*, p. 13 (Epworth Press, 1936).

the elements in his environment which hinder his happiness. He begins to tame the jungle. He does battle with wild beasts and snakes. He woos the soil to produce crops. He channels the angry river to irrigate his land.

There are elements, however, which he cannot master, like storm and flood, whirlwind and earthquake and the more serious diseases like cholera, plague and insanity. So he seeks to placate what he cannot master. He endows these mighty expressions of untameable power with the existence of spirits. Thus the local gods are born, manufactured from his own imagination, stimulated by terror and awe. Even in early Judaism, Jehovah was a storm-god who lived on the top of Mount Sinai.

In this primitive society rules emerge. If a man steals his neighbor's cow he is punished by the tribe. The word "stealing" now has a meaning, and stealing does not pay. If he steals his neighbor's wife the whole tribe rises against him and imposes a penalty because tribal life cannot be made to work without rules. The word "adultery" has a meaning, and adultery does not pay. So some things a man does are "right" but others are "wrong." Conscience, at first the lowly child of fear of consequence, either from gods or men, or fear of intolerable separation from the tribe, is born, and with it the first feelings of guilty fear.

It must have been perceived in very early days that a greater sanction was needed than a man's sense of guilt, derived only from the fear of what the tribe could do to him. So, in some primitive cultures, the help of the gods was called in. The medicine man would threaten the adulterer or thief that terrible things would descend upon him if he did not confess and make restitution. Thousands of years before the word "psychology" was born, the power of suggestion was made to play on the fears of men in regard to supernatural agencies, and the support of the "other world" was added to the disapproval of the tribe against the defaulter. Heaven was on the side of righteousness. And it may well be that since

know nothing. Only towards midday would our living atikokania appear.[21] The Palaeozoic Age, with its primitive life,
would claim a further eight hours, while the mysterious
saurian of the Mesozoic Age would only disappear from the
screen at 11:15 p.m. The last three-quarters of an hour of this
extraordinary long film would be devoted to the description
of the Cainozoic Age. And five seconds before midnight
would at last appear, for the first time—man! On a geological
clock of twenty-four hours, the history of man takes up the
minute fraction of five seconds!" [22]

To be too pessimistic about man, then, with his wars and
his apartheid nonsense, his brothels, his slums and his cruel-
ties, mental and physical, would be more foolish than would
be the attitude of a father, who, finding his children of three
or four years of age quarrelling in the nursery, regarded them
as hopeless and not worth further trouble or education.

Progress is certainly not inevitable, but we can, in Tennyson's phrase:

> *Move upward, working out the beast,*
> *And let the ape and tiger die,*

or, as I would rather say, make them our friends, joyously
serving us. Fortunately we have not been left alone. Into the
human nursery came a little child, who grew up, depending
on and trusting God as no one else has done before or since.
He revealed what God *must* be like and what man *may* be
like, and he pledged himself to stand by his little brothers
until they too achieved God's age-long purpose on this minor
planet; until *all* the sons of men realized their possibilities and
became the sons of God.

[21] "The first trace of life which geology unearthed in a Proterozoic
limestone in Ontario . . . is an enigmatic ponifera which, under the name
of Atikokania Lawsoni, can be taken, perhaps incorrectly, for the original
form of life," R. Gheyselinck, *The Restless Earth*, p. 69 (Scientific Book
Club, 1939).
[22] R. Gheyselinck, *The Restless Earth*, p. 101 (Scientific Book Club,
1939).

When all this has been said, I feel that the modern tendency to try to *understand* man's sinful behavior, instead of merely condemning and seeking to frighten or to punish him, is to move forward. I know we can go too far and try to whitewash what is plain "sin"; to seek to excuse really bad behavior and to account for it in terms of infantile environment, traumatic experiences, psychological complexes and the like. But I regard it as a sign of progress that we are at last doubting the value of the cane and tawse in the schoolroom and the birch and the hangman's rope in the jails.

Further, I would plead that there is such a thing as moral as well as mental illness, though sometimes a person is the victim of both. My friend, the Rev. Dr. Frederic Greeves, in a thoughtful book, *The Meaning of Sin*, disapproves of my own point of view, and includes me among those who "are eager to assert that man only *sins* when he knows that he is doing what is evil; they have little to say about the sins of ignorance. Perhaps the most hopeful word that can then be said about this non-sinful moral imperfection is that we are not to be blamed for it." [23] But by the definition of sin which I hold in common with many others—some of whom, like St. Augustine and Dr. J. A. Hadfield, are quoted at the beginning of this chapter—I want to ask how anything can be labeled "sin" if we cannot be blamed for it?

There are those who suffer from mental illness—Broadmoor Asylum is full of them—who, if released, would happily murder. They do evil but they do not *sin*. Tested by the McNaughten rules they are not guilty, for they see no moral situation and make no moral choice.

Very common are men and women who, for various reasons, do what in others would be called "sin," but which, though evil in its results, is not sin in the sense defined. I have a friend who has been jailed three times but who, I am persuaded, is suffering from a moral blind spot. Others, who

[23] *Op. cit.* p. 66 (Epworth Press, 1956).

suffer from complete homosexuality, or who are in the category of kleptomaniacs or alcoholics, suffer from moral disease. *Sin* is the result of desire. The alcoholic does not want to get drunk any more than the neurotic wants to be ill. "The dipsomaniac can no more resist the temptation to drink than the epileptic can resist his attacks." [24] Both are usually the victims of unconscious factors which drive them into behaving as they do and both need psychiatric treatment.[25] Similar are the cases of those who feel compelled to blaspheme or to think "impure" or sacrilegious thoughts.

It is worth quoting Hadfield's three tests for differentiating between moral disease and sin. "First, the moral disease has a *compulsive character* not characteristic of the sin, which is more deliberate. Secondly, sin is under the control of the will, whereas the victim of moral disease finds his will absolutely impotent to resist it. Thirdly, the sinner, as such, does not want to be cured, whereas the victim of moral disease, if he realizes that cure is possible, is anxious to obtain it. The psychotherapist as such rarely meets with 'sinners,' and this for two reasons: first, because the sinner does not want to be cured, and therefore does not seek cure, and also because psychotherapy is not the appropriate form of treatment.

"It will be recognized that a very large number of disorders at present considered sins really come under the category of moral disease. A reference to the three 'tests' just made will confirm this. Indeed, it is probable that most evil actions of everyday life—vanities, aggressiveness, evil obsessive thoughts, persistent habits—which are the despair of those who have them and those who treat them, are at least partially due to moral disease, and, if this is the case, our methods of treatment, whether on the religious and moral side, or on the legal, need very radical revision." [26]

[24] See Dr. W. L. Northridge's fine book, *Psychology and Pastoral Practice*, p. 157 (Epworth Press, 1938).
[25] See Dr. J. A. Hadfield, *Psychology and Morals*, p. 48.
[26] J. A. Hadfield, *op. cit.*, p. 49.

Hadfield adds that "to blame the victims of moral disease produces the most disastrous results," but he is rightly ready to admit that originally the patient may well have been to blame for taking to drink to cover his feeling of failure, and so on in other cases, though even so he warns us that the early steps which led to the development of "moral disease" may have been taken before the patient was fully responsible for his choice. We must not readily condemn these unhappy people even if the first steps which led to downfall were their own fault. After all, treatment not blame is indicated for a patient brought into hospital after a street accident, even if it were caused by his own carelessness in crossing the street.

After much thought, I cannot help feeling that the church harps far too much on sin. I know and feel the difficulty. After preaching for fifty years I know that some men need to see their behavior as sinful. But I believe that far more are only too ready to disparage themselves. Again and again, the religious service adds a further burden to that which men are carrying, the burden of guilty feeling. I feel that in our services there should be a greater emphasis, not on man's wickedness but on God's loving and forgiving grace, on the joy God meant us to have and the thrill of belonging to him. A church service should offer men wings to carry them, not load them with more burdens to carry.

Says Professor Jessop in his fine book, *Law and Love*: "It is often said nowadays that the Church is losing her power because she no longer talks enough of sin. It seems to me, on the contrary, that the word 'sin' has been over-used. The fulminating use of it in the pulpit is a cheap way of imitating the externals of prophecy, and the lavish application of it, in our meditations, to all our faults, is a sure way to morbidity and a common way to religious mania." [27] F. D. Maurice, with that in his opinion "it made the sinful man and not the

God of all Grace the Foundation of Christian Theology." [28]

How rarely did Jesus talk about sin or sins! Dr. Greeves truly writes, "As far as the Synoptic records inform us, our Lord used the noun only on six occasions and the verb on three occasions, allowing for parallel accounts. Were our Scriptures limited to the Synoptic Gospels the word *sin* would not be as dominant as it is in the Christian vocabulary. . . . When we speak about 'our Lord's attitude to different kinds of sin,' or about 'the sins which Jesus condemned' we are, in actuality, putting the *word* on His lips." [29] Paul used the words for sin ninety-one times,[30] and seems obsessed by the idea of sin. In fact my own opinion is that the epistles commonly attributed to Paul, and especially the letter to the Romans, have, in their references to sin, unduly over-burdened the whole Western world for centuries, as well as misleading it to believe that before God can forgive his own children someone must be made to pay a mythical "price of sin," a confusion still continued in our Communion service as we have seen (p. 117).

Nothing that I have written is intended to make light of sin. It is the darkest shadow on our fragment of the universe. My predecessor at the City Temple, Dr. Parker, picturesquely called it "a raised hand, a clenched fist and a blow in the face of God." It hurts and hinders the greatest lover of our souls. But I would fain deliver the modern layman from false thinking about it based on Paul's less inspired and obsessional point of view, and the clouded thought with which Jewish blood sacrifices and ancient mystery religions have hindered vision.

As Edward Barker says in his excellent book, *Psychology's*

---

[28] F. D. Maurice, *Theological Essays* (1871), p. xvi. Quoted from Greeves, *The Meaning of Sin*, p. 181.

[29] Greeves, *op. cit.*, p. 102 and footnote and p. 103. See also C. Anderson Scott in *New Testament Ethics*, p. 27 (1936).

[30] Dr. C. Ryder Smith, *The Bible Doctrine of Sin*, p. 142 (Epworth Press).

Impact on the Christian Faith:[31] "The Synoptists make no mention of atonement . . . it has been declared over and over again that the moral nature of God required the sacrifice of Christ on the Cross because sin must somehow be paid for . . . [but] the benevolent father in the parable of the prodigal requires no sacrifice, or atonement, or propitiation, or means of justification before he can accept back his son to the family fold. . . . With Jesus, forgiveness is the free and unconditional gift of God."

We close the chapter with a hundred questions unanswered. Why did God choose to set man in situations so fraught with evil and why has evil still such power? Why are there things like the disasters of Nature, earthquake, storm, flood and lightning, that wreck the happiness of millions? Why is there such a thing as cancer or progressive muscular atrophy or insanity? Why is man so prone to sin and why are some sins so attractive and the battle for virtue so loaded against victory?

All we can do is to rejoice in man's slow victories over some of the things that have destroyed him, and support his efforts to overcome evil in every way we can. We can rejoice that man is not left to himself to grapple with sin but has a Savior and a Deliverer who will see him through and who is committed to him as a faithful husband to an erring wife. We can try to clear our minds from the fogs of earlier thinking which still linger and distort our vision, live a day at a time, follow all the light we can get, and realize that hope and faith and love will never be repudiated and confounded. Let us humbly admit that there are many questions we cannot answer, but let us hold tightly to the certainty that he who humbly walks with God, though he suffers and sins and fails and doubts, will win at last and finds his way home, with hopes fulfilled which he never dared to formulate, and dreams realized that seemed too good to be true.

[31] Pp. 44-45 (George Allen and Unwin, 1964).

CHAPTER XII

DEATH AND SURVIVAL

"Nothing really matters except the answer to the burning question, 'Am I going to live or shall I vanish like a bubble?' What is the aim and issue of all this strife and suffering?"

Malinowski

"If only 1% of the money spent upon the physical and biological sciences could be spent upon investigations of religious experience and psychical research it might not be long before a new age of faith dawned upon the world."

Professor Alister C. Hardy, F.R.S.

"In the past fourteen years, long consideration of the march of scientific and material events has convinced me of the certainty of a personal immortality . . . Every material and scientific signpost points to the finality of death. Yet I believe we are immortal."

Professor Ian Aird, F.R.C.S.
(Hammersmith Post-Graduate Hospital)

DEATH AND SURVIVAL

LET us first rest our minds in the affirmation that natural death is as normal as birth and as much within God's plan. Paul wrote an unfinished sentence to the Romans which has been quoted earlier (p. 237), "Therefore as through one man sin entered the world, and death through sin; and so death passed unto all men, for that all sinned. . . ." J. B. Phillips translates, "This then, is what happened. Sin made its entry into the world through one man, and through sin, death. . . . As a result of one man's sin, death by natural consequence became the common lot of men. . . ." [1] Paul does not make it clear whether he meant spiritual or natural death. I should hotly contest the former, for I believe that the annihilation of even one soul spells a defeat of God's purposes, a denial of Christ's teaching [2] and a closure of heaven against those who love the "lost" soul. As Tennyson makes a mother cry: "And if he be lost. . . . Do you think that I care for *my* soul, if my boy be gone to the fire?" [3]

If physical death is meant, Paul's sentence is nonsense, for death, like disease and pain, was a fact in the earth long before man arrived. It is true that with us, more than with the animals, death is often preceded by pain and suffering, by anxiety and foreboding, but I am convinced that more and more we must come to see death in a new way and make terms with it, thinking of it not as a penalty or punishment

---

[1] Romans 5:12 ff.   [2] Luke 15:4, 8, "until he find it"   [3] Rizpah xvi

but as a blessing, not as a calamity but just a milestone, not as an end but as the beginning of a wonderful experience much more worth calling "life" than anything we have yet imagined.

One alleged communication from "the other side" speaks for them all. "We lead such a wonderful life compared with that on earth. Nothing I could say from this channel would give you an idea of its reality. It is so much more wonderful, bright and enjoyable than we can express." [4]

Over a long period of years I collected evidence about dying which I have set out elsewhere and will not repeat here.[5] I could not find one situation in which the experience of passing was other than a thrilling and beautiful experience. For most people, unconsciousness supervenes before death. They die in their sleep or in a coma. But sometimes they are conscious almost to the end. Some, like my own sister, recover even after they have had a glimpse of glories beyond the gates of death, and they are disappointed, as she was, at having to return. Others seem about to enter a new and glorious life. Let two experiences summarize the point. William Hunter, the world-famous doctor, said, as in 1783, he lay dying, "If I had strength enough to hold a pen I would write how easy and pleasant a thing it is to die."

The other bit of the vast evidence I have collected is the more impressive since it comes from one who had little contact with religion. I quote from an article by Mr. W. C. Edgar called, "The Adventure of Dying" from *The Spectator*.[6] I should first explain that he was a journalist who was advised to have a very dangerous operation, the outcome of which was highly dubious. He was amazed at the advice he received

[4] Etta, the sister of the Rev. C. Drayton Thomas purporting to communicate with him after her death. (*Beyond Life's Sunset*, p. 30, Psychic Press, 1949).

[5] See *Why Do Men Suffer?*, pp. 208 ff., chapter 12, "Is Death a Calamity?" (Abingdon Press, 1936), and *That Immortal Sea*, pp. 214 ff. (Abingdon, 1953).

[6] February 11, 1928.

from a surgeon to undergo this operation because he felt in perfect health. Thus he did not enter the experience, as so many patients do, with depleted bodily strength or with a mind possibly distorted by a long period of pain and anxiety. He had a local anaesthetic, and as he lay on the table he said to himself, "I am going to bring to this occasion the instincts of my craft. This is a very interesting event, in which I am going to take the leading part. I am about to enter the famous 'valley of the shadow of death,' and few have returned therefrom to tell the tale. My wits are all about me, I am not drugged into unconsciousness. I am able to see and hear and reason clearly, and will be to the end. I am going to make careful notes of this adventure and afterward set down all its details." He then goes on to describe the sense of ebbing and flowing life, and says, "I became absolutely convinced, beyond the shadow of a doubt, that this life element in me was indestructible, and that whatever happened to the body in which it had heretofore existed, it would survive and henceforth be imperishable." He then makes a more striking statement still. He tells us that his bias was in favor of going on into the unknown rather than returning to natural life. It was only the remembrance of his family and friends, and loyalty to the efforts of the surgeon, that made him exert himself in a powerful wish to live. His physician afterward told him that his heart had been alarmingly affected, and that several times he (the physician) thought he was about to go. They both concluded that the heart action represented first the desire to slip away, and then the powerful effort to remain living. He says, "The absolute certainty that death was not the end but merely a new beginning, was preeminent in my mind." He says another thing which will be of interest to us: "Had I lived a blameless moral life, which I had not, I could not have felt less remorse for the past. There was no regret for lost opportunities, no reviewing of life's history, no concern whatever for a reward or punishment, only a strong abiding sense of calmness and peace, and that I was in the hands of an infinitely benign power which cared for me and would protect me from all that was ill; a power whose attributes were goodness and mercy. The whole scheme of life on this earth, death, and the certain life to come, seemed to have meaning and purpose, to be harmonious, natural, and, above all, beneficent."

That is a piece of disinterested evidence which is worth a very great deal.

I think if I were asked what makes me believe in man's survival of death I should put first that kind of evidence. The journalist, whose experience I have just quoted, recovered, but sometimes in the course of a long ministry one has experiences of those who actually die, which, though they could be challenged and otherwise interpreted, are most convincing to the onlooker.

The minister will often visit a sick person in his last illness and will go on doing so patiently, week after week, though both know there is little hope of recovery. Toward the end, a patient may be so ill and weak that he cannot lift his head from the pillow or even open his eyes. In parentheses it should be said that those who watch should take great care to say no distressing word. The sense of hearing is the last sense to go off duty when man sleeps or dies. At one point in his evolution his safety depended on hearing a strange approach. Long after a patient is unable to move a limb or even open his eyes, he can *hear*.

As the last shadows fall, again and again the watcher by the bedside will see a strange, new light in eyes now opening easily, and the expression of those eyes is one of supreme joy and happiness. Then, in a way almost startling, the patient will sit up—he who could not raise his head—stretch out his arms and call the name of a beloved, dead it may be, a score of years before.

My beloved father-in-law, when dying, was sure that a daughter who had been dead for years was with him in his bedroom. Some of my own experiences in the death-chamber support this conclusion. Rosalind Heywood, watching a dying man, saw him suddenly sit up. She writes, "His face lit up. 'It's Annie,' he cried, gazing in joyous recognition at someone I could not see, 'And John! . . . Oh the Light! the Light!' " [7]

If that is a trick of the patient's brain or nervous system, if it is the hallucination of a disordered mind, all I can say is that it is strangely convincing to the watcher. Having seen that more than once, I for one am in no doubt about man's survival of death or of his reunion with those he loves.

On this point I questioned a friend of mine who, for four-teen years has been a sister in charge of a ward in a famous hospital. She wrote as follows: "Death has lost all fear for me by having been with so many people as they passed through that experience. More than this, the certainty that life goes on has increased, not diminished, by each encounter with death, as has also my certainty that the loving purposes of God are not defeated by it either." In another letter she wrote, "After twenty years in hospital I am absolutely con-vinced of one thing and that is of life after death." [8]

This is evidence which we cannot lightly set aside, but, of course, for the Christian, the attitude of Jesus is final. "Not for a moment," said Dr. Albert Schweitzer, one of the greatest men in the world and one of the finest Christians, "have I had to struggle for my conviction that in Him is the supreme spiritual and religious authority." [9] What a note of authority there is in his words to one whom we miscall "the dying thief!" [10] Jesus is not dealing with a great saint. And a dying man talking to a dying man does not hedge or bluff. If Jesus had said, "Well, maybe we shall meet again, I hope so, indeed

[7] Rosalind Heywood, *The Infinite Hive*, p. 83 (Chatto and Windus, 1964).
[8] A ward sister working for many years at University College Hospital, London, who has read the typescript above and approved its publication.
[9] J. K. Mozley, *The Theology of Albert Schweitzer*, p. 104.
[10] Luke 23:43, "miscall," because he was not a burglar or a highway-man, but a political revolutionary, a Sinn Feiner, one might say, a patriotic Jewish fanatic.

I have faith that it may be so," that would have been as far as many would go today. But no! He, who knew more about the unseen than any of us, could not have used more definite language. Nothing could have been more direct than the promise, only recorded by Luke the physician, "Today, thou shalt be with me in Paradise," or, as Phillips translates, "I tell you truly, this very day you will be with me in Paradise."

Certainly it would seem irrational to produce, on one of the minor planets, after millions of years, a being of immense possibilities called "man," who realizes only too clearly that those possibilities are never ended by the time he dies, and that some of them—like praying, worshiping and loving— have only then just begun to function, and then to deny expression to those possibilities by extinction. It would be the same kind of irrationality as would be the case if every baby died at birth. Within the foetus in the womb are the structures of ear and eye, of taste and smell, harbingers of a fuller life beyond the gates of birth. So man, groping on a material planet with powers within him that cry out for a non-material and spiritual world, is only rational in supposing that his hidden powers have meaning, function and glorious exercise in a life beyond the gates of death. His present concept of beauty, truth and goodness have, on earth, no adequate context. They cry out, hurting us in doing so, for a far wider context, in which they could find a fuller functioning. Thus we weep with frustration, loneliness and homesickness, sometimes, when ineffable beauty possesses the senses but cannot be adequately registered by them. Surely it is rational to suppose that the feeling of hunger, in a world that makes sense, means that there is food somewhere; that the urge of sex means that somewhere there is a mate. "I demand survival for self-fulfillment," man cries. With the Harvard philosopher William James, man, in his old age, cries, "I am just getting fit to live." With Victor Hugo he says, "I feel immortality within myself," and with Emerson he feels that "the blazing evidence of immortality is our dissatisfaction with any other solution," and whenever we attend the funeral of a loved one we *feel* that man cannot be "just an animal that dies alone in a hole."

I am not a spiritualist, but I am a member of the Society for Psychical Research, and I do not see how any unbiased student can close his mind to the evidence in that difficult but fascinating field. Let it be granted that alternative theories like telepathy may account for some phenomena which, in the past, have been supposed to support the idea of survival. And certainly let us acknowledge that the whole field of inquiry has been bedevilled by tricksters, liars and frauds; by the self-deceived and by those who seem incapable of refraining from distortion, exaggeration and unfounded interpretation when they report some psychic phenomena. But when allowance is made for all this, there is enough evidence left to convince me, at any rate, that communication has been established with the so-called dead. I have myself attended séances where every possible alternative has been considered, and where the explanation of the evidence which asks least from credulity is that of survival after death.

I will give three or four well-authenticated cases and indicate where others may be found. The first, called The Chaffin Will Case, is famous and has been commented on in the *Journal of the Society for Psychical Research*.[11] I feel with many others that the most reasonable interpretation of the facts is the one given in the following quotation from Dr. Raynor Johnson's book, *Psychical Research*.[12]

[11] Vol. 42, No. 717, September 1963, where C. T. K. Chari, of the Madras Christian College, surmises a fanciful hypothesis to account for the phenomena. I find it quite unconvincing.
[12] R. C. Johnson, M.A., Ph.D., D.Sc., *Psychical Research*, pp. 154-5. He writes (p. 149), "In some instances it would seem to me that the hypothesis of communication by a surviving discarnate personality is *much* the more probable explanation." (English Universities Press, Teach Yourself Books, 1955.) See also C. D. Broad, Litt.D., F.B.A., *Lectures on Psychical Research*, pp. 137-9 (Routledge and Kegan Paul, 1962).

The Chaffin Will Case [18]

"This is a much-quoted case, and is given below in a very condensed form. As a lawsuit was involved, the facts were subject to careful scrutiny and testing.

"A farmer, James L. Chaffin, who lived in North Carolina, made a will on November 16th, 1905, in which he gave the farm to his third son Marshall, leaving his widow and other three sons unprovided for. On January 10th, 1919, he apparently repented of this and made a second will, which was unwitnessed, but which would, according to the state law, have been valid provided there was proof that it was in the testator's own handwriting. The new will read as follows:

'"After reading the 27th Chapter of Genesis, I, James L. Chaffin, do make my last will and testament and here it is. I want, after giving my body a decent burial, my little property to be equally divided between my four children, if they are living at my death, both personal and real estate divided equal; if not living, give share to their children . . . etc.'

"He placed this second will between two pages of an old family Bible which had belonged to his father, folding the pages over so as to mark the place. No one knew of the existence of the second will, and the eccentric farmer took no steps to indicate its existence except that of stitching up the inner pocket of his overcoat with a roll of paper inside it bearing the words: 'Read the 27th Chapter of Genesis in my daddie's old Bible.' This posthumous treasure-hunt did not apparently eventuate after the old farmer's sudden death on September 7th, 1921. The third son, Marshall, obtained probate of the only known will—the first one—on September 24th of that year. In June, 1925, the second son, James started to have vivid dreams of his father. In one of these the old man appeared to stand at his son's bedside wearing his black overcoat and to say to him: 'You will find my will in my overcoat pocket.' Being convinced by this, James visited his brother John, who lived twenty miles away and had taken possession of the coat. On discovering the roll of paper with its message, James went with his daughter and two other witnesses to his mother's home. They found the old Bible, after considerable search, and the second will at the place indicated. In December, 1925, a lawsuit took place, and the second will was admitted to probate.

"Commenting on this: the period of three-and-three-quarter years which elapsed between the farmer's death and the son's dreams makes most unlikely any explanation which assumes that the initiative was with the son James. If his subconscious mind, without any stimulus from the conscious mind, exercised an extra-sensory or "psi" faculty and found what his father had done (the dream-figure of the father being merely a constructed vehicle to convey the information), why did it wait nearly four years? The same pertinent question applies to any suggestion that the old farmer's intention leaked telepathically into his son's mind but remained there latent for this period. In my judgment the circumstances point to the initiative by the surviving discarnate mind of the farmer."

It may be added that to all the attempts of a lawyer, Mr. J. Mc. N. Johnson, to make the relatives admit the possibility that one or the other of them might have had normal but subconscious prior knowledge of the facts, they answered: "Such an explanation is impossible. We never heard of the existence of the will till the visitation from my father's spirit." [14]

Another case reported by the Society for Psychical Research impressed me as genuine because of the number of people who "saw" the dead person, including a little child whose evidence sounds too simple to have been concocted.

The Case of Captain Eldred Bowyer-Bower [15]

"Captain Bower, aged twenty-two, was shot down in his plane in France on March 19th, 1917. The case is remarkable

[14] See Prof. C. D. Broad, *op. cit.*, p. 139.
[15] *Proceedings of the S.P.R.*, Vol. 33, pp. 167-76 (1923).

in that *a number of 'appearances' to different people* took place, three approximately at the time of death and the other two in December, 1917. The most remarkable was to his half-sister, Mrs. Dorothy Spearman, who was at the time staying in a hotel in Calcutta. She did not, of course, know of Eldred's death, or even that he was out in France again, as he had been home several months and had only returned there three weeks before he was killed. Her baby was baptized on the day of Captain Bower's death, and he was to have been the child's godfather. The following extract is from a letter to Captain Bower's mother (January, 1918), written by Mrs. Spearman:

" 'Eldred was greatly on my mind when baby was born and I could only think of him. On March 19th, in the late part of the morning, I was sewing and talking to baby; Joan was in the sitting-room and did not see anything. I had a great feeling I must turn round and did, to see Eldred; he looked so happy and had that dear, mischievous look. I was so glad to see him, and told him I would just put baby in a safer place, then we could talk. "Fancy coming out here," I said, turning round again, and was just putting my hands out to give him a hug and a kiss, but Eldred had gone. I called and looked for him. I never saw him again. At first I thought it was simply my brain. Then I did think for a second something must have happened to him and a terrible fear came over me. Then again I thought how stupid I was, and it must be my brain playing tricks. But now I know it was Eldred, and all the time in church at baby's christening he was there, because I felt he was, and know he was, only I could not see him. All the time I thought why do I feel like this when Eldred is safe . . . ?'

"About the time of his death a little niece of his, not quite three years old, appears to have had some visual impression of him. On the morning of his death she came up to her mother's room about 9:15 a.m. (the latter being still in bed), and said, 'Uncle Alley Boy is downstairs.' Although her mother told her he was in France, she insisted she had seen him. The third contemporary impression was received by Mrs. Watson, an elderly friend of Captain Bower's mother, who had not written to Mrs. Bower for eighteen months but felt impelled to write a letter to her *on March 19th*: . . . 'Something tells me you are having great anxiety about Eldred. Will you let me know?' "

I should like to add an example vouched for by Professor J. B. Rhine of Duke University, where he is the director of the Parapsychology Laboratory.

"To the students of extra-sensory perception (E.S.P.), the most significant type of case-history where the question of survival is concerned is one in which the information transmitted to the living person was known only to the deceased, or one in which the *method* of transmission is beyond the capabilities of the person through whom the information comes.

"A professor at Northwestern University received the following case from one of his students which is noteworthy on both counts.

" 'One evening when I was a boy of four, before I knew anything of school or the alphabet, my mother was working at her desk in our hotel, and I got hold of a note pad and began scribbling on it. Mother, noticing what I was doing, told me to stop and play with something else.

" 'The next morning my mother saw the papers with my scribblings and was about to throw them away when the day clerk, who had taken shorthand at night school, told her they looked like shorthand. He insisted on taking the papers to a teacher for examination. They *were* shorthand, the old-fashioned square-type shorthand.

" 'On those papers was a message to my mother from my father who had died two weeks before in New York, while my mother and I were in Oregon. It started "Dearest Be-

263

loved," and spoke of a letter that had not been posted. It was an urgent letter containing information about Father's safety-deposit box in the East. His death had been sudden, and Mother had not known the location of that box.

" 'My father had always called my mother "Dearest Beloved," and as a young man had learned the old-fashioned method of shorthand. Mother still has those pieces of paper, and the message has been verified by other people, too.'

"To a scientist, does such a story offer acceptable proof of life after death? No, but it is in line with scientific research that has proven that there is something in man that has a wholly different set of properties from those of his physical body—and it is this finding that makes survival a logical possibility." [16]

Many of us must have collected a few cases similar to these. I am myself fascinated by an experiment, which cannot yet be concluded, by which Dr. Thouless has arranged a message in code which, while he is still alive, he challenges anyone to decipher by telepathy or otherwise. If after he is dead, he provides the clue by means of a medium, his experiment will exclude telepathy from the living, so often dragged in as an alternative to survival of the dead, and offer valuable evidence that he is still alive, for so far, at any rate, no one has been able by telepathy to make anything of the message.

Outstanding to me is the work of my friend, Miss Geraldine Cummins. Her book, *The Road to Immortality*,[17] purports to have been communicated by F. W. H. Myers after his death. I find it strangely satisfying. Further, she uses in it words like "polyzoic," "polypsychic," "metetheric," telaesthesia" *which an independent witness found in Myers' great two-volume work,* "Human Personality and Its Survival of Bodily Death,"

---

[16] Quoted by special permission February 20, 1964 from *Guide Posts* (Guideposts Associates, Inc., Carmel, New York, 1963).

Note also the case quoted on p. 133 from *The Silent Road*, by W. Tudor Pole.

[17] Aquarian Press, 1955.

AFTER *Miss Cummins' script was completed.* These words and ideas were quite unknown to Miss Cummins at the time of writing, and are quite outside the range of her own vocabulary and ideas. Her own interests are in drama and fiction. She was quite unaware of the existence of Myers' book, and yet she used, during trance, the unusual words and ideas found in it. This seems good evidence to me. Students in this field have no shortage of this kind of evidence,[18] and the testimony of Sir Oliver Lodge stands for many who are coming to believe in man's survival of death. After fifty years of research and experiment he wrote:

"Surely it has led most of the investigators, and certainly it has led me, to realise on a basis of actual fact that death is not the end of mental activity, that the mind can function apart from bodily organs, that memory is not limited to the brain, and in fact that individual personality and character survive the loss of the body. The grounds for this clear and definite persuasion have grown in cogency during my lifetime until now I have no doubt at all."

Dr. D. Frazer-Hurst comments: *"This testimony, based on half a century of study is very impressive,* and may be favorably contrasted with the curt dismissal of the whole subject by many who have given to it neither time, thought nor study." [19] Paul Beard's conclusion seems to be that "reasonable truth-seeking intelligences are indeed at work trying to reach us."

If this evidence be accepted, it makes of death a mere milestone, not the end of a journey. It will always be sad, because we love to have our dear ones around us in bodies like our own. Yet if they had gone off to the ends of the earth and

[18] See a valuable book of evidence by Paul Beard called *The Search for Survival* (Hodder and Stoughton, 1965), especially his vivid account of alleged messages from the dead about the unreliability of the famous airship, R. 101, *before* she sailed and met with disaster.

[19] Dr. D. Frazer-Hurst, "The Church and Psychical Research," being the concluding chapter of *The Bridge of Life* (Mullen, Belfast, 1960), reprinted by The Churches' Fellowship for Psychical and Spiritual Studies.

left us here, though we should miss them terribly we should be happy in our hearts for them, and we must try to feel like that when they die. Both for myself and for my loved ones, I doubt if death makes any more difference to God's plans for me than whether I live in London or New York. This seems to be borne out in the literature of the subject which tells us repeatedly that one of the earliest difficulties which confront the dead is to realize that they are dead (see p. 323). Death itself seems not to make a great difference. Certainly man's eternal destiny is not determined by the act—often the accident—of dying. Spiritually, and apparently mentally, he goes on where he left off, save for the hamperings of the flesh, which—it should be remembered—may have hampered his mind, since while in the flesh his thinking is governed and filtered by a physical brain. In an etheric body, then, in some form by which we may know one another and express ourselves, I believe that all men, whatever their religion or lack of it, pass on into another phase of being, to another class in God's school.

If death is only that kind of milestone, in an age-long journey, the shock of a great calamity is lessened for us, as I think it should be. Again and again we read of earthquakes, floods, hurricanes and volcanic eruptions which sweep away thousands of lives. The theological problem is not made greater by the number of the people who perish. When one child is swept away by the tide on the beach near my present home, the *problem* is the same, though the shock of hearing that thousands have physically perished is greater. But if those who perish are in the same case as those who catch a steamer for a distant shore, then, while sadness remains, and they had made no choice to depart, our minds can stand up to the loss of their physical presence. They have only moved from one room in the Father's house to another.

Holding this view, as I do, of the relative unimportance of death in God's plan for us, I am a convinced member of the

Voluntary Euthanasia Legalisation Society.[20] This is such a controversial matter that it would take too much space adequately to set out all the arguments for and against. I had the honor of arguing the matter at the Oxford University Union recently and the debate, very much in favor of my position, went on for hours. But I sincerely believe that those who come after us will wonder why on earth we kept a human being alive against his own will, when all the dignity, beauty and meaning of life had vanished; when any gain to anyone was clearly impossible, and when we should have been punished by the State if we kept an animal alive in similar physical conditions.

If proper safeguards are strictly imposed—and the Society to which I have referred has drawn up a careful scheme with all the dangers and risks in mind—I for one would be willing to give a patient the Holy Communion and stay with him while a doctor, whose responsibility I should thus share, allowed a patient to lay down his useless body and pass in dignity and peace into the next phase of being. Having in mind the mental agony through which I have watched relatives of a patient pass while their loved one endures a long, incurable, useless and intolerably painful illness, easy death, so far from being cowardly and selfish, would be reasonable, liberating and altruistic. One young wife who watched her husband die of cancer of the brain wrote to Dean Matthews of St. Paul's Cathedral, who is also a member of the Euthanasia Society, saying: "I am thirty-eight. I feel like an old woman. To stand helplessly by and see the one we love best in all the world suffer terribly with no chance of recovery is sheer hell." [21]

---

[20] Particulars obtainable from the Secretary, 13 Prince of Wales Terrace, London, W.8.

[21] *Voluntary Euthanasia, The Ethical Aspect,* Very Rev. W. R. Matthews, K.C.V.O., D.D., D.Litt., Dean of St. Paul's Cathedral, p. 7 (Euthanasia Society, 1950).

Dr. Leonard Colebrook, F.R.S., the Chairman of the Euthanasia Society, in a pamphlet called, *A Plan for Voluntary Euthanasia*, writes of a man of seventy who had a very severe stroke. As he slowly recovered consciousness, he intimated his wish to die. Medical men and nurses fought for his life and he was gradually nursed back to a state of half-living, completely paralyzed on one side and with total loss of speech. This condition continued *for fifteen years* during which he had frequent recurrences of urinary infection, pneumonia, incontinence, bed sores and gall-bladder trouble—a human wreck. To me it seems cruel and wicked to refuse such a patient his reiterated request to be allowed to die. Lord Amulree, in a recent article in the journal *Crucible*,[22] quoted *The Lancet* in which a leading article stated, "A clinician who persistently seeks to sustain a parody of life may end in serving nobody and nothing except pride in his own technical competence." Lord Amulree added, "It seems only fair to the patient and to his relatives that all should feel sure that the doctor will not continue to keep *living*, as distinct from *alive*, a body from which all personality has for ever departed."

For similar reasons, I have come to regard even suicide as justifiable in certain cases, and I am glad that at last it is no longer a crime in England to take one's own life. To do so *might* be selfish and cowardly. It might be committed in a temporary mood of depression and this would be wrong. But it might also be an act of courage and self-sacrifice. When Captain Oates—a valued colleague of Captain Scott in his epic journey to the South Pole—found that frost-bite in his feet was holding up his companions, he walked out into the blizzard to lay down his own life and was rightly labeled, "a very gallant gentleman." No one would criticize the man who, after a shipwreck, leapt to certain death in a stormy sea because a raft containing women and children was already over-

[22] Journal of the Church of England Board for Social Responsibility.

filled. When incurable disease supervenes, often with severe pain and distress, and the patient sees that he is an increasing burden and hindrance to others, I cannot see why it is necessarily wrong for him, after thought and prayer, quietly to take his own life.

"Human life is sacred. The State cannot condone the taking of life," we are told. What hypocrisy this can be! My generation was decimated by the 1914 war when my fellow second lieutenants knew that the average length of life in France for a young officer was two days. The State until recently sanctioned and indeed ordered the taking of the life of a young, healthly man who could be made a useful citizen, if he were found guilty of capital murder! Is life treated as if it were sacred? It is often begun accidentally through ten minutes' passion on the part of parents, and a doctor will end it at birth if a mothers' recovery is at stake.

"Death," we are told, "should be left to God." We do not leave birth to God. We space births. We prevent births. We arrange births. Man should learn to become the lord of death as well as the master of birth.

I am tempted to laugh when pious men say, "Leave it to God." I want to show them the parts of my garden that I have left to God! A friend of mine left a broken elbow to God instead of calling in those who would have cooperated with God, and now my friend cannot lift his arm. Faith in God includes faith in those who help God. God has given us brains to use that we may cooperate with him and with others to master evil, and prolonged, incurable suffering is an evil both for the sufferer and for all those who watch others in long drawn-out agony. "There might be a miracle of healing discovered tomorrow," some say. I am glad my doctor is not one who waits for miracles, and when my house catches fire, I shall not pray for a miracle but ring up the fire brigade. That, be it noted, is a more religious attitude than leaving God to put the fire out. It is "loving God with all one's mind,"

269

which Jesus called part of the "first commandment." [23] Man is meant to be the master of his environment, of which, so often, suffering is part. Prolonged suffering is not God's intention. This we know from the work of Christ; and though life is sacred, yet, in the cases to which I am referring, nothing sacred is left, and no "noble reaction to pain" is possible. Drugs make it impossible, and every kind of deterioration sets in.

Lord Horder once said, "The good doctor is aware of the difference between prolonging life and prolonging the act of dying. He must do the first but need not do the second." It has always seemed to me unfair to "leave it to the doctor" attending the case. Incidentally, the patient is at the mercy of the doctor's private views. A Roman Catholic physician, I am told, is not allowed to end a patient's agony or to assist that end. But Lord Horder's distinction is very artificial. If a doctor gives an overdose of narcotic, holding in his mind the idea of ending the patient's life, then he is ethically in the wrong. If he gives *the same amount of narcotics* holding in his mind the idea of easing pain he is ethically correct. [24] This is absurd casuistry. Anyone can see through it.

The last Euthanasia Bill foundered in the House of Lords in 1936, though it had the approval of the Archbishop of Canterbury, largely because it involved such stringent safeguards that the patient would be intolerably distressed by the legal formalities. But if voluntary euthanasia becomes law, which I sincerely hope will be the case, those who take advantage of it and adopt it will not end "life." They will hasten a new and happier phase of it. There is no such thing really

---

[23] Mark 12:30; Matthew 22:37; Luke 10:27. It is significant that the original command in Deuteronomy 6:5 reads, "Thou shalt love the Lord thy God with all thine heart, and with all thy soul, and with all thy might." *It was Jesus who added, "and with all thy mind."*

[24] See *Voluntary Euthanasia—The Next Step*, by Professor Granville Williams, Quain Professor of Jurisprudence in the University of London, p. 3 (published by the Euthanasia Society, 1955).

as "loss of life," unless God himself annihilates a soul. Death is not only a door closing. Another door is opening.

Thousands of elderly people, even those who have comparatively good health, secretly long to put off the body with its laboring breath, its hardened arteries, its permanent tiredness and its creaking joints and muscles. They long to feel really fit and well and alive, unhampered by pain and physical disability. Dying must mark a difference like that between riding a creaking push-bike up a steep hill on a rough road against a bitter winter wind, and then driving a new Rolls-Royce on a perfect tarmac road in the Italian Riviera on a bright summer morning in June!

Jesus was very reticent about what life after death may be like. I suppose men could no more have understood or imagined it than a man born blind could appreciate our description of a sunset. Perhaps we need more faculties, or ability to perceive other dimensions, and perhaps this is why, on the whole, spiritualistic revelations seem disappointing and trifling. "I have no idea what it [the next life] will be like," said the late Archbishop William Temple to his wife, "and I think that I am glad I have not, as I am sure it would be wrong." [25] But I think another reason for our Lord's reticence may well have been a concern lest men, dreaming of a nonphysical life, should too readily develop dissatisfaction with this one and wrongly seek to enter the next before their work here was done and while they still might have done it.

Jesus was certain of the next life. When he referred to Abraham, Isaac and Jacob, who had been dead for centuries, he is reported to have added, "And God is not the God of the dead, but of the living: for all live unto Him." [26] And on the mountain of transfiguration it is reported that he had fellowship with Moses and Elijah. It must have been Jesus

[25] Frederick A. Iremonger, *William Temple, His Life and Letters,* p. 626 (Oxford University Press, 1948).
[26] Matthew 22:32; Mark 12:27; Luke 20:37-38.

himself who gave the two strangers these names.[27] The more I meditate on the message of Jesus and the meaning of life, the more certain I become that the whole universe is full of living presences, and that we, who would have been terrified of being born, if the event had not been shrouded by our undeveloped imaginations, need have no fear of dying. We are in the hands of the same infinite Love; the same wise, purposeful Planner. He who arranged human birth so that loving hands welcomed us and all that we needed was given, will not have overlooked that the next phase will be strange at first. So, he says, "I go to prepare a place for you." "Rejoice, for all is well." "If it were not so I would have told you." [28]

---

[27] Luke 9:28 ff., note verse 32.
[28] John 14:2, and Matthew 28:9, where the word translated "All hail," means "Rejoice," and is a *report* as well as an exhortation.

CHAPTER XIII

JUDGMENT AND HELL

"A man who was entirely careless of spiritual things died and went to Hell. And he was much missed on earth by his old friends. His business manager went down to the gates of Hell to see if there were any chance of bringing him back. But, though he pleaded for the gates to be opened, the iron bars never yielded. His cricket captain went also and besought Satan to let him out just for the remainder of the season. But there was no response. His minister went also and argued, saying, 'He was not altogether bad. Let him have another chance. Let him out just this once.' Many other friends of his went also and pleaded with Satan saying, 'Let him out. Let him out. Let him out.' But when his mother came, she spake no word of his release. Quietly, and with a strange catch in her voice, she said to Satan, *'Let me in.'* And immediately the great doors swung open upon their hinges. For loves goes down through the gates of Hell and there redeems the damned."

(Source unknown)

"Philosophy filtering out delusions from her theory of life, in dread of superstition gave religion away to priests and monks, who, rich in their monopoly, furbish and trim the old idols, that they dare not break for fear of the folk and need of good discipline."

Robert Bridges
(The Testament of Beauty)

XIII

JUDGMENT AND HELL

THE modern layman can exclude from his mind the idea of a set day of judgment. Many harbor the terrifying idea that after death, perhaps when the history of this little planet is over and it hangs like a lifeless moon in the sky, all who have ever lived on it, having "slept in their graves till the resurrection," will be hauled before a bar of justice. This will be "the dreadful day of judgment when the secrets of all hearts shall be disclosed." [1] God in awful majesty will occupy the "throne of justice" and everyone will be assigned either to heaven or to hell.

Such a travesty should be dismissed with the derision it deserves. C. S. Lewis, in the last book we shall have from his lucid and able pen and only published after his death, amusingly imagines God saying to Gabriel the archangel on the "day of judgment," "Gabriel, bring me Mr. Lewis' file." [2]

Reason should help us to get rid of this bogy about a day of judgment and a final discrimination between the damned and the blessed, since no line can possibly be drawn between men, all of whom are sinners, so that those on one side of the line are justly treated to an endless punishment and those just on the other are worthy of everlasting bliss. Besides, what of those who have never heard of Christ, little children dying

[1] This terrible language is quoted from the marriage service in the Prayer Book. Fortunately the bride and bridegroom are much too happy to notice the threat!

[2] C. S. Lewis, *Letters to Malcolm: Chiefly on Prayer*, p. 78 (Harcourt, Brace & World, 1963).

in infancy, Old Testament saints who lived too early, devout men and women in other religious faiths—Gandhi for instance—whose lives are more nearly Christian than those of most church-goers? "In every nation," said Peter bravely, "he that feareth (his god) and worketh righteousness is acceptable to Him." [3]

The only basis for this widely held superstition of a day of judgment is the parable of the sheep and the goats in Matthew's Gospel (Chapter 25). But as Leckie has so convincingly shown, this passage—which has no parallel in any of the other three Gospels—is lifted almost bodily from the apocryphal book of Enoch. Having quoted the almost identical parallel from Enoch, a book not considered sufficiently inspired for inclusion in the Bible, Leckie adds, "Surely it is evident that both [passages] owe their form to a common imaginative tradition. . . . *No one could infer from these prophecies that our Lord distinguished between different types of sinners.*" [4] Further it is often overlooked that in Matthew's prophecy there is an important introductory verse: "Before Him shall be gathered *all the nations.*" Clearly, individual *men* could not be separated in the way suggested, but there are nations who have gone into "eternal" or age-long obloquy because, in Toynbee's phrase, they were "instruments which God could no longer use." [5] The parable is not

---

[3] See Acts 10:35. *New English Bible* translates, "in every nation the man who is godfearing and does what is right is acceptable to Him."

[4] J. H. Leckie, D.D., *The World to Come and Final Destiny*, p. 110 (T. & T. Clark, 1918), where the passages from Enoch are quoted. See also my *After Death*, p. 54 (Epworth Press, 1923). Italics mine.

[5] The word *"aionios,"* translated "eternal," is used about the fate of both sheep and goats. It does not mean endless. Tennyson uses it in 'In Memoriam' (xxxv) in the sense of "agelong," and speaks of streams

> . . . *that swift or slow*
> *Draw down aeonian hills, and sow*
> *The dust of continents to be.*

The word *"kolasis,"* translated "punishment," means "pruning," clearly something done to promote subsequent growth. Dr. F. Spencer (Oxford), translates verse 46 as follows: "These will go away to the corrective punishment of the age but the righteous into the life of the age." There is no suggestion of endlessness.

one about men but about nations, but in any case I find it quite impossible to believe that he who said of those who put him to *death*, "Father, forgive them, they know not what they do," ever said of those who merely exposed him to *hunger*, because they were callous of the needs of his little ones, "Depart from Me ye cursed into the eternal fire which is prepared for the devil and his angels for I was hungry and ye gave Me no meat" (25:42). The "inasmuch" passages sound authentic on the principle enunciated earlier in this book,[6] but the violence is a reflection of the same spirit which made the disciples ask Jesus to call down fire from heaven on the Samaritans because the latter did not receive the former hospitably.[7] Perhaps Matthew was the spokesman. Indeed, that kind of attitude has lasted many centuries. Narrow-minded and intolerant men have often desired that those who differed from them should be tortured, or, at any rate suffer, e.g. the members of the Inquisition, and the mediaeval barons who built their dining halls just above their dungeons so that the groans of tortured prisoners might enhance the pleasures of the diners at their revels and orgies of triumph.

Paul, with his legalistic training, contributed to the false picture of a judgment hall. "We must all be made manifest," he says, "before the judgment seat of Christ, that each one may receive the things done in the body, according to what he hath done, whether it be good or bad." [8] We may put this down to Paul's obsession with sin and guilt and punishment in a legal set-up quite foreign to any teaching of Jesus.[9] The pictures Jesus painted of a lost sheep, a lost coin, a lost son and so on, were as far removed as possible from this kind of legalism. The fourth Gospel reports him as saying, "If any man hear my sayings and keep them not, I judge him not; for *I came not to judge the world* but to save the world . . .

---

[6] See page 66   [7] Luke 9:52-55   [8] 2 Corinthians 5:10
[9] C. E. Barker has worked this idea out excellently in *Psychology's Impact on Christian Faith*, pp. 44 ff., 130 ff. (Allen and Unwin, 1963).

the word that I spake, the same shall judge him in the last day." [10]

That sentence, so full of insight and so unlikely to have been made up, leads us along an avenue of thought which seems to me to reflect the Master's teaching on judgment and to offer a place where the modern man can rest his mind in regard to this important subject.

There is not one judgment day, surely, but a thousand! Every time we confront beauty, truth, goodness or love, our response to them judges us.

The matter is summarized in the delightful story of a visitor to a famous art gallery containing only pictures of established and famous greatness. Said the visitor to an attendant, "I don't think much of the pictures." Said the attendant, very courteously, "Excuse me, sir, *the pictures* are not on trial!" If I listen to Beethoven's music, perfectly played, I may find it a meaningless noise, but such a conclusion is a judgment of me, not of Beethoven. And when Pilate hauled Jesus to his judgment hall, what took place, as all the world admits, was a judgment of Pilate, not of Jesus.

So, as man, day after day, is brought into contact with beauty, truth, goodness, the three ultimates of spiritual reality,

> . . . he ever bears about
> A silent court of justice in his breast,
> Himself the judge and jury, and himself
> The prisoner at the bar. . . . [11]

Anyone who has sat on a public platform or in a pulpit during a public meeting or a church service, sees that the words being spoken are judging their listeners. The response of the latter reveals the judgment. The listener may be somnolent, bored, merely tolerant, or mentally excited. He may be thrilled, comforted, helped, frightened, challenged or stimulated. Far more than those sitting near him realize, his very face registers the

[10] John 12:47-48.   [11] Tennyson, "Sea Dreams."

verdict. The words are judging him. As the viewer in the art gallery is judged not by an art critic but by the pictures themselves; as the listener at the concert is judged by the music, so, when we pass the milestone of death and enter a word where presumably the environment is more spiritual, it will itself judge us with a judgment with which we must agree, for we pass it on ourselves and, incidentally, a judgment which, if thought to be unfair, unjust, useless or irrelevant—and the old idea of hell was all these—could have no real value in the education of the soul. We cannot pretend to *ourselves* to love music if we are in truth bored. We cannot pretend to love the things of God if they bore us. So the same "heaven" could be a hell of boredom to one man and the very height of bliss to another, just as in the same concert two men may sit together, one in rapture and one waiting for the interval and the chance of a drink! And though they are friends and sit together, between them is a great gulf, fixed, at any rate for the time being, since neither a love of music nor a love of God can be injected instantaneously to bring delight to one unable to make any response. "In all these things, between us and you there is a great gulf fixed that they which would pass from hence to you may not be able, and that none may cross over from thence to us." [12] The words were spoken before the cross and they need not be taken to mean that deprivation of happiness is fixed forever. I do not believe this. The unmusical man at a concert could begin to learn music. If the concert is going on forever, and he cannot get out, he would be wise to do so!

Strangely enough, on the very morning when I was writing these words, I received a letter from a complete stranger in America saying, "The idea that a person needs to prepare himself spiritually in order to be at home in the spiritual world after death was entirely new to me and so satisfying, in that it actually made me feel that life *is* worth living."

[12] Luke 16:26.

We may, of course, think of Christ as Judge in the sense that we judge our own lives *in the light of his.* Says Newman in "The Dream of Gerontius,"

> *The shame of self at thought of seeing Him,*
> *Shall be thy keenest, sharpest Purgatory.*

and Whittier has the same idea in the hymn we have all sung:

> *We test our lives by Thine,*
> *Thou judgest us;* Thy purity
> Doth all our lusts condemn.

We find the same attitude in the recorded life of Christ. He recognizes that adultery is sin, but when the trembling woman is thrust into his presence he says, "I don't condemn you," not because adultery doesn't matter, but because she has already condemned herself, and to say more would destroy the healing forgiveness of his loving kindness and leave a gulf between them.[13]

So when another woman of doubtful reputation gate-crashes at the party where he is the guest, Jesus does not play the Judge, though other guests do. He does not pretend that she is not a sinner or that sin doesn't matter. But he praises her love and offers forgiveness.[14] Will he have changed if and when we are confronted by him after death?

When he dined, at his own request, with Zacchaeus,[15] who, on his own confession was a twister, a cheat and an extortioner, no word of condemnation was spoken by Jesus. Zacchaeus condemned himself. The very presence of Christ made the day a judgment day—but there was no pompous judge on a throne uttering a verdict and a sentence. Zacchaeus was himself judge, jury and prisoner. Jesus hinted that he had been lost (19:10), but, while the onlookers called him a sinner (19:7), the only name Jesus called him was a "son of

---

[13] John 8:1-11   [14] Luke 7:36-50, note verse 47   [15] Luke 19:1-10

Abraham," the proudest name a Jew could claim, and one that restored his self-respect in a moment, made him believe in himself and set his face toward higher things. The lost was found that very day. Will Jesus have altered when he invites us to what John called the marriage supper? What kind of feast is it if it is full of condemnation and judgment?

If, by the phrase "the day of judgment" we mean an experience after death, when, free from the physical body we first contemplate reality with a clearer and more immediate sense of a divine encounter, then it may truly be said that for thousands of people who have thought little of themselves and dreaded death and its "afterwards" ("after death the judgment"), the day of judgment will be the happiest day they have ever known. For the first time, perhaps, they will be completely understood. Compassionate omniscience will know the hard, steep path they have trodden, the alluring power of the temptations of the flesh, now put aside, the hidden impulses of good, the secret longings for holiness, the brave silences and the hidden pain. They will find themselves believed in for the first time, in a way that releases them finally from the bondage of past sins and the exaggerated guilt-feeling which has tied them down for so long. With new life and belief in themselves, free from anxiety and worry, they will mount up with wings as eagles and begin a new life with all the old fears and dreads and anxieties behind them and remembered only as one remembers a bad dream.

All this, of course, does not make light of sin nor take all meaning from the word translated "hell." How are we to understand this word and its use in the Gospels?

We must at once throw over as unworthy of God any vestigial ideas remaining in our minds that anyone, whatever he believes or does, is landed in some kind of endless torture after death.

It is surely probable that Jesus, viewing the burning of rubbish in the valley of Hinnom, called Gehenna, used it, as he was so fond of using the things men saw every day, to point certain lessons. All that flame could consume in the valley of burning was consumed. But there was always a valuable residue, ashes used for cultivating soil or clinkers for making roads. True, the flames never went out, because, daily, new material was dumped on to the burning mass by the dustmen of Jerusalem. But, equally truly nothing of value was destroyed. The fact that a fire burns for a long time does not mean that it is acting upon the same material all the time. It can only consume what is inflammable. Hell may last as long as sinful humanity lasts, but that does not mean that any individual will remain in it all that time. The time of purging can only continue until purification is reached. And a God driven to employ an endless hell would be a God turned fiend himself, defeated in his original purpose.

The Gospel writers, like our own grandfathers, distorted the words of Jesus, impelled to do so by that age-long streak of malice in man which makes him desire that those who don't agree with him and follow his teaching shall suffer.[16] How revolting, cruel, sadistic and absurd the caricature about hell can become may be judged by a few quotations: "The Catholic Catechism," drawn up by Cardinal Gasparri, "for children who have made their first communion," with its imprimatur dated 1948, says: "In Hell the devils, and with them the damned, are deprived for ever of the beatific vision of God and are tormented with real fire and other most grievous pains." A writer in *The Sunday Times* of January 3, 1965, quoting this, adds: "According to this the Church teaches that God resurrects the bodies of the damned, solely to torment them." An essay, called *A Night of Hell*, by a Roman Catholic writer, describes a girl who in her earthly life had been inordinately fond of dress. In hell, therefore, she was condemned to wear forever clothing consisting of burning flame. I quote: "The blood was boiling in her veins, the brains were boiling in her skull, and the marrow in her bones." "The

[16] See p. 277.

existence of Hell is still taught as part of the Faith, without accepting which, no Catholic can see God—a god whom, if he believed what he was told, no one in his senses would wish to see. Dr. Arendzen in *The Teaching of the Catholic Church* (1952) tells his readers, 'If all that was ever written or painted or carved, expressive of the tortures of hell, could be brought before us at a glance, it would certainly fall immeasurably short of the truth.' A book published in 1964 intended for Roman Catholic children in grammar schools speaks of the physical fires of hell and the wicked writhing in envy and remorse for all eternity." [17]

Nor was such absurd, but to simple minds terrorizing, teaching confined to Roman Catholic teachers. We have read of a Scottish Divine, who, preaching to children, tore a slip of paper from his notes and, holding it in the candle by his elbow, informed his hearers that so their fingers might burn in hell if they did not keep them from mischief! I read that Lecky, the historian, told of a theologian who said that without doubt "infants not a span long crawled about the floor of hell," and that Jonathan Edwards, the American theologian (1703-58), who ministered in Northampton and who preached that God destined some people to eternal torture, said that if children were "out of Christ" they might *appear* innocent but were "not so in God's sight" but were "infinitely more hateful than vipers." Edwards had twelve children so perhaps he was plagued by the little "vipers"! [18]

Nowadays we rightly despise such superstition, and cannot accept as true of God behavior for which a man would be imprisoned or sent to a criminal lunatic asylum, but I could give case after case from the files of our City Temple Psychological Clinic where cruel and absurd views of God have set up illness of mind or body or both, in living men and women.

---

[17] *Objections to Roman Catholicism* (written by seven Roman Catholics), p. 20 (Constable 1964). The quotation is from the contribution by Magdalen Goffin.

[18] *Encyclopaedia Britannica*, Vol. 8, pp. 19-20.

We are bound to use words like "flame" (Mark 9:43), and "darkness" (Matthew 8:12) concerning what Browning called in "The Ring and the Book":

> ... *that sad, obscure, sequestered state,*
> *Where God unmakes but to remake the soul,*

but these conditions, however we describe them, are not, as it were, imposed from without by an angry God getting his own back. They are inherent in the development of a once controllable situation. If a sane and seeing man, having read many notices warning him of a cliff edge, keeps straight on in daylight toward it and falls over, we do not say, "How cruel of God thus to contrive man's pain!" We say, "Why didn't the man look where he was going and heed the warnings?"

If a man, morally heedless, spiritually insensitive, who thinks only of himself, who callously treads down others on his way to his own "success" or self-indulgence, and who is blinded by his own comfort, passes into another world without any heed to his own soul, may not the words "truth" and "fire" be synonymous? For myself, I feel that the truth, which I might have known and heeded, will envelop me with scorching—and, I hope—purging power. If I have hurt others, may I not have to identify myself with the suffering I have caused them and bear its fiery discipline before I can make spiritual progress? If I have deliberately turned from the light by which I might have walked, may I not find that I cannot yet bear the light in a clearer world, and may I not myself seek, for a period, the outer darkness where there is weeping and the awful, sorrowful remorse of those who need never have lost their way? Indeed, if a thing like lustful, sexual pleasure has mastered my earth life, may I not find it hard, even without a body, to escape the fantasies of the mind? May I not seek out kindred spirits, indulge in orgies of imagination, and postpone yet again any real awakening to, and desire for, the glory of the vision of God?

But God will never desert the soul. Let me add the next line to the quotation from Browning, given above.

> ... *that sad, obscure, sequestered state,*
> *Where God unmakes, but to remake the soul*
> *He else made first in vain;* which must not be.

Always there will be the chance to turn and love and live. The nature of the soul demands it. The nature of God proclaims it. The compassion of Christ guarantees it.

I realize that the logic of the situation demands the admission that *if* a soul finally turned from God it would perish. "There must be room in the Church, both for those who believe that some will actually be lost, and also for those who hold that the Love of God will at last win penitence and answering love from every soul that it has created." [19] Our human knowledge denies that any living thing can go on living indefinitely if it is permanently cut off from its environment. The eye, if in unbroken darkness indefinitely, loses its power to see, and so on. On maintaining communication with light depends its life. "We keep open," says C. W. Emmet, "the solemn possibility that final dissolution will be the ultimate end for such souls as have completely lost the power to recognize and desire goodness and respond to the love of God." [20] And Dr. Edwyn Bevan in *Symbolism and Belief* (p. 101) describes hell as "the darkness outside, the outer rim where being fades away into nonentity." Bishop Gore spoke of the possibility of "such a dissolution of personality as carries with it the cessation of personal consciousness." [21] But Love not logic rules and has the last word, and we must be allowed to hold the faith that though much may have to be suffered and, perhaps, many lives lived, the Good Shepherd at last

[19] *Doctrine in the Church of England*, ed. Archbishop Temple, p. 219 (S.P.C.K. 1938).
[20] C. W. Emmet, *Immortality*, p. 216 (Macmillan, 1918), cf. also pp. 170 ff. especially 208-9.
[21] *The Religion of the Church*, pp. 92 ff.

will bring every soul into the fold, for he himself gave men the picture of the Good Shepherd not content with 99 per cent of successes, but seeking the lost sheep *"until He find it"* (Luke 15:4).

No words used in the Gospels can legitimately be twisted to mean unending punishment, and indeed, such an expression is self-contradictory. The main motive of punishment surely is to reform the sufferer; in school, to make a better scholar; in the State, to make a better citizen. If the *punishment* goes on forever when does the sufferer benefit by the punishment or use the lessons he has learned so painfully? If hell were endless it would be valueless.

Yet for myself I do not throw over the imagery of fire. I cannot, for our Lord introduced it, however his followers may have distorted it. And there is a compliment implied in the very use of the word "fire." Wood, hay and stubble are *destroyed* by fire.[22] Gold is refined by it. Since destruction cannot be God's plan, his use of a discipline comparable with fire points to man's character being of the nature of gold which benefits by it. Nor does one forget that the refiner of gold carries the purifying process to the point at which he can *see his own face* in the molten metal.[23]

And while there is much in the Roman Catholic idea of Purgatory which I cannot accept, such as indulgences and ability to shorten it by costly gifts, I know my own heart well enough to know that there is very much in my nature which must be "burned away" before I can become all that I want to be and am capable of being. And surely the latter is God's plan and my goal; to be made all that he can make me, and to become at last one with him in an unbroken unity of communion and purpose.

Dr. Austin Farrer well says, "Purgatory was rejected by

---

[22] Cf. 1 Corinthians 3:12-15.
[23] Cf. Psalm 17:15, "I shall be satisfied when I awake in Thy likeness."

our reformers and undermining the Sufficiency of Christ's atonement; for it was taken to be the serving of a sentence by which the guilt of Christians was in some way worked off. Such an objection has no force against the teaching that we have a pain to pass through, in being reconciled to truth and love. And we may as well call this pain purgatorial, having no other name to call it. It seems strange indeed that so practical and pressing a truth as that of purgatory should be dismissed, while so remote and impractical a doctrine as the absolute everlastingness of hell should be insisted on. Nor is it that ultimate fire is scriptural, while remedial fire is not. Remedial fire was taught plainly enough by St. Paul to his Corinthians." [24]

Of course, the human soul will always have the power to reject God, for choice is essential to its nature, but I cannot believe that anyone will finally do this. To enter the next phase after death feeling very "out of it" and not even wanting to be "in it," in fellowship and love with others; to take no steps to "*see* the Kingdom of Heaven"—to use a phrase Jesus seems often to have used—to have no aspiration toward the heights of being, even when their glories are more fully revealed, seems impossible to me. If it were successful, there could be no perfect heaven for anyone, for we cannot complacently enjoy God if *one* of his sons or daughters is finally lost, and he himself defeated in his aims, for as Paul wrote to Timothy (1 Timothy 2:4), "He willeth that *all* men should be saved and come to the knowledge of the truth." It may take some aeons, as we think of time, or even many reincarnations, but we have the highest authority for believing that the Great Shepherd himself will not be content if one of his sheep is missing from the final fold.

What I think will be hell to most of us will be the slow realization, in a further life or lives, of how much sin has hurt

[24] Austin Farrer, *Saving Belief*, p. 154 (Hodder and Stoughton, 1964).

and hindered the loving God. Studdert-Kennedy, in one of his books,[25] tells of a father who in fits of drunkenness used to beat his little son whom in sober moments he loved dearly. The little lad lay dying, and the father, now sober, watched by the bedside. In his delirium, the child lifted his tiny hands, and, shielding his face, cried out in an agony of fear, "Don't let him hit me, Mother, don't let him hit me." The father knew then what his drunkenness meant to the lad. When we sin, we are drunk, blind drunk. We "know not what we do," as Jesus said. In the sober light of the spirit world we shall begin to know what our sin cost God. We shall see sin as the "crucifying of the Son of God afresh," [26] as the "raised hand, the clenched fist, and the blow in the face of God." [27] I never think of the after-life as *all* suffering or *all* pleasure, but very much like this life with light and shadow intermingled. But periods of self-discovery there must be and they may well be "hell" as we remember, and, with a new power of spiritual insight, re-assess, the sins we so glibly committed. Forgiveness will restore the relationship between ourselves and God, but as we remember our sins and assess the costliness of restoration, surely an experience of a burning sorrow will sting our hearts with purging pain. We read of a "book being opened" and ourselves judged (Revelation 20:12), but the book will be the book of our own memory and the judge our own awakened conscience.

> *I sat alone with my Conscience,*
> *In a place where time had ceased;*
> *We discoursed of my former living*
> *In a land where the years increased.*
> *And I felt I should have to answer*
> *The questions it put to me,*
> *And to face those questions and answers*
> *In that dim eternity.*

[25] *Rough Talks of a Padre*   [26] 1 Hebrews 6:6   [27] Joseph Parker

And the ghosts of forgotten actions
  Came floating before my sight,
And the sins that I thought were dead sins
  Were alive with a terrible might.
And I know of the future Judgment,
  How dreadful so 'er it be,
That to sit alone with my conscience
  Would be judgment enough for me! [28]

But for every sin forgiveness is offered.[29] In every heart repentance, recovery and progress are possible as truly after death as before it. What is there in the trivial incident of dying to prevent this? When we catch from Christ even a glimpse of what we can be made, by grace through discipline, and by grace through sunshine, we shall understand a phrase that used to puzzle me from the old saints and scholars: "The soul will run to its punishment." [30] Yes, burning may well be the way to bliss. If so, God help us to run to the fire!

An old legend puts the matter vividly: A man dreamed one night that he was allowed to pass into the next world. When he arrived, an angel invited him to visit heaven and hell. Together they went through all the courts of heaven, and the things they saw were very wonderful and very beautiful. But the heart of the visitor was ill at ease for he thought to himself, "This is all very fine, but how can they enjoy it while their brethren suffer in yonder torment?" And the angel read his very thoughts and said, "Would you like to see the place they call hell?" And, trembling a little, the visitor said that he would. So it came to pass that they drew near the gates of hell. The flames were terrible, and so great a heat was thrown

---

[28] Bishop Charles W. Stubbs, formerly Bishop of Truro.

[29] I have discussed the so-called unpardonable sin in *When the Lamp Flickers*, pp. 44 ff. (Abingdon Press, 1948). In my opinion there is no such thing.

[30] Cf. Plato's phrase, "The soul will run eagerly to its judge," and that of Hegel, "The sinful soul has a right to its punishment." See also my *Psychology, Religion and Healing*, pp. 325-27 (rev. ed.).

out that the visitor thought, "We shall not get near enough to see anything." And again the angel read his thoughts and said, "But can you *hear* nothing? And to his surprise the visitor heard strange and beautiful music coming from the heart of the fire. And he said to his angelic guide, "Sir, tell me, what wondrous songs are these which the souls in hell itself are singing?" And the angel whispered softly in his ear, "They are the songs of the redeemed."

CHAPTER XIV

REINCARNATION AND
RENEWED CHANCES

"Read not to contradict and confute nor to believe and take for granted, but to weigh and consider."

Bacon

"It is Plato's doctrine, and none more defensible, that the soul before it entered the realm of Becoming existed in the universe of Being. Released from the region of time and space, it returns to its former abode, 'the Sabbath, or rest of souls,' into communion with itself. After a season of quiet 'alone with the Alone,' of assimilation of its earthly experiences and memories, refreshed and invigorated, it is seized again by the desire for further trials of its strength, further knowledge of the universe, the companionship of former friends, by the desire to keep in step and on the march with the moving world. There it seeks out and once more animates a body, the medium of communication with its fellow-travellers, and sails forth in that vessel upon a new venture in the ocean of Becoming.

Many, no doubt, will be its ventures, many its voyages. For not until all the possibilities of Being have been manifested in Becoming, not until all the good, beauty and happiness of which existence allows have, by the wayfaring soul, been experienced, not until it has become all that it is capable of becoming—and who can tell to what heights of power and vision it may climb?—is it fitted to choose for itself the state and society which best meets its many requirements, as its natural and enduring habitation."

W. Macneile Dixon
(The Human Situation)

"If we watch ourselves honestly, we shall often find that we have begun to argue against a new idea even before it has been completely stated."

Wilfred Trotter
(The Herd Instinct)

"I could well imagine that I might have lived in former centuries and there encountered questions I was not yet able to answer; that I had to be born again because I had not fulfilled the task that was given to me. . . . A creative determinant must decide what souls will plunge again into birth . . . It is possible that any further spell of three-dimensional life would have no more meaning once the soul had reached a certain stage of understanding; it would then no longer have to return, fuller understanding having put to rout the desire for re-embodiment."

C. G. Jung
(Memories, Dreams, Reflections)

XIV

REINCARNATION AND
RENEWED CHANCES[1]

PART of our preparation for heaven may be that we have to come back to earth in another human body and try again. Said C. S. Lewis, "I believe that if a million chances were likely to do good, they would be given." [2]

It seems quite a shock to some people even to contemplate such a possibility, but it seems a very reasonable, even if unprovable, idea to me, and it would be unspeakable arrogance on the part of us in the West to dismiss without examination an idea current since the sixth century B.C., and held tenaciously by all Buddhists and Hindus, that is by about five hundred million people, many of whom are deep thinkers, saints, mystics and profound scholars.

Presumably we should all agree that if there is a life after this one, then this one is intended as a preparation for the next. Passing the tests which this life imposes is surely the only way of qualifying for the next phase. And there are some tests we can only undergo while we inhabit a body of flesh. If a man falls victim, say, to sexual immorality, to drug addiction, or to drunkenness, will he be able, by dying, to evade

[1] The substance of this chapter was originally delivered in 1957 as a lecture to the City Temple Literary Society, and then published as a pamphlet by my friend, Mrs. Peto, 16 Kingswood Road, Tadworth, Surrey, from whom it may be obtained. It is also available on the City Temple bookstall. 40,000 copies sold show the wide interest in the subject.

[2] C. S. Lewis, *The Problem of Pain*, p. 112 (Macmillan Co., 1943).

the challenge of mastering these tests? If he refuses to succor needy men in this life, will he, with all his selfishness unpurged, be let loose among those who have led a life of self-negation and self-sacrifice? It seems to me that such an arrangement would be as unjust and unsatisfactory as allowing the medical student who failed his first anatomy examination to proceed to the operating theatre; to allow the divinity student who could not pass the entrance examination to a theological college to take over the work of a church and preach in the pulpit, or the failed law student to plead in the courts. Can we really skip the tests of life in the flesh on earth and pass on to the higher forms in God's school for the soul?

At any rate, the matter is worth our inquiry. Some words from Plato's *Phaedo* often come to my mind, "It appears to me, Socrates, probably as it does to you with regard to these matters, that to know them clearly in the present life is either impossible or very difficult; on the other hand, however, not to test what has been said of them in every possible way, so as not to desist until on examining them from every point of view one has exhausted every effort, is the part of a very weak man." [3] "To suppress speculation would be a violence done to our nature as unnatural as if we were to prohibit ourselves from looking up to the blue depths between the stars at night," [4] or, to quote a blunt phrase from the book of Proverbs, "He that answereth a matter before he heareth it, it is folly and shame unto him." [5]

Of course, if it were clearly demonstrated that belief in reincarnation contradicted some *essential* teaching in Christianity one would have to consider and reconsider where the truth really lay and wait for further light.

Dr. John Whale says that the idea of reincarnation "is incompatible with the very genius of Christianity and is therefore no part of the Christian answer to the problem of evil,"

[3] Plato, *Phaedo* 85.
[4] *Autobiography of Mark Rutherford*, p. 255.
[5] Proverbs 18:13.

294

and "there is not a shred of evidence for this doctrine in the New Testament." [6]

With great affection and respect for my friend, John Whale, this is far too sweeping a statement. In John 9:2, we read that a man *born blind* was brought to Jesus with the question, "Master, who did sin, *this man* or his parents that he was born blind?" If *this man* could possibly have developed blindness through his sin, and yet have been *born blind*, then clearly the sin must have been in a previous life. [7]

I know that Jesus is nowhere reported as affirming reincarnation, but, though an argument from silence is precarious, he surely would have denied words which he believed to be false, as he did on another occasion, when life after death was under discussion, [8] and not allowed a falsity to prevail in the minds of the disciples through his silence, since, as John 9:2 shows, he did not allow the disciples to conclude that sin, either in this life or an earlier one, caused blindness.

We note a similar silence—when corrective speech would have been so easy—on the occasion when our Lord himself asked his disciples: "Who do men say that the Son of Man is?" And they said, "Some say John the Baptist, some Elijah, and others Jeremiah or one of the prophets." [9] Is it not extraor-

---

[6] J. S. Whale, *The Christian Answer to the Problem of Evil*, p. 55 (Student Christian Movement Press, 4th edition, 1957).

[7] It is worth staying in a footnote to make it clear that Jesus' answer, "Neither did this man sin, nor his parents but that the works of God should be made manifest in him," does not mean that the poor man had had to put up with blindness from birth in order that Jesus should be given an occasion to exhibit his powers! The full stop should be put after the word 'parents,' but the translater had no punctuation in the manuscript before him. Thus we should read: "Neither did this man sin nor his parents." (Full stop.) "But, that the works of God should be made manifest in him, we must work the works of Him that sent Me while it is day." It is as though Christ said, "Sin does not come into it. Let us not discuss that but let us get him cured before nightfall. That is the priority on this busy day."

[8] Mark 12:24.

[9] Matthew 16:14, Mark 6:15, and especially Luke 9:8-9, "Some were saying that John had been raised from the dead, others that Elijah had appeared, others again that *one of the old prophets had come back to life*" (New English Bible).

dinary that he did not tell them not to talk nonsense? At any rate, we cannot avoid the conclusion that the idea was a common one in his day and that he allowed its assumption to go unchallenged.

A significant passage is found in Matthew 17:9-13 (cf. Mark 9:11 ff.) after the Transfiguration, when Jesus exhorts the disciples, "Tell the vision to no man, until the Son of Man be risen from the dead." The disciples point out that the Scribes have always said that, "Elijah must first come." Jesus is reported as saying, " 'Elijah is come already. . . .' Then understood the disciples that *He spake unto them of John the Baptist.*" It would be difficult to explain such a passage other than by supposing that they regarded John the Baptist as a reincarnation of Elijah, and were led to do so by the words of Jesus if the latter are accurately reported.[10]

My own conclusion is not that reincarnation is proved, or that it is an essential part of Christian belief, but I do find that the evidence makes it probable, that Jesus never denied it, that there is nothing in it which is out of harmony with his teaching, and that it was probably part of the thought-structure of all the contemporary minds of his day. One prominent sect, the Essenes, definitely taught it, and Josephus makes reference to it as if it were commonly accepted. He writes, "They say that all souls are incorruptible but that the souls of good men are only removed into other bodies." [11]

It is important, as we examine the idea of reincarnation, to

---

[10] The impression the disciples had during the Transfiguration that Elijah was there on the mountain does not conflict with this view. Apart from mistaken identification concerning the appearances of "Moses" and "Elijah" many students of the occult hold that for each of us in the unseen is a root personality which can project itself, or even be incarnate, in other entities while at the same time it remains itself in the unseen. A rose bush may have its roots in one element, the soil, and its flowers in another, the sunshine. Each incarnation may be a flowering or expression of a deeper, more complete entity, a fundamental "self" in the real world, as, I suggest, are the various flowers that develop from one root which remains deep in the soil.

[11] *De Bello Judaico* 2:8.

realize the immense support for what I have written above which is provided by the fact that it was accepted by the early church for the first five hundred years of its existence. Only in A.D. 553 did the second Council of Constantinople reject it and only then by a narrow majority. If some view of reincarnation had not been widely held in the early church it would have been pointless to discuss it in a church council. It would be like the Church Assembly or the Methodist Conference discussing Palmistry or Astrology. Origen, a great scholar of the church (A.D. 185-254), accepted it.[12] Augustine (A.D. 354-430), an even greater authority, accepted it, and speaks of his infancy that "succeeded another age of mine that died before it." [13] St. Jerome supported it in his *Letter to Avitus,* Reference to *The Catholic Encyclopedia* informs me that St. Francis of Assisi (1181-1226) accepted it.[14] And belief in reincarnation, according to a priest writing in *The Liberal Catholic* is accepted by many Roman Catholics and has never been declared heretical by any Ecumenical Council.[15]

An important question to ask is whether the idea of reincarnation helps us to answer some of the questions which all thoughtful Christians ask, without denying any of the Christian affirmations. My own view is that reincarnation offers a key here to unlock many problems.

1. The Christian affirms that God is just, that ultimately life is just, that justice is what we call an "eternal value." It will be vindicated at last. No one—if we may put this point popularly—will be able to turn round finally on God and say, "Life wasn't fair to me. I had an unfair deal. I never had a chance."

Now if we take this life as we often see it, how terribly

---

[12] In *De Principiis* and *Contra Celsus.*

[13] In *Confessions* 1:6, p. 6 (Everyman edition, J. M. Dent).

[14] 1909 edition, Vol. 10, pp. 236-37 under heading "Metempsychosis" and "The Esoteric Tradition" by Dr. G. de Purucker.

[15] See Robertson, *Church History,* Vol. I, p. 157, and Hefele, *History of the Councils of the Church,* Vol. IV, pp. 223 ff.

unfair and unjust it seems. I have known people who, humanly speaking, have never had a chance. They have either been born with defects that appear to mar their lives, or else have met with a whole series of misfortunes that shut them off from the happiness others know.

I think of Betty Smith, born into a prosperous home, surrounded by every opportunity, given an ideal education, loving and marrying a man well able to keep her in the same kind of environment, giving her half a dozen happy, healthy children, and passing into middle and later life with full health and every possible amenity.

Then I think of Jane Jones, born blind, or deaf, or crippled, into a poverty stricken home, where a drunken father makes life a hell for everyone. Jane cannot escape, can never marry and have her own home, can never be given the things Betty enjoys, and dies early, let us say, of malignant disease. Some will recall Helen Keller and similar cases, but how few they are. Others imagine that "things will be squared up in heaven." Is Betty, then, to suffer in another life because she was happy on earth? What would that do in the matter of justice? Nothing. And certainly it would do Jane no good. Nor is she vindictive or mean enough to desire it. Is Jane to be "rewarded" or "compensated"? But what kind of *compensation* makes up for half a century of earthly misery? We cringe when we hear of a grant of money given to a man wrongfully imprisoned. How can that make up to him for the mental distress, the wasted years, the misery and pain to all his relatives . . . ? These things cannot be "made-up" for.

Is human distress just luck, then? If so, how unjust is life! Is it God's will? Then how unlike any human father he must be, for a human father who thus exerted his will would be clapped into jail, or into a lunatic asylum.

But if we accept the idea that all these inequalities are the result—in a cosmos of cause and effect—of earlier causes, the product of some distant past, the fruit of earlier choices, then our sense of justice is preserved. The body then, though born distorted, is not a greater mystery than the mangled body at the foot of a cliff, mangled because its owner did not look where he was going. We often *do* see suffering which is clearly the result of *recent* folly or ignorance or sin. None of these, but, indeed, their opposites are the "will of God," viz. wisdom, knowledge and holiness. What if *all* apparently unjust suffering is the result of either recent or older folly, ignorance and sin? "Whatsoever a man soweth, that shall he also reap" may indeed be a law that runs back for the sowing to lives before this and for the reaping to lives after this. This is the fundamental basis of the eastern idea of karma. The matter is not usefully thought of in terms of rewards and punishments, but of causes and effects, and refers to good as well as to evil happenings in our lives.

2. The idea of reincarnation seems to explain prodigies. Consider the ability of a child like the Italian, Giannella de Marco, aged eight years. The London *Times* of March 13, 1953, reported that Giannella conducted the London Philharmonic Orchestra at the Albert Hall, London, in works by Weber, Haydn, Wagner and Beethoven. I quote from *The Times*: "She plies a clear, generous beat and plainly has the music at her finger-ends . . . There is an unnerving maturity in her intellectual accomplishment . . . Her musicianship is surely to be admired, but it were better if, at eight years of age, such gifts were allowed to unfold gradually and quietly."

Speaking of child musicians, the London *Evening Standard* (September 23, 1953) described a girl of four years of age, Danielle Salamon, who played the piano before she could talk, can play Mozart's works and has composed several pieces of music and written the scores in a book. She is the daughter of English parents living in South Tottenham, London.

Similarly we learn of Sir William Hamilton, who started to learn Hebrew at the age of three, that at the age of seven he was pronounced by one of the Fellows of Trinity College,

Dublin, to have shown a greater knowledge of the language than many candidates for a fellowship. At thirteen he could speak thirteen languages. Among these, besides the classical and modern European languages, were included Persian, Arabic, Sanskrit, Hindustani and Malay. At fourteen he wrote a complimentary letter to the Persian Ambassador, who happened to visit Dublin, and the latter said that no one in Britain could have written a document in the Persian language. At six he would look up from his toys and answer a difficult mathematical problem, and at eighteen the Astronomer Royal of Ireland, Dr. Brinkley, said of him, "I do not say that this young man will be the first mathematician of his age. I say he *is* the first mathematician of his age." [16]

We could all contribute stories of these infant prodigies, but how are we to account for them? Mozart wrote a sonata when he was four and an opera when he was seven. Marcel Lavallard had a picture accepted by the Paris Salon when he was twelve. A boy called Zerah Colburn, in his eighth year, could solve difficult mathematical problems. On being asked how many minutes there are in forty-eight years, he gave the correct answer without making a mark on paper.

Is it an accidental group of genes that makes a little girl of eight a musician far in advance of grown men and women, who have slaved for many years in that field? Is it a piece of luck that a boy of fourteen can write perfect Persian? If so, life seems unjust as well as chancy. Or is it that they have been here before? Plato believed whole-heartedly in reincarnation, and his famous "Theory of Reminiscence" asserted that "knowledge easily acquired is that which the enduring self had in an earlier life, so that it flows back easily." In the dialogue, *Meno*, Socrates shows that an untutored slave boy knew mathematical facts which in this life had never been taught him "He had forgotten that he knew them . . . To Socrates it was self-evident that the boy's capacity was the

[16] See Dr. Raynor Johnson, *The Imprisoned Splendour*, p. 379 (Hodder and Stoughton, 1953), quoted from *The Ancient Wisdom*, by A. Besant.

result of an experience he had had in a previous lifetime." [17]

We see the problem less definitely, but puzzlingly, in other fields. In the same family some children seem to have a strange wisdom, to be "old souls," to have a maturity beyond their years or an appreciation of some forms of art, whereas some adults behave like silly children, and we find grown women reading nothing but *Peg's Weekly* and grown men made peevish and irritable by losing at "Scrabble." Confucius, that wise old philosopher and founder of a religion which millions still follow, distinguishes those who are "born wise" from those who "learn by toil" (Analects 16:9).[18]

I should imagine, for example, that a man like Hitler might well have to come back and "learn by toil." It is incredible that he can by now be a bright angel making progress in a purely spiritual realm! One speculates that he will be found either among the devils, or that, when light comes to him, he will *choose* to come back, perhaps as a slave in a Siberian mine, and seek to "work out his own salvation," and to find his way to the graduation class in God's school.

I think it possible, not that *all have* to come back, but that *some* have to, and that many *may* be allowed to return when it dawns on them that such is for them the path of progress, though in earth-language a thousand years may separate the incarnations.[19] Perhaps they are even allowed to choose their venue. They will doubtless choose in a way which gives them maximum opportunity, so they will choose parents with the right make-up. What looks like heredity, then, may be partly wise choosing on the part of a spirit, eager in new circumstances to realize his possibilities.

Bach was born into a very musical family, but why put this down merely to heredity when many great musicians

[17] Dr. Ira Progoff, *The Symbolic and the Real*, pp. 48 ff. (Julian Press, New York, 1963).

[18] Quoted by T. F. Glasson and also by Sir John Pratt in *China and Britain*, p. 65.

[19] See the quotation from Jung opposite the opening of this chapter, also his *Memories, Dreams of Reflections*, pp. 45, 222, 239, 293, 295, 297.

have had unmusical children? Clearly there is nothing inevitable about musical heredity. May the soul now called Bach have chosen the kind of vehicle and environment needed for its further progress and adequate expression? The soul may determine the heredity as much as heredity determines the soul.

The intelligent Christian believes that God is working out a plan in the lives of all men and women, and that the consummation of this plan will mean that his will is "done on earth as it is in heaven."

Now if every birth in the world is the birth of a new soul, I do not see how progress can ever thus be consummated. Each would have to begin at scratch and pass away from the life of the earth seventy or eighty years later. How then can there be progress in the innermost things of the heart? We can pass on *some* wisdom and, in outward circumstance, those who follow us can in some ways go on where we left off. They will not have to rediscover electricity or atomic energy. But they *will* have to discover, for example, each for himself, the vital supremacy of love and how to master selfish desire. Each child is born a selfish little animal, surrounded, it may be, by the enlightened, but not able in character to begin where the most saintly parent left off.

An illustration is provided if one goes back to revisit one's old school. When I did this I found better lighting, better blackboards, better maps, better desks, but two boys were standing outside the headmaster's study waiting to be caned, just as I used to do. The progress is in outward things. It cannot be in inward things as long as naughty boys keep joining the school.

How can a world progress in inner things—which are the most important—if the birth of every new generation fills the world with unregenerate souls full of untamed, animal tendencies? There can never be a perfect world unless gradually those born into it can take advantage of lessons learned in earlier lives instead of starting at scratch. True, the number of prodigies is small and so is the number of saints, but there may well be other planets more adapted than this is to be their classroom. It may be that we must relinquish the idea of *this* earth being the venue of the perfect society.

These thoughts make me agree with the late Dean Inge, no mean thinker, who said of the doctrine of reincarnation, "I find it both credible and attractive."

One wonders why men have so readily accepted the idea of a life *after* death and so largely, in the West, discarded the idea of a life *before* birth. So many arguments for a one-way immortality seems to me *cogent* for a two-way life outside the present body.

Naturally men ask for proof. The doctrine may be attractive, but can it be proved? This is a fair question and it is not proof to say that the doctrine is in harmony with Christian thought, that it provides an answer to many problems, or that it is held by a great number of scholarly men.

The answer must be that there is no proof. Yet, when one adds together some strange pieces of evidence, one is impressed by their cumulative effect.

Let me turn to some of these strange, but true, happenings.

A. We find people writing accurately about matters they have not studied and could not have experienced in their present life. Joan Grant, for instance, wrote books on ancient Egypt with amazing accuracy of detail, afterwards verified by scholars, and she actually claimed that in an earlier incarnation she had been an Egyptian princess. I have discussed the matter with her and I find it very difficult to explain the facts by any other theory.[20]

B. Again there is the familiar phenomenon which many people have experienced that "they have been through certain experiences before." Readers of the life of Shelley may re-

[20] She is the author of many books including *Winged Pharaoh, Life as Carola, Lord of the Horizon, So Moses Was Born,* and an autobiography, *Time Out of Mind* (published by Arthur Barker, Ltd., London, 1956).

member that when walking with friends in a part of the country which he had never before visited, he suddenly said to a companion, "Over that hill there is a windmill." As they breasted the hill and saw the windmill, Shelley fainted with emotion.

There may be other theories to account for this kind of experience, clairvoyance, for instance, or the alleged wandering of the self during sleep, or different speeds of recognition in different areas of the brain, but reincarnation offers itself as one possible hypothesis.

John Buchan, in his volume of reminiscences called *Memory Hold the Door*, says: "I find myself in some scene which I cannot have visited before and which is yet perfectly familiar; *I know that it was the stage of an action in which I once took part and am about to take part again.*" Clearly Buchan believed that the explanation of such an experience was reincarnation.

Dr. Hereward Carrington, a most trustworthy psychical researcher, tells of a man who visited a castle which he had never read about or seen before, and who stopped before a brick wall and said, "There used to be a door here." No visible evidence of such a door existed. No one present supported the statement, but subsequent enquiry proved that there had been a door at one time, but it had been built up years before. Many stories of this kind exist and point to reincarnation as a possible explanation.

C. Again, there are the remarkable experiences of those who seem to recognize one another, and who are convinced that they have known one another in an earlier life.

I met a married couple in Australia who told me their amazing experience. The lady had many psychic experiences by which she felt certain that none of her girlhood's boy friends would have any special significance for her, but that if she waited, her true mate would turn up. When she was in her middle thirties, she met her present husband at a public function, and both had an overwhelming and simultaneous conviction that, in an earlier life, they had been man and wife. They have now been happily married for over twenty-five years and both are convinced that this is their second incarnation. A year or two before meeting her husband, the lady had a vivid waking-dream of being in bed after the birth of a child whom she never saw. In the dream, her husband had to leave her in this distress to go on a forlorn and dangerous expedition on behalf of his King. The poignancy of parting was terrible, and in the waking-dream—experienced, let me repeat, a year or so before she met her husband—the lady wept bitterly. When she met her husband, she knew that he was the father of this child and the hero of this dream.[21]

D. Side by side with such an experience we can put one like this: Captain and Mrs. Battista, Italians, had a little daughter born in Rome, whom they called Blanche. To help look after this child they employed a French-speaking Swiss nannie called Marie. Marie, the nannie, taught her little charge to sing in French a lullaby song. Blanche grew very fond of this song and it was sung to her repeatedly. Unfortunately Blanche died and Marie returned to Switzerland. Captain Battista writes: "The cradle song which would have recalled to us only too painful memories of our deceased child, ceased absolutely to be heard in the house . . . all recollection of (it) completely escaped from our minds."

Three years after the death of Blanche, the mother, Signora Battista became pregnant, and in the fourth month of the pregnancy she had a strange waking-dream. She insists that she was wide awake when Blanche appeared to her and said, in her old, familiar voice, "Mother I am coming back." The vision then melted away. Captain Battista was skeptical, but when the new baby was born in February, 1906, he acquiesced in her being also given the name Blanche. The new Blanche resembled the old in every possible way.

[21] Quoted from *The Imprisoned Splendour* by Dr. Raynor Johnson, who in Melbourne, introduced me to the two people concerned.

Nine years after the death of the first Blanche, when the second was about six years of age, an extraordinary thing happened. I will use Captain Battista's own words:

"While I was with my wife in my study which adjoins our bedroom we heard, both of us, like a distant echo, the famous cradle song, and the voice came from the bedroom where we had left our little daughter Blanche fast asleep . . . We found the child sitting up on the bed and singing with an excellent French accent the cradle song which neither of us had certainly ever taught her. My wife . . . asked her what it was she was singing, and the child, with the utmost promptitude, answered that she was singing a French song . . .

" 'Who, pray, taught you this pretty song?' I asked her.

" 'Nobody; I know it out of my own head,' answered the child, and she ended by singing it gaily as if she had never sung another song in her life."

The Captain ends with a sentence which, short of calling him a liar, it is hard to set on one side. "The reader may draw any conclusion he likes from this faithful narrative of facts to which I bear my personal witness. For myself, the conclusion I draw from them is that the dead return." [22] I should want to say, "It looks as though, in certain circumstances, the dead are permitted to visit the world again in another body."

Recently a widely read Sunday newspaper, *The People,* reported an experiment in hypnosis, which seems to me to bear on our theme. [23] A Liverpool physician, whose name I have since learned, hypnotized a Lancashire housewife called Annie Baker, who had never studied French or been to France and whose education did not extend to any foreign languages. Under hypnosis she spoke perfect French, although, the doctor assures us, "she had not the slightest interest or knowledge of the French language, the French

---

[22] Quoted from *The Problem of Rebirth,* Hon. Ralph Shirley, pp. 54-55 (Rider).

[23] April 19, 1959. Quoted by special permission.

Revolution or France itself for that matter." [24] The patient referred to the death of Marie Antoinette as if it had just happened, and gave her own name as Marielle Pacasse, and that of her husband as Jules. On waking she spoke of a "dream," as hypnotized patients often do. But when she was questioned *in French,* she said she could not understand a word of what was being said. While in hypnotic trance she gave the name of a street, in which she purported to have lived, as the Rue de St. Pierre near the Notre Dame Cathedral. When the representative of *The People* made enquiries, he found no such street, but verified that there had been a street of that name in that vicinity one hundred and seventy years ago.

Under hypnosis the woman said she did not understand what tea was. It was almost unknown in France a hundred and seventy years ago. The name Marielle is rare now, but was much in vogue in 1794.

These strange facts would have an adequate explanation if the woman Annie Baker were a reincarnation of a Frenchwoman of the seventeen hundreds. The writer of the article comments: "Perhaps dead people's souls can be reborn in living human people."

A highly educated lady has written to me[25] of some experiences which she had with her son, David, "a charming, but unusual, boy who showed psychic tendencies from a very early age."

I quote from his mother's letter: "From four years he spoke of an invisible playmate—whom he called his Little Princess. In any difficulty he would say: 'I must ask my Little Princess.' We identified this figure later with my husband's ancestors —and do indeed believe he could see and hear her.

"At the age of seven he went to Rome with me to visit my grandmother—who stayed in Italy a great deal. On this

[24] Letter from the doctor to Mrs. M. C. Peto, dated October 28, 1959.
[25] Letter written in London under date October 28, 1959.

307

occasion we met a noted archaeologist who took us to see a newly excavated Roman villa on the outskirts of Naples. David became extremely excited, and ran about till he found a Roman bath. The edge of the bath was made of polished blue tiles about five inches square. These tiles were engraved with the signs of the Zodiac. David knelt down, and called out: 'Here's our bath, and our tiles—mine had a bull on it and the fish was Marcus'.' As he said the name 'Marcus' he burst into floods of tears and called out: 'Take me away, Mummy, take me away—it was all so terrible, I can't bear it.'

"On another occasion we were visiting some caves in Guernsey which had been used at one time as prisons for French soldiers. David tapped on the wall stating that there was another cave there where a young man had been walled in. He said he *had watched it being done*. The existence of this cave was denied by the authorities. But as David persisted, giving the name of the prisoner, we asked for information.

"Eventually, steps were taken and the walls were tapped for any thin place which could have been the outline of a door. The door was found: it had been bricked up. Stretched out on the floor was the skeleton of a man. When the archives were searched, the name David had given was correct.

"These incidents were so much a natural part of David's life that it is very difficult to sort them out as anything unusual. But about the age of fourteen I accompanied him to to look at some mummies in the British Museum. I felt it was asking for trouble, but, to my surprise, David was quite calm. He approached a sarcophagus and after looking at it, he remarked that there should be three initials on the underside of the case and that they were in a sort of white paint.

"I asked him if he could draw these initials. He took a pencil and paper and drew three Egyptian birds. 'That was my name,' he said, 'but you weren't there then. I was a kind of inspector; I had to mark the coffins if they were satisfactory.'"

After considerable trouble this was found to be correct. The three birds were discernible.

These strange happenings seem to have no adequate interpretation other than that of reincarnation, which in some people of an unusual psychic make-up are remembered from one life to another if sufficient stimulation occurs.

I may add that David's mother has a University degree in a scientific faculty, but had no knowledge of the occult nor of psychic matters until after David's death at an early age in 1935.

It would not be fair to advance any of these illustrations if they were isolated. I can only vouch for the fact that the literature of this subject abounds in similar well-authenticated stories. Paramhansa Yogananda in his *Autobiography of a Yogi*, tells a striking story of a similar kind to that of Captain Battista. Men feel they have visited a place before, that is common enough (a striking instance is that of Shanti Devi of Delhi, who described, and later identified, buildings in a city, Muttra, which she had never visited, five hundred miles from Delhi), but they manifest information that they have not acquired in this earth-life, like Joan Grant's detailed knowledge of life in Egypt three thousand years before Christ. Men confront a wall and "remember" there was a door in it, which turns out to have been true centuries earlier. Geniuses show powers which could not have been acquired at such an early age, and a child of six, who has never learned French, sings a French cradle-song which no one has taught her. All these stories have numerous parallels. There is room for doubt, of course, but not of all of them added together. And to the doubter the challenge is rightly made: "Very well; given that these things happen—and that cannot be doubted—what is your own explanation?"

The poets, in a matter like this, ought to be heard. It is interesting to note their testimony.

Here for example, is the Poet Laureate himself—John Masefield:

> I hold that when a person dies,
> His soul returns again to earth;
> Arrayed in some new flesh-disguise
> Another mother gives him birth.
> With sturdier limbs and brighter brain
> The old soul takes the road again.

Says Dante Gabriel Rossetti:

> I have been here before,
> But where or how I cannot tell;
> I know the grass beyond the door,
> The sweet, keen smell,
> The sighing sound; the lights around the shore
> You have been mine before,
> How long ago I may not know;
> But just when at that swallow's soar
> Your neck turned so,
> Some veil did fall—I knew it all of yore.

Browning has no more moving poem than the one addressed to the beautiful girl of sixteen, Evelyn Hope, who died, but whom he claimed as a twin soul:

> Just because I was thrice as old
> And our paths in the world diverged so wide
> Each was nought to each, must I be told?
> We were fellow mortals, nought beside:

He replies to his own questioning:

> I claim you still for my own love's sake.
> Delayed it may be for more lives yet,
> Through worlds I shall traverse not a few;
> Much is to learn, much to forget
> Ere the time be come for taking you.
> But the time will come.

I must be content with very few selections from the poets, but one could add F. W. H. Myers, both on his own account and when he translates Virgil. Both support reincarnation.

Tennyson meets a friend and is sure that they have been friends in an earlier incarnation.

> So friend, when first I looked upon your face,
> Our thoughts gave answer each to each, so true
> Opposed mirrors each reflecting each,
> Although I knew not in what time or place,
> Methought that I had often met with you,
> And each had lived in others' mind and speech.

Tennyson returns to the same idea again:

> As when with downcast eyes we muse and brood
> And ebb into a former life or seem,
> To lapse far back in a confused dream
> To states of mystical similitude,
> If one but speaks or hems or stirs a chair,
> Ever the wonder of it waxeth more and more,
> So that we say, All this hath been before,
> All this hath been, I know not when or where.

Walt Whitman, Longfellow, Swinburne, W. E. Henley, Morris, Rudyard Kipling—all have been quoted in support of reincarnation. It is an impressive witness, and to the poets, Dean Inge, in *God and the Astronomers* (p. 290), tells us we can add J. E. McTaggart, Professor of Mental Philosophy at Cambridge, in *Some Dogmas of Religion*, Maeterlinck, Ibsen, Lavater, Schopenhauer, Hume, Goethe, and in the ancient world Cicero, Seneca, Pythagoras and Plato. A belief held by so many and by such distinguished thinkers is not to be brushed lightly aside, especially when it throws light on some otherwise very dark problems, though I admit, of course, that some alternative hypothesis—such as access to

311

an imagined cosmic pool of memory—may yet explain the phenomena.[26]

Of course we must be ready to answer some of the criticisms made of reincarnation.

1. To quote Dr. Whale again, I find he objects to it because, he says, "my alleged pre-existence can have no present moral meaning simply because I am debarred from remembering anything about it." [27] What a preposterous statement! So, if some drug were now given to Dr. Whale, blotting out the memory of his youth, any indiscretions of that youth could have "no present moral meaning." He forgets that they would just as effectively have made him and molded him to be what he is, as if he remembered them. A judge is not often ready to excuse a prisoner of all moral responsibility if he asserts that "he can't remember anything about it now!"

None of us can now remember his earliest years. But any psychologist will stress their importance and the effect they had upon us. Much psychological treatment of the disorders of mature life is focused on recovering to memory the forgotten incidents of childhood, either by psycho-analysis, dream interpretation or drug injection, including the latest amazing treatment with lysergic acid.[28] But this recovery is only a way of treating disorder. Blessed forgetfulness is better while we are still in the flesh. The brain is of more value as a means of forgetting than as a means of remembering. Its withholding is more beneficent to mental health than is its ability to fill consciousness with mental material. It is a useful valve which prevents the conscious mind being overwhelmed.

These childhood incidents happened, not to another, but

[26] For those interested, a splendid anthology called, *Reincarnation*, with 400 selections by Joseph Head and S. L. Cranston, is now published by The Julian Press, New York, 1961.

[27] *Op. cit.*, p. 54.

[28] Lysergic Acid (LSD 25) is a drug first prepared from ergot in 1938. It makes easier the recovery of early memories but also produces hallucinations. Mescalin prepared from Peyote has similar effects. See Huxley, *Doors of Perception*, De Ropp, *Drugs and the Mind*, Newland, *Myself and I*, and Dunlop, *Exploring Inner Space*.

to us, and, though now forgotten, determined many of our present reactions to life. The very pattern of adult life is a form of stored memory. We do not need to remember mental impressions to be influenced by them. The *fruit* of experience does not depend on memory.[29]

It is a tendency of the normal mind to forget the unpleasant incident, given a comparable degree of impact at the time, and I am glad that I have forgotten many unhappy incidents of childhood in this life. Certainly I am glad I have no memory of an earlier one save perhaps those strange, fleeting sensations of indescribable, and quite inexplicable joy, stimulated by some trivial incident like the sudden melody of a blackbird singing in the rain, or the sight of the first primrose in a wood, or a piece of music which one hears for the first time—in this life—and yet feels through "shadowy recollections," one has always known! [30]

So, though,

> *Our birth is but a sleep and a forgetting! . . .*
> *Though inland far we be,*
> *Our souls have sight of that immortal sea*
> *Which brought us hither.*[31]

[29] At the same time, living people can be found who claim to remember an earlier life. See *The Evidence for Survival From Claimed Memories of Former Incarnations,* Ian Stevenson, M.D., Chairman of the Department of Neurology and Psychiatry, School of Medcine, University of Virginia, U.S.A., published by M. C. Peto, 16 Kingswood Road, Tadworth, Surrey.

[30] Some research has been done with the tunes very young children hum to themselves. They have sometimes been found to be tunes from the masterpieces of great composers which the babies could not possibly have heard before. Do we love them because we knew them at happy moments in earlier lives? On the other hand, Dr. Guirdham in *The Nature of Healing,* p. 93 (George Allen and Unwin, 1964) ascribes certain symptoms to an earlier life of the patient. Edgar Cayce of Kentucky claimed to trace the origin of many illnesses to earlier lives and, in trance, to have access to these facts. See *Venture Inward,* Hugh Lynn Cayce (Harpers, 1964).

[31] Wordsworth's "Ode on the Intimations of Immortality from Recollections of Early Childhood," written in 1802-6.

2. A second objection seems to have more point. It runs thus: "But I count on meeting my dear ones again after death." "Supposing," writes a friend of mine, "that my dear one has gone back to be an Italian organ grinder and I am robbed of the joys of reunion." More seriously a friend writes, "Didn't Christ promise to be with the dying thief that same day in Paradise? Supposing the thief was reincarnate in some other body."

Christ did thus speak and the words are among the most precious in the world. For me they take away all fear of not meeting my loved ones again. But no one in all the literature of reincarnation suggests that it follows the earth-life at once. Much has to be learned on a different plane first. It may be, however, that—counting in earth time—after a hundred or a thousand years or so, the soul may feel that the only way to progress—a progress for which he increasingly hungers—is to do what I have called "taking again the exams that he failed on earth." Joan Grant, whose books I recommend as fascinating, particularly her autobiography called *Time Out of Mind*, puts five thousand years between her two incarnations. Dr. Alexander Cannon, in his book, *Powers That Be*, speaks of an average interval of a thousand earth-years between each earth-life, during which interval astral life is lived on other planets.[32]

3. A third objection is, to my mind, not nearly as cogent as it can be made to sound. "But," says the objector, "I should lose my identity in a number of incarnations."

I don't think you will, any more than you have lost it already half a dozen times. You are William Tompkins, let us suppose. All right. You are the little, runny-nosed Willie Tompkins who got punished for being late at school. Do you want to keep your identity with him? You are the Will Tomp-

---

[32] It should not be forgotten that the references in Hindu Scriptures to constant births and deaths often refer to this life. A. K. Coomaraswamy says, "Man dies and is reborn daily and hourly in this present life." See *Eastern Religions and Western Thought.*

kins who wrote those wet verses and slipped them into the hand of that girl of sixteen with blonde plaits. Do you want to assert your identity with him? You are the William Tompkins who got sacked for being unable to account for money received on behalf of the firm. Do you feel robbed if he passes out of your sense of identity? You are W. Tompkins, with rheumatic joints and poor hearing and peering sight, whose body is now a nuisance. Try this experiment: Say "William Tompkins, William Tompkins, William Tompkins" over to yourself aloud a hundred times. Imagine a hundred thousand angels all round you doing the same thing. All heaven chanting "William Tompkins!" Is it really important that the whole personality of Tompkins should go on for a hundred, a thousand, ten thousand, a hundred thousand years? Still William Tompkins . . . !

An actor in his lifetime plays many parts and wears many costumes. I don't want to be "identified" with one part, let alone one costume called "my present body." I am a very different person—in body, mind and spirit—from the man I was a score of years ago. I want to be the player who has been made a better actor by every part that he has played, and I want the *play* to be a success, not just my acting, and life is God's play, and—in parentheses—no one can wisely judge a play by one act. Surely William Tompkins living at 18 Slugger Row, Wigan, is only a temporary expression of an immortal soul able to be expressed in other incarnations. The Buddhists, I think, would say that the same *person* is not reborn, but that there is a river of consciousness, and that our present life is but a reach of the river.

Our true identity will not be lost, the pure gold of the ego will be maintained, purified, please God, and strengthened. But why this emphasis on separateness? I have a hunch—and it can only be that—that we may lose our separateness in a new context of closer relationship; glad to be nameless members of a team.

I don't want to be one note sounding on alone. What a

315

nauseating thought. If I could be one note in a glorious symphony, would it not be well for separateness to be lost in symphony?

And, to use the favorite figure of the Buddhist, would it really matter if I were lost like a drop of water in the ocean, if I could be one shining particle in some glorious wave that broke in utter splendor and in perfect beauty on the shores of an eternal sea?

CHAPTER XV

HEAVEN AND GOAL

"I have been a foolish, greedy and ignorant man;
  Yet I have had my time beneath the sun and stars;
  I have known the returning strength and sweetness of the seasons,
  Blossom on the branch and the ripening of fruit,
  The deep rest of the grass, the salt of the sea,
  The frozen ecstasy of mountains.
  The earth is nobler than the world we have built upon it;
  The earth is long-suffering, solid, fruitful;
  The world still shifting, dark, half-evil.
  But what have I done that I should have a better world,
  Even though there is in me something that will not rest
  Until it sees Paradise . . . ?"

Johnson in *Johnson over Jordan*
J. B. Priestley

XV

HEAVEN AND GOAL

SOME years ago I was the guest of a layman in the North of England whose office, if not name, would be known to every reader, so that I will not mention either. After a meeting at which I had spoken, followed by a reception at his lovely home, he asked me if I was tired. When I gave him the expected negative, he placed me in a comfortable chair in his library and told me one of the most remarkable stories I have ever heard, but without calling a good man a liar, or self-deceived, or imaginative to the point of delusion, I cannot rebut his testimony.

He said that on coming into that very room late one evening, he found a man sitting in the chair I occupied who greeted him with, "Don't be alarmed! You don't know me or I you, but I know you have steady nerves and an honest mind, and I want to use you to get some ideas across and I don't know how else to do it." Seeing the astonished look on my host's face the visitor went on, "You see, I am dead, but I want to say some things to you which will remove the fear of death from any who read your report of what I am going to tell you. Let me start at the beginning. Last week I was knocked down by a bus here in X and instantly killed. *But I did not know I was dead.*[1] So I went—as I thought in the

[1] The relevant literature shows that this is a common experience of those who meet a sudden and violent death. Cf. repeated sentences in W. Tudor Pole's, *The Silent Road;* e.g. "My friend had been drowned, but evidently was quite unaware of the fact" (p. 27). "He was standing in the road outside his own gate trying to get in. He still had no idea that he was dead . . ." (p. 28).

same body—to my office as usual. There I found my partner anxiously looking at his watch and saying to the typist, 'I can't think what has happened to Mr. ———' (meaning me), 'he is never late.' Hearing this, I said, 'Don't be silly, I'm here beside you.' He made no reply but repeated, 'I hope nothing has happened to him.' Whereupon I again said, 'What's the matter with you, William? Can't you see I'm here with you?' But again my partner made no reply and seemed entirely oblivious of my presence. At this point, someone I did not know appeared, having apparently glided through the door, and spoke to me. He said, 'Your trouble my friend is that you are dead and you don't know it. I'm dead too and I'll look after you.' Whereupon he took my arm and we seemed to float right through the door. I never saw my office again. I found myself absurdly happy; happier than I have ever been in my life, and I said to my new friend, 'Is this heaven?' 'Well,' he said, 'unless your mental attitude alters, it is happy enough, but there will be some experiences you will call hell, or at least purgatory. We are on a journey my friend. We are on a journey!' " [2]

From time to time my northern host entertained his visitor in his library and wrote out the substance of the interviews. About that I will say no more now. [3]

---

[2] Cf. W. Tudor Pole, *The Silent Road*, pp. 10-11, "During our conversation I happened to look at his hat and, to my surprise, found that I could see the mirror through it. Only then did it dawn on me that my visitor was not bodily present in the accepted meaning of the term."

[3] Skeptics may like to know that the *Daily Telegraph* of August 28, 1964, printed the first hand experience of a leading land agent who went down to the school last half-term to see his sons. I quote:

"While near his own old room in the Timbralls he took the opportunity to see if it had changed after two decades.

"He found things much the same and was soon in deep, reminiscent conversation with his former Dame. Even in her dress the woman who cared for the well-being and food of the boys had not changed at all. With natural pleasure he related the events to his wife, who was waiting for him.

"Recently he dropped in to see his former house master, now curator of a National Trust house, and recounted this meeting. 'Maybe,' said his old tutor, 'but Mrs. ——— died three years ago.' "

Several things of immense interest emerge for me. Again and again the literature of the subject offers us well-authenticated accounts of those who, after a sudden and violent death, continue to function on our plane of being. They are able to produce on our consciousness the same impression which they made when alive in our world, and they themselves are slow to realize that they are what we call "dead." One soldier killed in battle communicated thus: "We went over the top. . . . It was twenty minutes before I realised that I had 'passed over.' During that time, although my physical body was lying on the field, I went on with the attacking party, *thinking I was still alive*. I then found that those around me could not see me and I went back and saw my body, lying dead." [4] To take another example of a soldier killed in battle: "I went out suddenly, in full strength, consequently it did not take long for me to awaken. . . . The shock was terrible. . . . I was at home in my father's house as much as ever I was, I heard every word uttered, saw the sadness, and, as it were, lived it. But *I could not make myself known*." [5]

Another point which emerges is that we have yet more evidence that the immediate after-death feeling is one of intense joy and freedom. [6]

Among the many messages from the other side which I regard as genuine are those purporting to come from the late F. W. H. Myers, one of the founders of the Society for Psychical Research and author of the big two-volume posthumous work, *Human Personality and Its Survival of Bodily Death*, [7] author also of the famous poem, "St. Paul." Through the well-known medium Mrs. Holland, he communicated this message after his death, "If it were possible for the soul to die back into earth again, I should die from sheer yearning

---

[4] Lilian Walbrook, *The Case of Lester Coltman*, p. xiv (Hutchinson, 1924).

[5] Dr. Hereward Carrington, *Psychical Phenomena and the War*, p. 23 (T. W. Laurie, 1918).

I owe both these illustrations to Dr. Crookall. *Op. cit.* pp. 26-27.

[6] See pp. 256 ff. [7] University Books, 1903.

to reach you, to tell you that all we imagined is not half wonderful enough for the truth." Ambrose Pratt, a close friend of my friend, Dr. Raynor Johnson, speaking through the dependable mediumship of our mutual friend, Miss Geraldine Cummins, said, "I was called from fairer realms than you can ever possibly imagine or even faintly conceive so long as you are in the flesh." [8] This seems the unanimous testimony of all who pass over if the authenticity of their messages is accepted.

A further point is that immediately after death we seem to possess a body very much like the fleshly one, except that it can easily move wherever thought directs it, and it can pass through what we call solid objects as Christ's resurrection body did. "The formulation of a clear wish to be in another place is itself sufficient to move the astral body with great rapidity." [9] This makes it hard for us at first to realize that we are dead, and of course it is just the kind of merciful provision we should expect to be made for us, lest the shock of passing from one mode of being to another at death be terrifying, as indeed, birth would have been if the imagination had developed enough for us to realize what was happening.

Many writers in this field tell us that interpenetrating our earthly body in this life is an "etheric" one which is very like it. Some think that in deep sleep we leave the first and adventure in the second. At death it does seem likely that we leave the earthly body finally, and manifest our presence and express ourselves in its etheric counterpart. "I postulate," said Dr. Raynor Johnson, "a psychic aether or 'substance' which partakes of some of the qualities of matter, such as localisation in space and retention of form), and which is yet capable of sustaining thought-images and emotions, something in short which is a bridge between matter and mind. . . . There is an aetheric duplicate of every material object. . . . An

[8] Raynor Johnson, *The Light and the Gate,* pp. 71-160 (Hodder and Stoughton, 1964).
[9] Raynor Johnson, in *A Religious Outlook for Modern Man,* p. 174 (Hodder and Stoughton, 1963). See the whole chapter entitled, "What is it like after death?" pp. 164-77.

aetheric world of this sort with its own phenomena and laws seems to me something we may be driven to recognise. Professor H. H. Price postulates it to account for hauntings and apparitions." [10]

A friend of my own, when very ill, although apparently attached to her body by something in the nature of a cord, seemed to hover above it and watch it with an almost disinterested detachment. She saw her husband come into the bedroom, bend over her, gently shake her shoulder and then rush to the telephone on a bedside table to summon the doctor. She watched the doctor prepare to give her an injection and as the latter began to take effect she seemed to be drawn back into her own physical body with something of reluctance, and shortly afterwards she opened her eyes and told the doctor and nurse that she had watched them at work. They pooh-poohed this and told her that since she had been unconscious and had nearly died, she must have been dreaming, but she was able to tell them in detail all they had done, where they had stood, and even what her husband had said to the doctor on the telephone.

Many occurrences of this kind have been reported and are recounted in the *Journal of the Society for Psychical Research* and in other literature.[11] Dr. Raynor Johnson quotes a number in his book, *The Imprisoned Splendour*.[12] With the editor's permission I quote a letter which appeared in *The Sunday Times*.[13]

"During the war, in the Western Desert, I was knocked unconscious by bomb blast and had the peculiar sensation of being out of my body, viewing the scene from a point about twenty feet above the ground. I could see and hear everything that went on. I could hear the aircraft as it came in on another

---

[10] Raynor Johnson, in *The Imprisoned Splendour*, p. 138; cf. p. 213.
[11] See Dr. Robert Crookall, *The Supreme Adventure*, pp. 14-30 (James Clarke, 1960).
[12] Pp. 218 ff.   [13] March 25, 1962

attack and the voices of my companions. I could see the dust clearing away from the explosion that had knocked me unconscious and my own body lying there on the gravel.

"The thing that still impresses me, although it may be just the result of a vivid imagination, was that I was still attached to my body by a cord, and I sensed that if that cord broke I would not be able to get back to my body and I would be dead. I remember the thought. 'I've got to get back,' and then the next thing I recall was that I was back in my body, consciously trying to force my eyes open. An odd thing was that although I could hear perfectly while I was unconscious and could tell my comrades what they had said during that period,[14] when I recovered consciousness I was stone deaf and remained so for two weeks afterwards. My hearing is still imperfect.

"This experience has convinced me that there is a part of a person that survives after death, for, even though I was not dead, the thinking part of me had succeeded in leaving my body, and I am certain that when I do eventually die, or rather, when my body dies, part of me will carry on—to where and to do what, I just don't know.

                                        Robert Andrew Hall."

These instances go to suggest that at death we may use for self-expression an etheric body not normally seen by others still living in the flesh, but in which we feel at home—so at home that we do not always realize that we are dead, or free from the flesh—and in which we are, for some hours at least, near the scene of our passing. "We must emphasise," says Dr. Raynor Johnson, "that the next world, or astral world, which the mind discerns after death, is quite as real to souls using astral senses, as the physical world is to souls using

---

[14] Note the point that the brain can "hear" without the ears being engaged, and we can "see"—or receive in the brain the impression of seeing —without the eyes being engaged.

physical senses. We must dismiss the idea that the after-death state is something vague and formless." [15]

It was reported that after his death President Roosevelt communicated through a medium that he had attended his own funeral. He commented on the unusual dress of one of the senators, a detail which he could not otherwise have known and which the medium did not know, and claimed that only his little dog had recognized him, and that the dog, on doing so, had rolled over on its back waiting to be tickled, and this, Roosevelt said, he had done. Strangely enough, one of the mourners at the funeral, who knew nothing, of course, of this communication, which was made later, said that he noticed Roosevelt's dog suddenly roll on its back as if someone were tickling it. It must be fun going to one's own funeral and listening to what is said, but the evidence would seem to be that quite soon after death one moves on into other experiences of joy, reunion and progress, and that it is a matter of some difficulty then to communicate sensibly with those still in a physical body.

Certainly there can be nothing in the incident, and often accident, of death which makes one ready for the final bliss of the end of the journey. We say and sing that our loved ones are "with God," but they always have been. God does not dwell more fully in heaven than on earth, not even in the "highest heaven." What alters is our capacity to know, love, appreciate and indwell God. We go on where we left off here into a world which may at first give us the illusion of solidity, but then let us remember that the solidity of this world is also illusion. This seemingly solid desk at which I sit is a whole universe of whirling electrons. "The large majority of human beings, when they die, are dominated by the conception that substance is reality. . . . Tom Jones, who represents the unthinking man in the street, wants to smoke and to play golf, so he smokes and plays golf. *But he is merely dreaming all the*

[15] Raynor Johnson, *A Religious Outlook for Modern Man*, p. 169 (Hodder and Stoughton, 1963).

time, or rather, living within the fantasy created by his strongest desires on earth. After a time . . . he longs for a new life. He is prepared to make the leap in evolution and this cloudy dream vanishes." [16]

Most thoughtful people have by now realized that the golden streets and the harps, the white robes and the eternal music are symbols we can discard. May we be delivered from a heaven that is anything like an endless church service, and if I and some of my friends are going to sing in the heavenly choir it will not be heaven for anyone!

Yet, though we throw over what may be felt to be outworn symbols, we ourselves can only speculate and use language which is also, of necessity, symbolic. Some things, however, seem certain.

1. It seems clear that the soul experiences a deeper quality of *joy* than the earth-life affords. John's symbolic language, just referred to, was meant to suggest joy. The word on Christ's lips when he came back from the dead was *"Chaireté,"* translated "All Hail!", but better, "Rejoice!" [17] This word has always seemed to me a report as well as a greeting. It is significant that in the literature of what is loosely called "spiritualism" one hardly ever gets a message that would seem to deny the happiness of the liberated spirit. The mystical experiences of all sorts and conditions of men, from the "ordinary man" to the saint, seem to be shot through and through with joy. C. S. Lewis' emphasis in his book, *Surprised by Joy,* is typical of all mystical writing, and he takes this joy to be a true foretaste of what lies beyond death. When C. F. Andrews tried to describe such an experience he said, "A veil seemed to be lifted from my eyes . . . waves of joy and beauty were bursting and breaking on all sides." A man who fell on to some rocks from a great height and was thought to be dying said later, "When my body finally

[16] Geraldine Cummins, *The Road to Immortality,* p. 49 (Aquarian Press, 1955).
[17] Matthew 28:9.

bounded against the rocks . . . I became unconscious without experiencing any pain whatever. . . . The moments when I stood on the brink of this life were the happiest I ever experienced." [18] All who report nearness to dying bear the same testimony.

2. A second promise, sure to be fulfilled in the after-life, must be that of fellowship. Those who really love will be drawn to one another even though their spiritual and mental achievements and stature may be very different. Jesus promised to be with a dying revolutionary with whom he could have had little in common. At the same time, a merely conventional relationship, even though it be of husband and wife, surely cannot force people to be together. Most of us, if we are honest, would rather find fellowship with close friends than with difficult relatives. For myself, I would rather spend eternity with a horse I knew in the desert of Mesopotamia than with a church official I knew in England! Indeed, if we have truly loved an animal we may have endowed it with survival power. Everything that can be said here is bound to be speculative. We do not know why the animal creation exists, or what purpose its creation achieves, but within the so-called group-soul the beloved animal may continue to exist, awaiting its redemption, or perhaps its reincarnation into some higher expression of life—perhaps as part of its owner's life.

Wrapped up in the thought of fellowship is that of humor. The power to worship, to use language, to be conscious of oneself, and to laugh, are the four great abilities which separate man from the animals and show his divine nature. Here is the image of God. Joy and fellowship can hardly exist without laughter. God is revealed in Christ, and he again and again resorted to humor. God, who presumably created the playfulness of kittens and puppies, must himself rejoice when man uses this God-given faculty. Recently, when a man died

[18] Dr. H. Carrington and J. R. Meader in *Death, Its Causes and Phenomena*, p. 315 (Rider and Co., Ltd., 1911).

who always brought laughter to people's faces wherever he went, one mourner said to another, "There will be some fun somewhere in Heaven tonight!" I do not suggest a heaven in which we gather, as it were, in corners, and tell each other funny stories! But our humor here may well be a foretaste of the mirth and gaiety of the life above.

3. Service to others I regard as fundamental in any happy human life. Surely where there is fellowship we must be able to serve and encourage one another. Service to one another is God's highest service and "His servants shall do His service." [19] Further, we may speculate that we shall also be able to minister to those we leave behind. As Dr. Raynor Johnson says: "Thought has the freedom of all levels, so that there may remain a constant awareness of the ideas and doings of souls in the flesh with whom one has some real affinity." [20] The last words one of my sisters spoke to me as she lay dying were, "I am sure I shall be allowed to help you from the other side." All I can say is that *someone* unseen has continually helped me, not least when I have been trying to write a letter, an article, a sermon or a book to help others. To what extent a sermon is partly made on the "other side" it is impossible to say. And why is one so consciously "guided" at times to make a visit, to write a letter or to send a book? Who sent that woman last night fifty miles to ask me a question the answer to which put her mind at rest? Why did that particular man make that particular journey to attend that particular service at which, all unknown to him beforehand, his particular problem was dealt with?

I must not enlarge on this, but again and again I have suddenly written down the name of one of my people and felt I *had* to visit his home, only to find that he was in some special need. Again and again, while preaching, I have altered the sermon or an illustration in it, only to find that the alteration was relevant to the need of a previously unknown listener.

[19] Revelation 22:3   [20] *Op. cit.*, p. 175

My own solution of the mystery is that unknown friends in the unseen, who see "with larger, other eyes than ours," convey to one the need they see.

> *Free from the fret of mortal years,*
> *And knowing now Thy perfect will,*
> *With quickened sense and heightened joy*
> *They serve Thee still.*
>
> *O fuller, sweeter is that life,*
> *And larger, ampler is the air:*
> *Eye cannot see nor heart conceive*
> *The glory there;*
>
> *Nor know to what high purpose Thou*
> *Dost yet employ their ripened powers,*
> *Nor how at Thy behest they touch*
> *This life of ours.*[21]

Heaven, then, is the goal which makes this life meaningful. We can ignore those who scorn such an idea and pretend that it is unworthy to have as one's motive what has been called "pie in the sky when you die." For one thing, I have never appreciated this scorn in regard to rewards. It seems a silly affectation to me. Says C. S. Lewis, "We are afraid that heaven is a bribe, and that if we make it our goal we shall no longer be disinterested. It is not so. Heaven offers nothing that a mercenary soul can desire. It is safe to tell the pure in heart that they shall see God, for only the pure in heart want to. There are rewards that do not sully motives." [22] Jesus never seemed to scorn rewards. The word seems often to have been on his lips. "Great is your reward in heaven," [23] seems an authentic word of his, and so does "he shall in no wise lose his reward." [24] One can hardly imagine a greater reward than

---

[21] William Charter Piggot (Methodist Hymn Book, 657).

[22] C. S. Lewis, *The Problem of Pain*, p. 145 (Macmillan, 1962).

[23] Matthew 5:12

[24] Matthew 10:42; Luke 6:35

to hear his voice say, "Well done, thou good and faithful servant." [25] As Austin Farrer put the matter in one neat sentence: "Heaven is not a cash payment for walking with God; it is where the road goes." [26] Should we scorn the lover and say, "He's always thinking of marriage"? That's where the road goes and what a rich reward of his wooing it becomes! We do not scorn the traveler because he longs to see the lights of home. It does not mean that the journey has been valueless. It does mean that the journey is meaningful.

It is just that element of meaningfulness which so many lives need and do not possess. On a long sea journey round the world I once meditated on what would happen if the captain, one day, in the middle of the Pacific Ocean, summoned us all to the saloon and said something like this: "There is plenty of food on board. Life will proceed as before. Meals will be served, games played, dances arranged, concerts provided, but I have decided not to make for a port. We shall just cruise round and round in the ocean until our fuel is exhausted and then I shall sink the ship."

Mark this. The next few days would *appear* just the same as those which preceded them. Only one thing would be different. The Captain's speech would have snatched from every mind the concept of purpose, meaning and goal. And, in my opinion, very soon afterwards, on a dark night, first one and then another passenger would jump overboard. The mind hates meaninglessness.

The parable may seem absurd, but the lives of some I know who believe in no hereafter, no God and no meaning in life, seem to fit it. The high rate of suicide of fit people would, I think, be lowered, as would the number of cases of mental illness—which is so often motivated by a desire to escape what seems like a meaningless existence—if a sense of purpose gathered life's events into a unity. What a difference there is between the beads on a beautiful necklace on a woman's throat, and those same beads, their connecting thread broken, lying, unrelated to one another, on the bedroom floor. When worn as a necklace, each bead, in itself small and insignificant, has a place and a significance. A single thread running through each holds the whole necklace together in a unity of beauty. Similarly no deed or event, trifling or tragic, lacks significance for him who believes in the purposefulness of God, not determining each detail, but running through every part and every event of his life.

To watch some lives closely is almost to be drawn into the dull apathy or the frenzied pleasure-seeking of those who live them. Thousands of people get up reluctantly, eat cornflakes and bacon, catch a bus, sit at an office desk, go out to lunch, drink a cup of coffee, catch the bus or the train home, eat a meal, yawn over the evening paper, watch television and go to bed, and the same tomorrow, and tomorrow and tomorrow. . . . Even weekends fall into a dull routine of their own, and a wet fortnight at Margate, during an English miscalled "summer," crowns a dull year! Who can wonder that youth rebels and cries out for life, and finds it in exciting and often unsatisfactory ways?

Listen to Aldous Huxley writing in *Ends and Means* about meaninglessness.[27] "The nature of things seems to have so constituted the human mind that it is extremely reluctant to accept such a conclusion [that life is meaningless] except under the pressure of desire or self-interest. Furthermore, those who . . . accept the doctrine of absolute meaninglessness tend in a short time to become so much dissatisfied with their philosophy . . . that they will exchange it for any dogma, however manifestly nonsensical, which restores meaning if only to a part of the universe."

What then is the meaning of life? Why are we here? These are the questions asked again and again whenever people can ask religious questions. My own answer is that life is a school

[27] P. 275 (Chatto and Windus, 1938).

ordained by God to train us, so that we may finally realize all our highest possibilities and attain at last the bliss of full communion with him and a sharing of his divine life. One of the oldest promises in the Bible is "Ye shall be as gods." [28] And Browning describes man as, "a god tho' in the germ." [29] Jung writes, "Like every other being, I am a splinter of the infinite deity." [30]

Life on this earth seems to me to be the lowest form in this school. In it we may rise to the top of the form or sink to the bottom. Those at the top are qualifying themselves for the next class. Those at the bottom may not qualify—as one remembers at school—to go up at all, but may have to come back (reincarnation) and take some of the exams again.

During this hard schooling of the earth-life, we all have to learn to be masters of the body, to serve other people, to turn our pain and sorrow and frustration into spiritual asset, to conquer bitterness and apathy, to accept forgiveness, not wallowing in guilt and self-despising, and to move onward and upward having learned from our sins and mistakes.

Or, we may liken life to a journey, the end of which we cannot see, and we have to learn how to be good travelers, to cooperate with fellow travelers, and learn how to cope with the hills and the mists, using all the aids offered, and especially the companionship of the One who promised to travel with us.

It is not the fashion now to sing hymns like the one containing the lines

> *I'm but a stranger here,*
> *Heaven is my home*

and certainly earth is not to me "a desert drear"! It is a very jolly place and I don't want to leave it. But everybody has to leave it, and for myself, as I get older, though still liable at

---

[28] Genesis 3:5 (RSV margin).
[29] "Rabbi Ben Ezra," xiii.
[30] *Memories, Dreams, Reflections,* p. 17 (Collins, 1963).

times to be frightened of the pain and dreary invalidism that may lie between me and the next phase, I rejoice secretly at the thrill of waking up in a new world without a body that aches or hurts somewhere, and without creaking muscles, stiff joints and hardened arteries!

Heaven can be very attractive to the elderly even though they know it is only the beginning of another journey. Of the end of that journey no man may even guess. And he who decides what he even *wants*—apart from asking what God has in store—only expresses his own immaturity as does the child who at seven decides he will be an engine-driver, but at seventeen is grateful that his father does not hold him to that choice. Many Christians will wonder whether they will be "with Christ." Paul could not decide whether he was really destined to serve his Master on earth or in heaven, "having," so he says, "the desire to depart and be with Christ, for it is very far better." [81] In a true sense we believe that Christ is with us while we are sojourners here on earth, and in this sense we shall still be with him and he with us in heaven. Having shed an earthly body which—if one may use the word —blocked the full revelation of his blazing majesty and power, it may be that the soul, at the beginning of the next life, could not bear his unmediated presence, and to enjoy the latter may demand from us aeons of "schooling." To see him in unmediated glory may well be an aspect of the goal of human life, but I think we shall have to be like him to see him as he is. Only the pure in heart may see God, and when we do see him it must surely be forever, and who among us is ready at death for that?

It is interesting in this connection that Sir Oliver Lodge, who lost his son, Raymond, in the First World War, asked him, through the medium, Mrs. Kennedy, "Raymond have you been let to see Christ?" The answer is interesting, "Father, I shall see him presently. It is not time yet. I am not

[81] Philippians 1:23.

ready. But I know he lives and I know he comes here. All the sad ones see him if no one else can help them ... I am not expecting to see him yet, father; I shall love to when it's time." [32]

On another occasion, Raymond tells them in a séance that he has been allowed to enter a higher sphere. He says: "I feel exalted, purified, lifted up. I was kneeling. I couldn't stand up. I wanted to kneel. Mother, I thrilled from head to foot. He didn't come near me and I did not feel I wanted to go near him. Didn't feel I ought. ... I've asked if Christ will go and be seen by everybody, but was told 'not quite in the same sense as you saw him.' I was told Christ was always in spirit on earth. People think he is a Spirit walking about in a particular place. Christ is everywhere, but not as a personality. There is a Christ and he lives on a higher plane, and that is the one I was permitted to see. ... I am proud to do his work, no matter what it is." [33]

On a third occasion when the famous Mrs. Leonard was the medium, Sir Oliver Lodge asked, "Have you ever seen that Person otherwise than at that time?" "No, I haven't seen him except as I told you; he says, father, that he doesn't come and mingle freely here, there, and everywhere. I mean, not in that sense; but we are always conscious and we feel him. We are conscious of his presence." [34]

There I think we must leave the matter. To summarize, basing my summary on religious truth and what seems to me the authentic findings of psychical research,[35] I believe that for everyone the actual experience of dying is one of great happiness, of immediate reunion with loved ones on the other side, and of tender, welcoming care from ministering spirits.

[32] Sir Oliver Lodge, *Raymond*, p. 207 (Methuen, 11th edition, 1919).
[33] *Ibid.*, pp. 231-32.
[34] *Ibid.*, p. 260.
[35] I would warmly recommend to those interested, the splendid summary of serious psychic research findings to be found in *The Supreme Adventure*, by Dr. Robert Crookall, Ph.D., D.Sc. (James Clarke, 1960).

Indeed, loved ones seem to attend the dying before death happens. Their presence has often been commented on.[36]

The body in which we manifest ourselves immediately after death will I think *appear to us* to be still material, and, indeed, may consist of highly attenuated matter on a different scale of vibration. There may be a form of "matter" which lies between the physical as we know it and the psychical. This may account for the difficulty some newly-dead people have of realizing that they are what we call "dead" (see p. 323). They wonder why the living do not respond when they speak, and yet they find they can pass through closed doors. One communicator tells how "for fun" he rushed at a door only to find he could pass right through it.[37]

The immediate life which follows death seems to be full of happiness and a sense of freedom and joy. It is what our Lord called "Paradise," though it can be marred for the so-called "dead" if those who remain on the earth-plane grieve too much. Sir Oliver Lodge's dead son, Raymond, said to his mother, through the celebrated medium Mrs. Leonard, "Don't grieve so much mother, you hurt me horribly." A boy communicator said, "I am bound to earth by the sorrow of my parents." A little girl who had died pleaded through a medium, "Oh, Mummie, don't cry so. It makes me so unhappy." [38]

[36] See Chapter XII, especially pp. 256 ff. Good evidence of this was given me by a ward sister who was nursing a dying woman in a London hospital. News of the suicide of her son was kept from the patient. One evening, however, the patient said, "Michael has been to see me this evening." Michael was the son who had taken his life, though the patient died in ignorance of this fact.

[37] "Suddenly I remembered what you said, that spirits can go through matter. I said 'Here goes,' and ran at the door—and passed right through it. I tried it two or three times. . . . I shall be at the funeral tomorrow. I am still mixed up with the earth." Alice Gilbert, *Philip in Two Worlds*, p. 89 (Andrew Dakers, 1948). The spirit takes time to leave the body and thus it is wise to leave a few days before cremation, otherwise shock is complained of.

[38] Crookall, *op. cit.*, pp. 155 ff. Raymond promised to be present at the family Christmas party but added, "No sadness, . . . Keep jolly or it hurts me horribly," *Raymond*, p. 205.

Following this immediate happy post-mortem experience there would seem to be a period of spiritual stock-taking. The soul meditates on its past life, all of which is now accessible in present consciousness, and we could call this the period of judgment, though it is a judgment of the soul by itself in the light of re-assessed values. A Methodist minister of great psychic insight, whom I knew, purporting to be in communication with his deceased father and sister, wrote that his dead father said, "No other person could be so just a judge as we ourselves can be when facing the truth. For many it is a terrible hour. . . . No torture which another can inflict is so terrible as the remorse which one's own best self inflicts when enlightenment comes. There is an instinctive feeling that one must work it out. . . . And this way of recovery is in helping others who have exactly similar limitations, difficulties or vices." [39] Following this may be a time of purgatory or self-discipline, since the soul suffers through its inescapable awareness of suffering caused to others in the earth life. Presumably the soul cannot find complete freedom unless and until it can receive the forgiveness of any who have been wronged, or made by it to suffer, in the earth-life.

Gradually it would seem as though the spiritual "body" or means of manifestation and communion with others loses anything akin to matter as we know it here, and becomes more spiritual and less in touch with the earth-life. It may be as different as the life of the butterfly is different from that of the caterpillar crawling on the grimy earth, or as the pure white lotus lily, flashing in the sunshine, is different from life in the slimy depths of a stagnant pool where it had its root-beginning. The means of manifestation of the soul would seem to be dependent on, and appropriate to, the soul's degree of progress. Some souls may return in a reincarnation. Some may have to. Some may want to. Some may not need or want to. Some, from the very heights of heaven, may be willing to

[39] Rev. C. Drayton Thomas, *Beyond Life's Sunset*, pp. 48 and 52 (Psychic Press, 2nd edition, 1949).

336

visit some inhabited planet and wear the "flesh" of those whom he makes his brothers in order to help and guide them. Perhaps we can account for some of the world's great teachers —and even Christ himself—by means of this speculation.

> *Ah, did not He the heavenly throne*
> *A little thing esteem,*
> *And not unworthy for my sake*
> *A mortal body deem? . . .*
> *So Love itself in human form*
> *For love of me He came . . .*[40]

If the soul continually makes the right choices, it surely must make progress, and it may be a disservice to try to get into communication with an advancing spirit, though a word-less communion is precious to many and may do no harm.

> *I watch thee from the quiet shore;*
> *Thy spirit up to mine can reach;*
> *But in dear words of human speech*
> *We two communicate no more.*[41]

At the same time I was impressed by the true story told to my wife by a reliable friend who lost his wife by death and in his great grief sought a message from her by attending a séance. The man had spent much time in seeking suitable accommodation, for he just could not bear to stay in the home in which they had been so happy together, and further, he could get no one suitable to look after him. At the séance his wife purported to give him this incomprehensible message: "You will be happy in the cat and fiddle room." The man, much mystified, went from one hotel to another, seeking accommodation, and then, at a hotel at which I myself have stayed, the proprietor said to him, "We have only one room left and you can have that. We call it the cat and fiddle

---

[40] Naryan Vaman Tilak, tr. by Nicol Macnicol.
[41] Tennyson, "In Memoriam" (lxxxiv).

room." Eagerly the man followed his host to a room bearing on the door a brass knocker in the form of a cat playing a fiddle. In that room the man settled happily, and, as far as I know, is still there. He had never before heard of such a room, or of this particular hotel, nor had he visited this town before. It is of interest to report another message which his wife purported to give him at the same séance, "Do not call me back too often," she said. So he did this only once a year on the anniversary of their wedding. It is interesting to note that the message fits in with many others which lead us to believe that it is difficult and costly for the dead to communicate with the living. "I found the earth-atmosphere *stifling*," one communicator is alleged to have said, "and I was glad to get back." [42] F. W. H. Myers, from beyond death said that he felt, in trying to communicate with the living, as though he stood behind a sheet of frosted glass which blurred sight and deadened sound, dictating to a reluctant and somewhat obtuse secretary. "A feeling of terrible impotence burdens me," he said. "I am so powerless to tell what means so much." [43]

I never advise bereaved people to attend a séance. If they are emotionally easily moved, the experience could be very disturbing, and, what is worse, there might be no message of any value, and there could be an *alleged* message that was trivial, upsetting, misleading or even hurtful. Also, the supposed message might only be a bit of telepathic mind-reading on the part of the medium, even if the latter were genuine. The whole subject must be much further explored and its laws understood by trained enquirers before it can be wise to counsel the bereaved normally to find solace at the séance. But I would not dissuade a balanced and objective seeker from doing so, because the church's answers to the bereaved are woefully disappointing and they seldom satisfy. Furthermore,

[42] *The Curtain Drawn*, p. 33 (Psychic Press Ltd., 1949). Crookall, *op. cit.*, p. 218.
[43] *Proceedings of the Society for Psychical Research*, Vol. 21, p. 208.

sometimes an authentic message seems to come through. I can witness to this from my own experience.

As for the ultimate goal of human life my mind cannot contemplate anything less than final bliss in a heaven of heavens for all souls. Though I know this could take aeons upon aeons to effect, as we reckon time, my mind cannot regard any other view as satisfactory. The nature of that final bliss is probably further beyond us than the healthy adult life of a millionaire living in a palace is beyond that of a sick baby in a slum! But Charles Wesley sang of even a "helpless worm" being redeemed, being made something else, being changed from one glory to another glory, and beyond that even the wildest speculation cannot penetrate. Here is the ecstasy of the spirit which has always eluded us and which is only very, very dimly foreshadowed in the feeling produced in us by great loving, great music, great art, great poetry or great preaching; that terrible, utterly lovely, supernatural, numinous Presence which would smash the brain if, unmediated, unshrouded and unfiltered, it invaded earthly consciousness. To be one with God, sharing in his life, all evil done away, in unspeakable and unimaginable glory, this I believe to be the final goal of every human life, a tiny part of the glory of God and the whole of the bliss of man.

CHAPTER XVI

CREDO AND COMMITMENT
(A Summary)

"Oh Christianity, Christianity,
That has grown kinder now, as in the political world
The colonial system grows kinder before it vanishes, are you
    vanishing?
Is it not time for you to vanish?
I do not think we shall be able to bear much longer the dis-
    honesty
Of clinging for comfort to beliefs we do not believe in,
For comfort, and to be comfortably free of the fear
Of diminishing good, as if truth were a convenience.
I think if we do not learn quickly, and learn to teach children
To be good without enchantment, without the help
Of beautiful painted fairy stories pretending to be true,
Then I think it will be too much for us, the dishonesty,
And, armed as we are now, we shall kill everybody,
It will be too much for us, we shall kill everybody."

Stevie Smith
("How do you see")

"I am confident that if a single ray of light reaches a man from
Christ, penetrates into his being and influences his way of living,
he is further along the road of true belief in Him than if he gave
his unreflecting assent to a multitude of orthodox propositions which
have no perceptible effect upon his conduct."

Rev. Dr. J. H. Oldham
(*Life Is Commitment*)

"God offers to every man the choice between truth and repose.
Take which you will, you can never have both."

Emerson

"What certainly is true is that there are many men who find traditional religion and spirituality completely meaningless, and that you
will find them among those who are completely committed to Christ
as well as among those who are not . . . We have reached a moment
in history when these things are at last being said openly, and when
they are said there is an almost audible gasp of relief from those whose
consciences have been wrongly burdened by the religious tradition."

Prism, September, 1962

XVI

CREDO AND COMMITMENT
(A Summary)

THIS final chapter is bound to be personal. My excuse is that I know that much that I have written in earlier chapters will be considered controversial, and I therefore want to end the book on a positive note, even if it must be merely a personal one. After spending fifty years of my life in expounding Christianity, trying feebly enough, to respond to its challenges, and to bring to its many problems such mental grasp as my limitations permit, I am quite convinced about what *I* regard as fundamentals, and having a great affection for the many lovable and splendid people who have either cut themselves off from the church or been made conscious of its disapproval, I would seek to draw them in and share my beliefs with them.

I grudge the word "fundamentalist" to those who are usually labeled with it, and I would share the word "agnostic" with those who are smeared with it. For me, the area of "fundamentals" grows smaller as I grow older, and the area of agnosticism—in which one says, "I don't know"—grows larger. But this, I think, is gain and, in a growing mind, inevitable. The speculations of men centuries ago have too often been paraded as certainties because "divine revelation" has been claimed for them. I want to keep my mind ever open to new truth from whatever quarter it may come, and I want to claim freedom to reject old ideas, however venerable and allegedly part of "revealed truth" they may be, if I cannot still

343

hold them without breaking the integrity of my mental processes. In doing this, I am aware of the reluctance one has to accept new ideas if they are presented by people one dislikes, or of whom one disapproves on other grounds. Similarly, I am aware of the temptation to accept too readily the views of someone whom I greatly admire or whose point of view is attractive, fresh and appealing. Again and again, a person with whose views I have at first violently disagreed has been the person from whom I have learned most, and conversely, a person whom I admire and love, and to whom I am attracted, has often expressed views with which I cannot agree.

Now, even though it involves repetition, let me summarize some of my own fundamental convictions without any thought of thrusting them on others, remembering the warning of A. N. Whitehead, the scientist, which holds for religion as well as science, that "the merest hint as to finality of statement is an exhibition of folly."

1. I believe in God. We are always being told that we cannot prove his existence or his non-existence. Yet the line of argument pursued earlier amounts to proof to me.[1] The universe seems, at the few points where I can breathlessly follow what is going on, to exhibit mind rather than accident, order rather than chaos. And if purpose is exhibited anywhere it must exist everywhere even when I cannot discern it. Such a Mind cannot, I hold, be denied the quality of loving, or else, unless all my values are false, I, who am the result of that Mind, am higher in the scale of values than It is, for, if I know anything, I know that love is "higher" in the scale of values than blind chance, let alone hate, cruelty or indifference. Such a Mind must be more than personal rather than less, for a person—a self-conscious center of thinking, feeling

---

[1] See pp. 78 ff. I realize, of course, that our modern difficulty is not so much establishing proof of God's existence, as providing evidence that God is relevant to the business of living. As a student said to Dr. George MacLeod, "You have proved your case up to the hilt. And *it doesn't mean a thing*." See *Only One Way Left*, p. 42 (Iona Community, 1955).

and willing—is "higher" in the scale of values than a thing. I agree that God is not *a* person in our separated sense, but, included within his infinite being, there must surely be the capacity to enter into relationships with men which they cannot call other than "personal." If I label this Mind the Absolute, or Ultimate Reality or Cosmic Reason or the Ground of Being, my words take me further from the truth, for they sound less personal than the noun, "Father," or the pronoun, "he." I cannot be in a personal relationship with a thing, and my own mystical experiences (such as that described on pp. 74 ff.), apart from the more convincing experiences of the saints, the existence of the world church, and the logic of missionary activity, point to the probability of such a relationship. I call this august Being, "Father," aware, of course, of the charge of anthropomorphism, but I am not likely to get a better word than Christ himself used.

When I meditate on this Being, a reverent agnosticism floods my mind at once. I believe he is loving, suprapersonal, everywhere available, all knowing, and finally can know no defeat of his purposes, but concerning his activities in his vast, mind-staggering universe I have no means of knowing more than a minute fraction, and whether he can be described as three in one or three million in one, who can say, and, if I may say so very reverently, what does it matter? Why must anyone or any body of men guess, and then thrust their guesses upon others for all time?

2. I also believe in the divinity of Christ, though I do not know what divinity means. All I know is that the evidence about him, the total impression that he makes on my mind from all four Gospels, from the researches of scholars and from the experiences of men and women for two thousand years, is that he stood in a special relationship with God and was indeed an incarnation of God in a fuller sense than any other known Being. Some may call him "man to the *n*th," and some "avatar." It is impressive that Jews, very strict monotheists, should speak, to him and of him, in words never used

345

The Christian Agnostic

about ordinary men, however revered, but it may be that all men will one day achieve the quality of divinity which he showed forth. So, says Browning:

> ... shall I pass, approved
> A man, for aye removed
> From the developed brute; a god though in the germ.[2]

Dr. H. R. Mackintosh wrote: "It was one of the underlying maxims of Luther that human nature has been created for participation in the life of God and *is destined to reach it* to a degree of which we can form no conception, save from the exemplary instance of Jesus Christ our Head." [3]

My mind is attracted to the idea that he may be one of a hierarchy of divine beings who, either by direct creation and endowment, or by attainment through many incarnations, or by both, have achieved what we call "divinity," for lack of any better word, and that, seeing the plight of man on earth, he volunteered to take our flesh and become our Savior. From such a hierarchy there may have proceeded other saviors on other planets, all "Sons of God."

> God may have other words for other worlds,
> But for this world, the word of God is Christ.

No one, short of information not available, can say that Christ is "the *only* begotten Son of God." One can only say "only" if one can exclude all other possibilities. There may be a "Son of God" on Mars. Further, as Dr. Geoffrey Parrinder has pointed out, "Jesus never used the title 'Son of God' about himself. . . . His own name for himself was 'Son of Man,' which identified him with the community and gave a hint of his sufferings. The New Testament also never clearly calls Jesus 'God.' It regards him as the 'Word' or 'Son of God' and 'Lord.' . . . The basis of the World Council of Churches

[2] "Rabbi ben Ezra," xiii.
[3] H. R. Mackintosh, *The Person of Jesus Christ*, p. 239. Italics mine.
346

which declares that Jesus Christ is 'God and Saviour according to the Scriptures' (the latter phrase added at the request of the Norwegian State church) is incorrect, if not heretical." [4]

At the same time I do believe that he was and is the Savior of our world, saving us, not from some vulgar hell, but from the despair which would fall upon man, if, conscious of all his sublime possibilities, he frustratedly saw no hope of attaining them.

The manner of this "saving" I have dealt with on p. 115 and in my book *A Plain Man Looks at the Cross*. It is surely by the pressure of love in all the ways open to endless loving. Certainly we can now give up the old transactional and substitutional views of salvation. As Dr. Nathaniel Micklem says, "To most men today the notion that our sins are forgiven or need to be forgiven 'by the blood of Jesus,' or by some mysterious transaction between two of the Persons of the Trinity, wherein one of them agrees to die for man and the other to forgive man's sins on the basis of this satisfaction, seems an unintelligible flight of fancy. . . . We pervert the idea of God if we allow ourselves to suppose that God did not and could not forgive sins apart from the death of Christ." [5] At the same time that death reveals the nature of God in such a way that I *want* to be forgiven and become sure that I can be.

The manner of his birth matters, in my judgment, not at all. The Virgin Birth never has been part of the essential Gospel, and Mark, Peter, Paul and "John" never even mention it. Both the genealogies of Jesus, Matthew 1:1-17, and Luke 3:23-38, as Dr. William Barclay points out,[6] trace the lineage of Jesus through Joseph and not through Mary in order to establish that Jesus was descended from David. Mary was descended from Aaron, not David. Dr. Barclay concludes,

[4] Geoffrey Parrinder, D.D., in *The Christian Debate: Light from the East*, p. 64 (Gollancz, 1964).
[5] Nathaniel Micklem, *Faith and Reason*, pp. 128, 130 (Duckworth, 1964).
[6] *The Mind of Jesus*, pp. 329-32 (Harpers, 1960).

"I do not think that we are intended to take the Virgin Birth literally" (p. 332), and Eric Ackroyd in a thoughtful article in *The Modern Churchman* writes, "If God were the begetter of Jesus in any way in which He is not the begetter of us all, then Jesus was not human, and Christianity—the religion of God-expressed-in-human-terms—falls to the ground. The creed's 'begotten not made' contains dangers no less grave than those against which it was intended to guard." [7] The fourth and latest Gospel not only describes the Jews as calling Jesus "Joseph's son," but describes Jesus' own followers as doing so.[8] One of our greatest New Testament scholars, Dr. Vincent Taylor, wrote, forty years ago, his great book, *The Historical Evidence for the Virgin Birth*. It was hailed by *The Expository Times* as "one of the best books ever written on the Virgin Birth because the author has not settled the matter before writing it." Dr. James Hastings, of the *Hastings Dictionary of the Bible*, added, "More than that, Dr. Taylor has not settled the matter when his book is written. And that is better still." [9] The historical evidence is quite inconclusive and as Sir Richard Acland said, "Every little mythological god and godling all round the Mediterranean world had to have some kind of wonder story about his birth." [10]

Many of the miracles of Jesus may be found to be explicable as our knowledge—especially in the field of psychical research—advances. Clearly, the wonderful is not evidence of the divine. But I am certain that, in ways we can only dimly perceive, he survived death, and, using an etheric body, proved his survival to his followers. In doing so, he proved the existence of a state of being not limited to matter as we know it, or to the normal perception of the senses. At enormous sacrifice this Divine Person is, I believe, committed to stand by humanity and work through it and within it until

[7] *The Modern Churchman*, April 1964, p. 163.
[8] John 6:42, "Surely this is Jesus, son of Joseph. We know His father and mother." (*New English Bible*), cf. Matthew 13:55, John 1:45.
[9] See *The Expository Times*, March 1964.
[10] Sir Richard Acland, *op. cit.*, p. 95.

it fulfills God's will. There seems to me no point in equating him with God, as Paul does,[11] since he himself did not do so. One who is "begotten of God" cannot be "on an equality with God." One is Creator, the other is created. Nor does one on an equality with God pray to God as Jesus did.

> *Oh Christianity, Christianity*
> *Why do you not answer our difficulties?*
> *If He was God He was not like us*
> *He could not lose . . .*
> *Oh what do you mean, what do you mean?*
> *You never answer our difficulties.*[12]

Incidentally, Jesus did not claim to be sinless.[13] He was so far above us in moral stature that we have no means of assessing sinlessness. It is, however, interesting to note the way in which all Christian writers *assume* sinlessness and then fit in the events of his life in ways based on that assumption. For instance, if anyone nowadays threw over the tables of tax-collectors or money-changers, we should say that he had lost his temper; if anyone else said to his friend, "Get thee behind me, Satan!" we should lift an eyebrow; if anyone else cursed a fig-tree for not having figs even though it "was not the time of figs" we should shrug our shoulders. Jesus is reported as rebuking a man for saying to him, "If thou canst! all things are possible to him that believeth" (Mark 9:23), yet he himself in the garden of Gethsemane is reported as using similar words, *"If it be possible* let this cup pass" (Matthew 26:39). For myself, such of these sayings as are not capable of explanation by the distortion of reporters simply make him the more human and lovable, but it is worth pondering that his perfection is not a fundamental of belief. It could not be,

---

[11] Philippians 2:6.

[12] "How do you see?" Stevie Smith in *The Guardian*, May 16, 1964.

[13] Luke 18:19, "Why callest thou me good? None is good, save one, that is God," or as the *New English Bible* translates, "No one is good except God alone."

for the simple reason that we cannot assess it. A man who cannot take off colored glasses cannot determine what whiteness is.

3. In regard to the Holy Spirit I retreat into agnosticism. Few Christians, whom I know, think of the Holy Spirit as a separate Person. If they did they would be worshiping two Gods, for two *persons* are two gods, and if they *equate* Christ with God, three Gods. They cannot, *in practice*, include three persons in one nature when they worship.

I suspect that the early church had to face the charge of tritheism and tried at the same time to rebut the charge and to weave into a system the references to the other Comforter in (only) the fourth Gospel (14:16). On the Trinitarian formula in Matthew 28:19-20, Dr. H. D. A. Major comments: "The Trinitarian baptismal formula, possibly introduced into the text of this Gospel because it was used in baptising in the church where this Gospel circulated, could hardly have been uttered by Jesus himself since the Christian church for many years after the death of Jesus never used that baptismal formula at all but was satisfied to baptise converts into the name of the Lord Jesus alone." And again, "The Trinitarian baptismal formula was not used until the Christian Mission had passed out beyond the boundaries of Judaism into the Pagan World." [14] So it was not necessary to believe in the Trinity in order to be a Christian! [15] Frankly, I have always thought that the doctrine of the Trinity was a bit of sheer speculation and I applaud St. Augustine's shrewd comment, "The answer 'Three Persons' is given, not that it may be spoken, but that it may not be left unspoken," and the great founder of Methodism, John Wesley, commented, "I dare not insist upon anyone using the word 'Trinity' or 'Per-

[14] See *The Mission and Message of Jesus*, p. 250 and p. 227 (Nicholson and Watson, 1937).

[15] Dr. James Pike, Episcopal Bishop of California is reported by the *New York Times* and the British *Church Times*, November 25, 1964, as saying bluntly, "The Trinity is not necessary."

son.'" The Methodist founder had a very clear idea of what was fundamental to Christian belief! When I was a theological student we were encouraged to see expressions of the Trinity in the threefold and lovely benediction which runs, "The Lord bless thee and keep thee; the Lord make His face to shine upon thee and be gracious unto thee; the Lord lift up His countenance upon thee and give thee peace." [16] The threefold, "Holy, holy, holy" in Isaiah 6 was pressed into the same argument, and of course the ancient benediction clinched the matter, "The grace of the Lord Jesus Christ and the love of God and the communion of the Holy Ghost be with you all" (2 Corinthians 13:14), though usually Paul was content with the "grace of our Lord Jesus Christ." [17]

For myself I see no need of the concept of the Holy Spirit as a third person in a Trinity. When the Psalmist cried, "Whither shall I go from Thy spirit?" [18] he had no thought of a third person. When Isaiah cried, "The spirit of the Lord is upon me," he had no thought of a third person in the Godhead, and *nor did Jesus when he quoted Isaiah.*[19] I must say I find as much truth as convinces me in the use of the word "spirit" in my favorite Psalm (139). Here, I think, a reverent agnosticism can be allowed. It cannot matter fundamentally whether one spells the word "spirit" with a small or with a capital S.

4. I believe intensely in *the* church, though as yet it has only made a beginning and a faint impact on the life of the world. A famous bishop is alleged to have said, "I believe in the Holy Catholic church and sincerely regret that it does not at present exist"! But it has had an unbroken history for two thousand years. Its missionary activity is the chapter in its history which enheartens me the most.[20] Christ surely meant

[16] Numbers 6:24-26.
[17] See Romans 16:20, 1 Corinthians 16:23, Philippians 4:23, 1 Thessalonians 5:28, 2 Thessalonians 3:18.
[18] Psalm 139:7   [19] Isaiah 61:1-2, Luke 4:18
[20] See the exciting record of changed lives and changed societies in *They Found the Church There,* by Henry P. Van Dusen (Charles Scribner's Sons, 1945).

351

the church to be the fellowship of *all* who love him and are striving to do two things: respond to life's challenges and demands in his spirit, and extend that spirit throughout the world. This would not only mean the dedication of private lives, but it would mean feeding the hungry, clothing the naked, housing the poor, killing the war-spirit, caring for the aged and the widow, healing the sick, fighting exploitation by the wealthy, ending the death penalty, understanding the young, preventing murder on the roads, and a dozen other good causes crying out for the expenditure of time, energy and money with a priority that pushes reaching the moon far down the list, and makes childish the insistence on "orthodoxy"—defined by pompous ecclesiastics.

When I realize that Albert Schweitzer and Billy Graham, Ronald Knox and General Booth, the present Pope and the present Head of the Salvation Army, the Leader of the Society of Friends and the President of the Methodist Conference, members of the one hundred and fifty Christian denominations in America and many a secret, silent Christian in remote Scottish glens where no church service is offered, in Chinese cities where Communist authority would prohibit a service, are all within THE CHURCH as Christ sees it, although their views are completely irreconcilable or reducible to the same creeds or formulae, I realize that, outside minimal fundamentals, what the individual believes, and the way he worships, should not bar him from recognition by his fellow Christians.

I regard the church on earth as a human copy of a divine original, a fellowship stretching across the world, back through time, forward to the unforeseen future and up into the unseen, where, "with angels and archangels and all the company of heaven" those who love Christ serve and adore and worship and move forward to the unimaginable unity with God which is his will.

5. I believe that the Bible is a marvelous library of writings which depict man's developing and increasingly successful

search for God, and which describe human experience in so doing. I believe the Bible to be a progressive revelation beginning with a conception of God which now is seen to be crude and imperfect, but which moves on until Christ is shown to be the best clue to God's nature which man has anywhere received.

I believe that the Biblical writers were often inspired, as when Paul wrote his great hymn of love in 1 Corinthians 13, but I believe that no view of inspiration can be held to prevent human error, prejudice or distortion. I believe the inspiration of some Psalms to be superb and of others lamentable and worthless; that the Bible would not lose anything vital if the Song of Songs were omitted and *The Pilgrim's Progress* inserted; that some passages of Browning are of far superior spiritual value than some passages of Leviticus, or of Numbers 31:15 ff. and Deuteronomy 21:10 ff., which are clear invitations to rape, or the opening of Deuteronomy 7 which is a complete denial of the spirit of Jesus let alone the lie in verse 15, "The Lord will take away from thee all sicknesses." I think William Temple's ideas of God were in many ways spiritually more profound and sensible than those in which Paul tells us, for example, that Christ will soon return, that we shall not all die but be "caught up in clouds to meet the Lord in the air" (1 Thessalonians 4:17, *New English Bible*)—a giddy and meaningless adventure—and that our relationship with God could not be put right without the sacrifice of Christ. No greater authority could be cited here than Dr. Vincent Taylor who writes: *"In no recorded saying does Jesus connect forgiveness with His death."* [21] Because of his own guilt complex Paul harps on sin and guilt interminably.

[21] Vincent Taylor, Ph.D., D.D., *Forgiveness and Reconciliation*, p. 13 (Macmillan, 1941). Dr. Taylor notes that Matthew 26:28, "unto remission of sins," is a comment added by the evangelist. It is quite unscriptural and false to sing, "He died that we might be forgiven," for the penitent was forgiven before Christ appeared (Cf. Psalm 103:3) though it would be true to say, "He died that we might *want* to be forgiven" or, "His death makes me certain that I can be forgiven."

I agree with Edward Barker, the psychotherapist, when he says, "The theological faith of St. Paul seems not to explain or clarify the concepts of Jesus but to distort them." [22] As Doctor Frederic Greeves reminds us, "As far as the Synoptic records inform us, our Lord used the noun [for 'sin'] only on six occasions and the verb only on three occasions. Yet the noun, verb and adjectival noun occur two hundred and seventy times in the New Testament, ninety-one times in St. Paul alone." [23] He adds, "Were our Scriptures limited to the Synoptic Gospels the word 'sin' would not be as dominant as it is in the Christian vocabulary." Christ's gospel breathes the very atmosphere of love, liberty, gaiety, forgiveness, joy and acceptance, and, in trying to understand God and his dealings with us, we must resolutely reject everything in the Bible which is out of harmony with the spirit and attitude of Jesus, as the total, reliable and authentic evidence about him which is available, conveys this to our minds.

6. I believe in God's providence and care. I know how hard it is for many to believe in either, but, if God is love, to deny them would be harder still. Secretly, many of us have had moments when, in our hearts, we have felt that, if we had had the power with which we credit God, we would have made a better world than this. With old Omar Khayyam we cry,

> Ah Love! could thou and I with Fate conspire
> To grasp this sorry Scheme of Things entire,
> Would we not shatter it to bits—and then
> Remould it nearer to the Heart's Desire! [24]

But should we do any better? Are there any possibilities that have not occurred to the Architect of the Universe who is also the Master of our lives?

[22] *Psychology's Impact on Christian Faith*, p. 130 (Allen and Unwin, 1963).

[23] *The Meaning of Sin*, p. 102 (Epworth Press, 1956).

[24] Omar Khayyam, ed. Fitzgerald, tr. 1:73.

Two dear friends of mine, an elderly man and his wife, were going with my sister to see Liverpool Cathedral. As they examined the exterior, the old lady said, as she poked at the stone with her umbrella, "I think they have chosen the wrong kind of stone. It's pretty, but it's too soft. It won't last." To which, with a twinkle in his eye, her husband answered, "Yes dear; but I expect the architect thought of that!"

In face even of the formidable mystery of pain we may say reverently, "The Architect of the Universe thought of that." Our very protests at natural calamity and human suffering reveal our standards. The fact that *we* care, proves that he does. A God who did not even care is no God at all, and no standards of ours can conceivably be higher than his.

When I look at the cross, I say to myself very quietly—and a strange awe and hush come upon me—"He thought of that." He knew it would cost that. And he went on because he had enough patience to believe it was worth even that. And he who hung there—he who had tried only to do his Father's will—might have railed at God and called the universe a failure, a devilish fraud, a foul obscenity. But he called God *Father*, even in the midst of his agony, and died in unbroken peace. And all the saints in their own way, and so many of them at cost of everything that human lives count dear, followed in his train.

It is impossible for us at our infant stage of development to get the suffering of the world—which has made so many men disbelieve in God—into the right proportion. I have sometimes imagined a mass meeting of toddlers with a chairman aged five. I imagine an angry discussion in which speakers prove that there cannot be love at the heart of their homes. It is alleged by one speaker after another that parents allow the existence of cats with sharp claws, furniture and dinner knives with sharp edges, paths covered with sharp gravel. How can love be said to rule when a toddler is put into a home situation carrying so many evidences that either parents don't care or they have no power to alter things? "Look at my cut knees," says the chairman, adjusting his bib. "Look at the scratch on my hand, and I only meant to play with the cat"!

In exactly this spirit, believing himself to have grown up, Richard Robinson writes, "A god who was all-powerful but left much misery in the world would not be all-benevolent. An all-benevolent god in a world containing much misery would not be an all-powerful god. A world containing a god who was both all-powerful and all-benevolent would contain no misery. Here, then, we have a mathematical proof bearing on a common religious doctrine. Anyone who is confident that he frequently comes across misery in the world may conclude with equal confidence that there is no such thing as an all-powerful and all-benevolent god. And this mathematically disposes of official Christianity." [25] Exit Christianity!! I must remind Mr. Robinson, in familiar words, that the Christian religion is "an anvil which has broken many hammers" and his so-called "mathematical proof" is inadequate to banish the faith of a believer, even when he suffers.

I believe that one day we shall view the suffering that now appalls us, as now we view the sufferings of our childhood. Then, we could see no meaning, no justification, no value in them, just as now we are often overwhelmed at the sorrow to which man is prone. As children we marveled at our parents' seeming callousness. They gave us sympathy, it is true, but they did not seem appalled and dismayed as we were. Were they neither good enough nor powerful enough to protect us from scraping our knees on the gravel paths, or falling down the stairs, or coping with the cat? Surely God has an answer and it must be bigger than our questions. Indeed, what a wonderful answer it must be if it answers, as it must, all the anguished questioning of man!

If we are patient, and try to learn his meanings, the more shall we help him in his mighty purposes; and I believe that

[25] Richard Robinson, *An Atheist's Values*, p. 124 (Clarendon Press, 1964).

those purposes are so vast and glorious, beyond all guessing now, that, when they are achieved and consummated, all our sufferings and sorrows of today, even the agonies that nearly break our faith, the disasters that well-nigh overwhelm us, shall, seen from that fair country where God's age-long dreams come true, bulk as little as bulk now the pieces of a broken toy, strewn long years ago upon a nursery floor, over which, thinking then that all our little world was in ruins, we cried ourselves to sleep.

7. I believe in prayer, namely that it is possible to have communion with God and that he can sometimes use our prayers to help others, when, with sincerity and love, we can realistically focus them.

8. I believe in the value of faith in the sense of trustful commitment to God whatever happens, using, of course, all available help, which is part of trusting God who revealed to man the ways of help. I believe in an attitude of mind by which having proceeded as far as the reason will take us, like a plane at the end of a runway, we soar in the direction of the evidence, seeking to land in a sense of certainty otherwise unreachable. To myself, I summarize my faith in God by saying that while things will happen to me as they happen to everyone, nothing can happen to me which God cannot weave into his purposes in a manner which, with my co-operation, will not advance his kingdom and my final well-being. The sense of meaning and purpose flowing through every life is of immense importance in my thinking. And it contributes to mental health. As a woman patient said to Jung, the psychiatrist, "If only I knew that my life had some meaning or purpose then there would be no silly story about my nerves."

9. I believe that sin is a dark fact of human life which cannot be dismissed by euphemistic psychological labels, and I realize that evil from various sources is rampant in the world, but I believe intensely in forgiveness, a restoration of relationship which has immense therapeutic power, both when the broken relationship has been between man and

357

God, or man and man as well. Sins (plural) are like the rash on the skin, the symptoms of interior dis-ease set up by the soul through making self the center around which all revolves. It is not just our sins we have to deal with, but we must let Christ reorientate our whole life and put us right at the center. Thus, he so deals with *sin,* that *sins* do not develop so terribly. The victory of Christ over all the evil and sin which assailed him enables me to believe that God's final victory over both is certain.

10. I believe that every soul survives death. In my opinion, this power to survive is inherent in the nature of the soul, though survival does not of necessity involve living for ever. The Greeks believed in survival before Christianity underlined it and placed the emphasis on its quality rather than its duration. When the Bible speaks of "eternal life" something different is meant, something to be assessed in terms of the quality, not the quantity of life, and something to be, in one sense, won, and, in another sense, accepted, as one is accepted into a fellowship like, say, the Royal College of Surgeons, so long as one has passed the tests. Without the tests one would feel "out of it" anyway. The word "everlasting" used about hell is used also of heaven, and both heaven and hell describe a temporary existence. Some souls, it may be, reenter an incarnate life and take its tests again. For all we know, life on other planets in other forms than "flesh" may be open to the spirit after death, and this may account for the very few people one knows who have any glimmering of having lived before. It may account for the shortage of prodigies. We need another word than "heaven" to describe the final bliss. It has been called "the beatific vision" or "the consummation of the ages," or "union with the Absolute."

11. I believe that after death the soul goes on spiritually where it left off, using an etheric body composed, perhaps, of a substance which is partly physical and partly psychical, but "of so etheric a texture as to be largely malleable by

thought." [26] It may well be that, as many cells make up a human body, so human persons belong to a group soul. We shall rejoice in our fellowship with others, especially those we love and those with whom we shall cooperate, and I hazard the guess that though we keep our identity we may lose something of our separateness

> *When that which drew from out the boundless deep*
> *Turns again home.*

12. All the evidence points to the thought that unimaginable bliss awaits those who give up once and for all the idea that there is any corner in the whole universe where they can live in any true sense without God, and who steadfastly set themselves to follow the upward path toward unity with God. Much may be suffered, but bliss at last seems to me certain for all. It may well be that, from such bliss in heavenly places, our Lord volunteered to enter the limited life of earth and suffer, in order that he might show, what, in God's sight, man might become, and what in man's sight God was like. I believe the main significance of the cross is that Christ by going to the uttermost—and while in the flesh the expression of uttermost loving is to love even unto death—revealed God's nature, and, at the same time, pledged himself to stand by humanity and to share humanity—for he is still human as well as divine—until the whole human race is won back into harmony with God's will. That is what I mean by "the redemption of the world by our Lord Jesus Christ." This would be a fitting climax to history, a "second coming" and perhaps, though not necessarily, the end of the world.

To that Person, so august, so high above me and yet so human, so lovable, so knowable, so utterly forgiving, understanding and ready to accept me, I desire to commit myself, and, affectionately and humbly, I invite the reader to do the same. If all the people in the world who, in their secret hearts,

---

[26] Crookall, *op. cit.*, p. 147. See also p. 54 and pp. 148-51.

love Christ, or at any rate admire his spirit, could declare their love and *act* together, there is no evil that spoils the world that could not be swept away.

Again and again, now, at the end of my life, I find myself going back in imagination to the way Christianity began. Men made an act of commitment. They committed themselves to Christ. A friendship began in which they not only, in a profound sense, found *him*, and through him, his Father, but also they found themselves. In an oft-quoted saying of Buber's, "real life is meeting," and this was real life. And what held it together was a love-relationship which was far more fundamental than any intellectual knowledge or theological suppositions, and it took them further. I expect doubts existed about many things until the end of their lives, but they were sure of him, and because of him, sure of love and of being loved. If only the church were a great fellowship of those who, loving him, really loved one another, it would not matter that they differed in their intellectual beliefs or worshiped him in different ways.

But no amount of conference discussion, appeals to authority, theological argument or biblical research and quotations can produce love. Those of us who are happily married know that the only way of producing love or proving love is by *commitment to a person*. In an ideal love-relationship we find evoked all we are capable of being. We find others who are hungry for love, and we can enrich their lives also and draw them into a love relationship, not based on their worth or on any qualifications, but on the fact that they are persons within the loving care and concern of God. *Complete* fullness of life for us all will be a love relationship with all mankind in which we, at the same time, depend on others and give to others.

"We need a return," said a writer in *The Times* (January 5, 1963), "not so much to 'Christianity'—that complex of doctrines, organisations, liturgies, traditions and even social habits, which would always be partly a man-made thing—as to faith in, and personal commitment to Christ Himself as the Lord of all life, the revealer both of man's meaning for God and of God's meaning for man."

Once such a commitment has been made, a wide margin of agnosticism is, in my view, permissible. "Hold to Christ," said Professor Butterfield, Vice-Chancellor of Cambridge University, and a Methodist lay preacher, "and for the rest be totally uncommitted." [27] I feel that, once such a commitment is made, one cannot go back on it finally, any more than a faithful husband, having established a love relationship with his wife, can go back on her, though she may often puzzle him and set up doubt and even irritation in regard to less important matters. Doubt, and the mental wrestling it engenders, are surely the way to a deeper and better grounded faith than is possible to those who can, with naïve facility, accept what is told them. "It is not like a child that I believe in Christ and confess Him," said Dostoevsky when he was criticized for the reactionary character of his faith. *"My hosanna has come forth from the crucible of doubt."* In my own little way, I feel the same.

Yet when all this is said, I respect and reverence the authority of Christ in regard to certain assertions, once I am persuaded that Christ really made them. He was so sure of God, so sure that God cared for the individual, so sure that the world's destiny was in the hands of omnipotent love. Am I in my heart to say to Christ, "You were wrong you know. There is no such being as God. He is a figment of your wishful imagination. I know better. There is no God, nor anyone who cares. Only in unaided man are man's hopes for himself or the world"? It was the horror of this alternative which played a part in the conversion of Professor Joad to Christianity after nearly thirty years of militant atheism.

Like him, I find the atheistic position untenable. If Christ was wrong I will be wrong with him, and go out into the meaningless darkness too. In a matter like religion every man has to come down on one side or the other, to say, "I am for," or, "I am against." "He that is not with me is against me," Christ is alleged to have said.[28] I admit a thousand doubts, problems and difficulties. If God is only a myth, a wishful thought, a projection of human fatherhood, a phantasy of infant thinking, then the atheists are right. But I have had moments which do not make sense unless God exists, and they have been the highest, most significant and most deeply joyous moments I have ever known. Sometimes, I believe, he unmistakably speaks to us in what must be called mystical experience. I do not mean visions or voices, although of course I do not dismiss them as necessarily illusional. It may be only in the love of another human being, the gratitude of one we tried to help, the feeling that there is something supernatural at the heart of a close relationship with another, the solemnity of the evening sky, the trust of a little child, great music if our mood is right, or great poetry or great art, the sound of a church bell far away, the silence in the lonely hills, the sermon of some dedicated spirit who has seen into the unseen.

Any such experience demands commitment, and commitment brings peace of mind; not the end of a journey but the end of wandering, not the end of a road but the end of searching for one, not the end of doubt and questioning but the discovery of a Friend in whose friendship nothing is felt to matter so much as maintaining the love relationship. Said David Sheppard, the cricketer, in the hour of a great commitment, "I walked back to my rooms in Trinity Hall late that night. I knew that it was more important than anything else in the world that I should become right with God. I knelt . . . and asked Christ to come into my life and to forgive me and to be my Friend and Master." [29]

[28] Matthew 12:30.
[29] David Sheppard, *Parson's Pitch*, p. 50 (Hodder and Stoughton, 1964).

I am permitted here to quote the final paragraphs of Dr. J. H. Oldham's great book, *Life Is Commitment.*

"I am not attempting here to discuss the difficulties attaching to Christian belief. I know that they are real and manifold. I am only pointing out that those who have encountered Christ and made a wholehearted response to that encounter have found an answer to the problem of man and truth. They have been given a faith which they do not have to carry, but which carries them. It is the testimony of Christians that amid all the uncertainties of relativism they have discovered that to which they may surrender themselves in complete trust. *They have encountered a reality which gives them confidence that the universe is trustworthy.* What they have known and experienced of love is something that they believe will hold firm in all the stresses and tests of life and prove stronger than death itself.

"That is one answer to the problem of man and truth. I do not myself know of any other answer in which my mind can rest. But it is inherent in that answer, as I understand it, that the answer must vindicate itself in open and free discussion, that all formulations of the answer made by fallible men are necessarily defective and incomplete and are in constant need of correction and enrichment by the contribution of the experience of all sincere seekers after truth." [30] So, Ruskin wrote to his father: "I resolved that I would believe in Christ and take Him for my Master in whatever I did . . . that to disbelieve was as difficult as to believe; that there are mysteries either way, but that the best mystery was that which gave me Christ for a Master. When I had done this I felt a peace within me which I had never known before. . . ."

In a small measure I have found that peace, and I think it can be made to grow. If *I* have found it, it is certain that anyone can. If the word "know" has any meaning, then, in a tiny, imperfect way, I have known God. I am certain of God

[30] J. H. Oldham, *Life Is Commitment,* p. 130 (Student Christian Movement Press, 1954). Italics mine.

and that God is love. I have had experiences, few, but convincing, which have no meaning apart from the faith that God is, and that a mysterious, loving omnipotence embraces all lives, gathers them all into a plan and will never desert them but will bring to them all utter peace and endless joy. There are still many things I cannot understand and many things that frighten me. And I know that I still have a very long way to go. I have had experiences that make me doubt, and even tempt me to cynicism so that I attempt, for days together, to leave God out of my life. How bleak and dreary, how lonely and miserable they are! I know Pascal's *"misère de l'homme sans Dieu."* And then, warmed of heart by some contact with love, by some word of another, printed, written or spoken, or even by the glory of a summer morning, or the quiet music of the sea at night, I come back, and his grace comes flooding in, cleansing, refreshing, renewing, uplifting, like the sparkling tide in a dull, muddy backwater. Then the whole earth fills with his glory, and once more I know that all is well. The mind recovers its resilience and gaiety, the soul finds its rest, and the will takes once more the upward road, and *knows* that the Great Companion is near, and that he will never weary of mankind, or regard a single soul as too unimportant, or too unworthy, to be his friend.

INDEX OF SUBJECTS

365

INDEX OF PROPER NAMES